FRONTIERS IN SELF PSYCHOLOGY

Progress in Self Psychology
Volume 3

FRONTIERS IN SELF PSYCHOLOGY

Progress in Self Psychology
Volume 3

Arnold Goldberg
editor

THE ANALYTIC PRESS

1988   Hillsdale, NJ   Hove and London

The Analytic Press

Distributed solely by

Lawrence Erlbaum Associates, Inc., Publishers
365 Boadway
Hillsdale, New Jersey 07642

Library of Congress Cataloging in Publication Data

ISBN 0-88163-066-7
LC Card No. 85-21875

Printed in the United States of America
10   9   8   7   6   5   4   3   2

Contents

Contributors

George E. Atwood, Ph.D., Professor of Psychology, Rutgers University; Coauthor, *Psychoanalytic Treatment; An Intersubjective Approach*

Michael Franz Basch, M.D., Professor of Psychiatry, Rush Medical College; Training and Supervising Analyst, Institute for Psychoanalysis, Chicago.

Beatrice Beebe, Ph.D., Associate Professor of Psychology, Ferkauf Graduate School of Psychology, Yeshiva University, Bronx, NY; private practice, New York City.

Bernard Brandchaft, M.D., Training and Supervising Analyst, Los Angeles Psychoanalytic Institute; coauthor, *Psychoanalytic Treatment: An Intersubjective Approach*

E. Virginia Demos, Ed.D., Director, Program in Counseling and Consulting Psychology, Harvard Graduate School of Education; coauthor of forthcoming book on infancy, affect, and development.

James L. Fosshage, Ph.D. Cofounder and Board Director, National Institute for the Psychotherapies; Faculty, Postdoctoral Program in Psychoanalysis, New York University.

Robert M. Galatzer-Levy, M.D., Faculty, Chicago Institute for Psychoanalysis; Lecturer in Psychiatry, University of Chicago.

Daniel Kriegman, Ph.D., Private practice, Newton and Cambridge, MA; formerly Clinical Director, Massachusetts Treatment Center for Sexually Dangerous Offenders.

Frank M. Lachmann, Ph.D., Faculty, Senior Supervisor, Training Analyst, Postgraduate Center for Mental Health, New York City.

Joseph Lichtenberg, M.D., Editor-in-Chief, *Psychoanalytic Inquiry*; author, *Psychoanalysis and Infant Research*

Leslie M. Lothstein, Ph.D., Director of Psychology, The Institute for Living, Hartford, CT; Associate Clinical Professor of Psychology, Department of Psychiatry, Case Western Reserve University, Cleveland, OH.

Arthur Malin, M.D., Training and Supervising Analyst, Los Angeles and Southern California Psychoanalytic Institutes; Associate Clinical Professor of Psychiatry, UCLA School of Medicine.

Russell Meares, M.D., Professor of Psychiatry, University of Sydney, Westmead, Australia; Director of Psychiatry, Westmead Hospital.

Lisa J. Moskowitz, M.A., Practicing Psychoanalyst; Fellow, American Institute for Psychotherapy and Psychoanalysis, New York City.

Louis W. Sander, M.D., Professor of Psychiatry, University of Colorado, Denver.

Doren L. Slade, Ph.D., Practicing Psychoanalysts; Fellow, American Institute for Psychotherapy and Psychoanalysis, New York City.

Robert D. Stolorow, Ph.D., Faculty, Southern California Psychoanalytic Institute; Coauthor, *Psychoanalytic Treatment; An Intersubjective Approach*.

Paul H. Tolpin, M.D., Faculty, and Training and Supervising Analyst, Chicago Institute for Psychoanalysis; Attending Psychiatrist, Michael Reese Hospital, Chicago.

Preface

With the third volume of our series in psychoanalytic self psychology, we join a new publisher and adopt a revised format. Our introduction for this book is written by Dr. James L. Fosshage, and future volumes will be introduced by various members of the community of self psychology. The articles in the collection have been gathered from a wide field of contributors after careful evaluation by our editorial board. We hope that we have been able to live up to the spirit of continued progress in the field.

Arnold Goldberg, M.D.
Editor

Introduction

James L. Fosshage

This volume focuses on various theoretical and clinical issues that are of central concern today for the leading clinicians and theorists of self psychology. These current efforts are a continuation of Heinz Kohut's contributions, beginning with his discovery of what he then called the narcissistic transferences and his formulation of his theory of narcissism, embedded within the drive model and viewed as a complementary theory to the drive-defense model (Kohut, 1971), to his subsequent development of a comprehensive psychoanalytic theory of self psychology, in which the consolidation and regulation of the self dominates the scene (Kohut, 1984). In keeping with these theoretical and clinical changes and in the hope of briefly orienting the reader in anticipation of the intriguing and enlightening chapters to follow, I wish to present in an outline form what I consider to be the central contributions of self psychology and some of the emergent questions that the contributors address in this volume. In this Introduction I can, of course, mention only a few of the authors who have contributed significantly to the issues at hand.

Foremost was Kohut's (1959, 1982) placement of the *empathic mode of observation*, that is, observing and understanding from within the patient's frame of reference, at the very center of psychoanalytic inquiry and as the definer of the field itself. The definition of psychoanalysis, from a self psychological perspective, is no longer wedded to a particular personality theory, developmental model or even to the clinical theory of the analysis of transference and resistance, traditionally considered to be the hallmarks of psychoanalysis. Rather, psychoanalysis is conceptualized, in Kohut's now well-known words, as "a psychology of complex mental states which, with the aid of the persevering empathic-introspective immersion of the observer into the inner life of man, gathers its data in order to explain them" (1977, p. 302). The emphasis on the empathic mode of observation implicitly reminded us of the potential influence of the observer on the observed and opened the door to an experience-near theory, minimizing, but never eliminating, the possible imposition of a theoretical framework onto the patient and the possible ascription of affects and motivational intentionality to the patient derived from the analyst's, not the patient's, subjective experience.

Kohut's most significant clinical discovery, enabled by the consistent application of the empathic mode of observation, was the *self-selfobject matrix*, wherein a person both within and outside psychoanalytic treatment utilizes another person to provide specific intrapsychic functions for the maintenance and regulation of a cohesive sense of self, which the person is otherwise, at the moment, unable to provide for himself or herself. This discovery provided a heretofore undefined specificity to a central dimension of object relations. It became clear to Kohut that selfobjects are necessary throughout life (that is, we need and utilize others to provide more or less specific self-regulatory functions in the maintenance of ourselves throughout our life span) and that we can speak, as Kohut (1984) and Wolf (1980) have pointed out, of developmental lines of selfobjects from the most primitive to the most mature. Currently we are in the process of understanding and conceptualizing the particulars of these various developmental lines, for example, the mirroring, idealizing, and twinship selfobject functions. The selfobject dimension in human relationships is now viewed as ever-present and, as Stolorow and Lachmann (1984/85) have pointed out, is always a facet of the transference that emerges into the foreground and recedes into the background according to the requirements of self-cohesion.

This crucially important conceptualization of the self-selfobject matrix has provided a field theory from which the analyst can no longer attempt to hide behind a supposedly anonymous blank screen, "objectively" analyzing the patient's intrapsychic conflicts over drives, defenses, and prohibitions. Instead, the analyst is an active participant attempting vicariously and introspectively to enter into and understand the patient's experience, but *always more or less affecting the patient both through the analyst's presence as well as through the analyst's particular ways of attending to and organizing the clinical data*—a most intricate and subtle interplay between analysand and analyst, which Stolorow, Brandschaft, and Atwood (1983; see also Atwood and Stolorow, 1984) refer to as the intersubjective field.

Correspondingly, the exquisitely detailed and refined infant research is elucidating the most subtle organizational interplay between infant and caregiver. The study of this "systems perspective of organization" (Sander, this volume) through the elucidation of the "interactive mutual influence patterns" (Beebe and Lachmann, this volume) and of "affect systems" (Demos, this volume) provides an additional empirical basis for our understanding of the development of psychological organization. This research is producing a fundamentally revised picture of psychological development (Stern, 1985) that profoundly affects our psychodynamic and genetic understandings and explanations and serves as a springboard for our understanding of the developmentally enhancing or detracting interplay within the analytic arena. For a simple yet noteworthy example of extrapolation from infant research, just as the infant requires periods of disengagement to experience "endogenous motivation" (see Sander's discussion), corresponding with Winnicott's "origins of the capacity to be alone," so it is for the analysand who needs at times to disengage from the analyst, not for defensive purposes (i.e., "distancing" from the analyst, a possible formulation from an object relations perspective), but for self-consolidating goals.

The emphasis on the empathic mode of observation and the recognition of the field that encompasses analyst and analysand has led to an important shift in transference interpretations, as delineated by Kohut, the Ornsteins (1980), Stolorow and Lachmann (1984), and others. Whereas traditionally transference interpretations have focused on the identification of the "distortions of reality" with the intent to correct the distortions through the insertion of the analyst's "realistic" view, from a self-psychological perspective the focus is on the elucidation and understanding of the patient's experience, the precipitants of that experience, including the analyst's role, the operative organizing principles, and the historical context for the development of these principles. In this way the patient's subjective world is elucidated and understood from within, without prejudgments about the nature of "reality."

Kohut has placed at center stage for the developmental model and the psychoanalytic treatment situation an experience-near concept, the *self*, what he referred to as "the core of personality" and as the "independent center of initiative" (1977). We might refer to this as the primary organization of experience including experiences of the self and of the other (Atwood and Stolorow, 1984; Stern, 1985). In contrast to the classical motivational model of libidinal and aggressive drives and object relations models of the striving and need for object attachment, from a self psychological perspective the primary motivational thrust is toward the consolidation and maintenance of the self according to its inherent "program of action" (Kohut, 1984). Correspondingly, emergent conceptualizations derived from infant research view the infant, not as incapable, drive-dominated, narcissistically focused, or even symbiotically attached, but at birth as an incipient self (Stern, 1985) or as an agent actively organizing his or her experience (see Beebe and Lachmann, Demos, Lichtenberg, and Sander in this volume). (In Kriegman's well-developed evolutionary biological analysis in this volume the empathic attitude and corresponding altruistic behavior, rather than a reaction formation, are viewed as historically primitive attributes that have evolved because of their adaptive advantage and because of selective pressures to serve as the basis for requisite parental responsiveness.)

These developmental and motivational models require a reassessment and a reformulation of defenses and their functions to include self-protective and self-preservative functions (Kohut, 1984). Psychotic delusions, rather than being a defensive turning away from reality, are reconceptualized as "a concretizing effort to *substantialize* and *preserve* a reality that has begun to disintegrate" (Stolorow, Atwood, and Brandchaft, this volume). Dreaming, rather than being seen as a drive-discharge phenomenon convoluted by defensive measures, is viewed as a mentational effort, predominantly imagistic in form, whose aim is to develop, maintain, and restore psychological organization (Fosshage, this volume). And, as I have written elsewhere:

> Probably because the model initially emerged in response to the psychoanalytic treatment of patients with severe self-pathology, the developmental model of the consolidation of the self has, to this point, predominantly focused on the formation and maintenance of the structural cohesion of the self. Consolidation of the self is not to be viewed as a static end point, requiring, subsequent to its establishment, only maintenance functions; for newly emerging developmental phases throughout our lives continually require [through waking and dreaming mentation] internal organizing, disorganizing, and reorganizing endeavors [1983, p. 5].

Thus, we are in need of a more complete developmental model that traverses the entire life span.

On the basis of these developmental and motivational models our concern over the separation process within the clinical arena needs to shift fundamentally to a focus on the self-consolidation process, for separation is an integral developmental component and consequence of self-consolidation. (Beebe and Lachmann suggest a shift away from focusing on differentiating from the other to the "dynamic interplay.") To expect a patient to separate even from a "noxious" object when that object is providing essential self-cohesive functions, is at best a misunderstanding and at worst a critically experienced communication and a potentially conflict-exacerbating and self-fragmenting intervention.

We know that patients in a psychoanalytic situation, given an incipient cohesive self and the necessary self-selfobject milieu, will, despite intense fears and self-protective needs, strive to repair themselves and to proceed with their developmental course. This knowledge releases us from the traditional overemphasis on defensive functioning and the analysis of resistances, sensitizes us to recognize the patients' developmental needs and strivings (in contrast to the classical model and its emphasis on the renunciation of so-called infantile demands), and facilitates, therefore, our empathic immersion and availability to our patients for the developmental requirements. Most likely it is these conceptualizations, particularly the incipient self, striving to repair and develop psychological organization through the search for viable selfobjects, that have recently enabled psychoanalysts to position themselves to understand and, therefore, successfully treat the most seriously disturbed. (See Galatzer-Levy; Slade and Moskowitz; Stolorow, Atwood, and Brandchaft; and the Discussions of Basch and Tolpin in this volume.)

Kohut concluded, especially by the time of his last book (1984), that the ultimate source of psychopathology was contained in the self-selfobject matrix. Arrests in the development of the self occur when there is not one but consistent selfobject failures. But what, as Goldberg (1981), Stolorow and Lachmann (1980), Stolorow and Brandchaft (1985), and others have asked, is the status of conflict in this model? Do we maintain complementary theories so that arrests in the consolidation of the self are more primitive problems and conflicts of the drive-defense model are the products of higher organization? The clinical evidence that *all* patients struggle with self issues contradicts this awkward theoretical amalgamation. The existence of two complementary models undoubtedly occurs with the emergence of a new model and demands a new synthesis. No one would deny that intense conflict exists, but we are in the process of redefining its ingredients. It is more likely that when intense unresolvable conflict persists, ultimately it reflects a problematic self-selfobject matrix that positions us not to rest in the clinical situation until we have discovered its origins, currently and developmentally.

Kohut (1984) entitled his last book with the question "How does analysis cure?" He emphasized the role of optimal emphatic failures. These failures are optimal in that the patient is capable of managing them by supplying the missing functions previously provided by the analyst, stretching, if you will, and consolidating their self-capacity. But Kohut (1982, 1984) also concluded that the very presence of empathy is therapeutic. Specifically, the very experience of being understood produces cohesion. Implicit in Kohut's work is that within this ambience empathic connections with previously rejected and negatively experienced aspects of ourselves are gradually established, resulting in transformations that we call structure building and structural change. In addition, infant researchers propose variations of a model wherein "characteristic patterns of interactive regulation organize experience" (Beebe and Lachmann, this volume) and, thereby, form psychic structure. We are, indeed, at the frontiers of understanding how the processes of structure building and structural change occur, processes that are essential to psychoanalysis and are currently being avidly investigated in the psychoanalytic situation and in the research of infants.

REFERENCES

Atwood, G. & Stolorow, R. (1984), *Structures of Subjectivity: Explorations in Psychoanalytic Phenomenology*. Hillsdale, NJ: The Analytic Press.

Fosshage, J. (1983), Developmental arrests and conflict theory toward a unifying theory: "The Case of Burton." Presented at meeting of National Institute for Psychotherapies Professional Association.

Goldberg, A. (1981), One theory or more, *Contemporary Psychoanalysis*, 17:626–638.

Kohut, H. (1959), Introspection, empathy and psychoanalysis. *Journal of the American Psychoanalytic Association*, 7:459–483.

———— (1971), *The Analysis of the Self*. New York: International Universities Press.

———— (1977), *The Restoration of the Self*. New York: International Universities Press.

———— (1982), Introspection, empathy, and the semicircle of mental health. *International Journal of Psycho-Analysis*, 63:395–408.

———— (1984), *How Does Analysis Cure?* Chicago: University of Chicago Press.

Ornstein, P., & Ornstein, A. (1980), Formulating interpretations in clinical psychoanalysis, *International Journal of Psycho-Analysis*, 61:203–211.

Stern, D. (1985), *The Interpersonal World of the Infant*. New York: Basic Books.

Stolorow R., & Atwood, G. (1983), Intersubjectivity in psychoanalytic treatment: With special reference to archaic states. *Bulletin of the Menninger Clinic*, 47:117–128.

———— & Brandchaft, B. (1985), Developmental failure and psychic conflict. *Psychoanalytic Psychology*.

_____ & Lachmann, F. (1980), *Psychoanalysis of Developmental Arrests*. New York: International Universities Press.

_____ (1984/85), Transference: The future of an illusion. *Annual of Psychoanalysis*, 12:19–37. New York: International Universities Press.

Wolf, E. (1980), On the developmental line of self-object relations. In A. Goldberg, ed., *Advances in Self Psychology*. New York: International Universities Press.

Self Psychology
and Infancy

Chapter 1

Mother–Infant Mutual Influence and Precursors of Psychic Structure

Beatrice Beebe
Frank M. Lachmann

There is a long-standing tradition in psychoanalysis linking child development and the organization of psychic structure. Recent research on mother–infant interaction in the first six months of life can illuminate the development of psychic structure, specifically the precursors of self and object representations and the emerging organization of infant experience.

We will focus on the prerepresentational origins of psychic structure and explore the relevance of early patterns of experience in the first six months of life, before representation and symbolic thought are established. Representation can be assumed to begin toward the end of the first year and to undergo major reorganization at one to one-and-a-half years, and only in the third year can symbolic functioning be assumed to be fully established (Piaget, 1954). The discussion of the prerepresentational origins of psychic structure will be limited to the relevance of the purely social exchanges between mother and infant. Such issues as self-regulation and the management of "alone states" will not be addressed. The infants studied were all

The contributions of Daniel Stern, M.D., Joseph Jaffe, M.D., and Robert Stolorow, Ph.D., are gratefully acknowledged.

developing in the normal range with an intact central nervous system.

Mother and infant generate ways of experiencing each other in the early months of life. How is this experience organized, and how is it represented? Our basic proposal is that early interaction structures provide one important basis for the organization of infant experience. These interaction structures are *characteristic patterns of mutual influence*, which the infant comes to recognize and expect. The dynamic interplay between infant and caretaker, each influencing the other to create a variety of patterns of mutual regulation, provides one basis for the representations of self and other.

MUTUAL INFLUENCE STRUCTURES

Mutual influence refers to a communication process in which influence flows in both directions: both mother and infant systematically affect, and are affected by, the other. Mutual influence does not imply equal influence. Each partner does not necessarily influence the other in equal measure or in like manner. However, each contributes to the regulation of the other's behavior.

A mutual influence model stands in contrast to a great deal of previous thinking, which focused on one-way influence and emphasized *either* the parent's influence on the child, or the child's influence on the parent (Bell, 1971; Cappella, 1981; Lewis and Lee-Painter, 1974). A mutual influence model can be seen as part of a "regulatory systems perspective" (Sander, 1977, 1983), where the organization of behavior and experience is seen primarily as a property of the infant-caretaker system at this age, rather than primarily the property of the individual. As Sander (1983) notes, conceptualizing the organization of experience with respect to a systems point of view is consistent with the psychoanalytic writings of Hartmann (1939), Erikson (1950), Spitz (1965), Winnicott (1974), Sullivan (1953), and Atwood and Stolorow (1984). For example, Erikson's (1950) epigenetic model described development as a sequence of levels of the organization of "fitting-together" of infant and caretaker. Spitz (1965) described the ontogeny of the self within an interactional framework. Atwood and Stolorow (1984) consider that the organization of experience, its structuralization, and its derailments, occur as a property of a dyadic system.

With increasing clarity the empirical literature on mother-infant interaction documents early mutual influence structures. Observations of mutual regulations have been made in every modality examined; for example, vocalization (Stern, Jaffe, Beebe, and Bennett, 1975; Anderson, Vietze, and Dokecki, 1977), gaze (Stern, 1974), general affective involvement (Tronick, Als, and Brazelton, 1980; Beebe, Stern, and Jaffe, 1979; Beebe and Kronen (in preparation); Beebe and Crown (in preparation) and timing (Jasnow, 1983; Beebe, Jaffe, Feldstein, Mays, and Alson, 1985). The relationships among mutual influences, infant experience, and psychic structure could be illustrated in any of these modalities.

The concept of mutual influence structures is illustrated in Sander's work on the regulation of sleep-wake cycles during the first weeks of life, and in Stern's work on the regulation of gaze during face-to-face play at three to four months. Sander and his co-workers have proposed that a basic regulatory core jells in the early weeks of life in relation to the caretaking environment. Without this basic core at the physiological level, the other dimensions of the infant's development will not proceed adequately (Sander 1977, 1983b). The concept of the basic regulatory core is derived from the regularities in the sequence and duration of infant sleep-wake and feeding states. Such regularities are established over the course of the first days and weeks of life only as mother and infant mutually influence each other to establish predictable sequences. Thus mutual influence is required in the establishment of the basic regulatory core: "The infant's wakefulness determines the activities of the mother, the activities of the mother determine in some degree the course of infant state over the interaction period, and the modifiability of infant state by maternal manipulation determines the mother's further activities" (Chappell and Sander, 1979, p. 106).

In studying the mutual regulation of gaze during face-to-face play at four months, Stern (1974) similarly documented that each partner influences the other. In evaluating the infant's influences on the mother, given that mother is looking at infant, the infant's initiation of gaze at mother increases the likelihood that mother will continue gazing. It is unlikely in this circumstance of mutual gaze that mother will avert her gaze. When mother and infant are gazing at each other, it is more likely that the infant will gaze away. In fact, it is the infant who makes and breaks mutual gaze, since the infant initiates and terminates 94 percent of all mutual gazes, while the mother tends to gaze steadily at the infant. In evaluating the mother's influence on her infant, Stern found that when the mother gazes at the infant, the likelihood that the infant will return her gaze increases. The most likely outcome of the pattern of each partner's responsivity to the other is mutual gaze.

HOW DO EARLY MUTUAL INFLUENCE STRUCTURES ORGANIZE INFANT EXPERIENCE?

Mutual influence structures organize infant experience through expectancies. The neonate has a remarkable capacity to perceive time and temporal sequence, to estimate the duration of events, and to develop an expectation of when events will occur (DeCasper and Fifer, 1980; DeCasper and Carstens, 1980). The neonate can detect a predictable relationship between its own behavior and the environment's response, which is termed a "contingent" response (Watson, 1985). Expectancy provides an experience of efficacy, in that the infant's actions produce consequences (see Lewis and Goldberg, 1969). This experience is postulated as one precursor of initiative.

A series of experiments by DeCasper on a group of infants (DeCasper and Carstens, 1980) showed that whether or not the environment provides contingent and expectable responses for the infants it does affect their attention, memory, emotions, and very capacity to learn. DeCasper used the infants' capacity to time events to teach them that if they paused longer (or shorter) between sucking bursts, they could turn on music. When the infants' expectations were confirmed, that is, when they slowed their sucking and music followed, then the infants' affect was positive. In a second experiment, the infants were taught to "turn on" music, and then their expectation that they would turn on the music was violated. They first learned, as in the previously described experiment, that by pausing longer (or shorter) between sucking bursts, music would follow. Then the experimenter *stopped* giving music contingent on the infants' behavior, and instead presented the music randomly. In this case, the infants' affect became negative: they grimaced, whimpered, cried, and in some cases stopped sucking altogether. In a third experiment, a new group of infants was *first* randomly exposed to music. Then the experimenter tried to teach the infants the same expectancy as in the first two experiments: that if the infants lengthened (or shortened) their pauses between sucking bursts, they could "turn on" music. In this third experiment, the startling result was that the babies could not learn this relationship. They did not seem to detect the contingency between their own behavior and the music, once having been exposed to the situation in which the music had a random relationship to their own behavior. The findings of this last experiment suggest that if the environment were completely noncontingent, which would be a very extreme condition, then the infant's very capacity to organize its experience within a dyadic relationship would be interfered with. Usually, however, mothers provide a tremendous amount of contingent stimulation (Stern, 1977; Schaffer, 1977; Tronick, 1982).

DeCasper's work also points to a new view of infant memory. What the neonate remembers is not simply an event, but a particular contingent relationship *between* its own behavior and environmental event. That is, the neonate remembers an interaction. This view of infant memory implies that memory is perfectly suited to structuring dyadic relatedness from birth on.

Neonates can thus learn, remember, and anticipate from birth. These capacities allow them to participate in numerous mutually regulated interactions from the beginning of life. Those interactions which recur over and over, and are thus characteristic, become generalized as structures that organize the infant's experience. Structures are understood in Rapaport's (1960) sense: configurations or patterns with a slow rate of change. These interaction structures, in which each partner is systematically influenced by the other, will include the infants's actions, perceptions, cognition, affects, and an associated pattern of proprioceptive experience.

HOW DO SELF AND OBJECT REPRESENTATIONS EMERGE FROM EARLY INTERACTION STRUCTURES?

Developmental theorists using different frames of reference have all conceptualized representation in a remarkably similar way (Werner, 1948; Piaget, 1954; Church, 1961; Schilder, 1964). They have all considered activity to be the primary factor in the creation of representations: the function of representation is fundamentally dependent on concrete actions. All have used the concept of action as including an associated sensoriaffective-proprioceptive experience. Representation is defined as interiorized actions, so that children can now do with mental images what before they did with their own actions. Representational capacity *begins* to be established at seven to nine months, although it is not completed until the third year.

We will build on this definition of representation to explicate the relationship between early interaction structures and self and object representations. These very same movements, actions, and gestures of early interactions between mother and infant, are the *same actions* which construct representations. Actions include everything the infant does—looking, attending, vocalizing, grimacing, turning away, and so on, and an associated proprioceptive experience. The different actions of the infant with the caretaker, and the different actions of the caretaker with the infant, create different interaction structures and ultimately different patterns of representations. What is represented is not simply interiorized action, but interiorized *inter*action: not simply the infant's action, nor simply the environment's response, but the dynamic mutual influence between the two (see Beebe, 1985). Interiorized interaction patterns include actions, perception, cognition, affect, and proprioceptive experience.

Self and object representations are not constructed only on the basis of early interaction structures. As mentioned earlier, self-regulation and the management of alone states (Sander, 1977) are understood to contribute as well to the construction of self and object representations. Furthermore, we assume that interactive patterns throughout the period of forming representations will continue to shape representations. This assumption uses a transformational model of development where earlier structures are understood both to shape and to be shaped by subsequent experience. However, as the representational process begins, at approximately seven to nine months, this construction will in part be based on the early interaction structures which are characteristic to this point.

This definition of representation differs substantially from the usual psychoanalytic usage. For example, according to Jacobson (1964), self and object representations evolve from memory traces of pleasure and unpleasure: "From . . . instinctual, emotional, ideational, and functional experiences, and from the perceptions with which they become associated, images of love objects, as well as images of bodily and psychic self, emerge" (p. 19). These images, which are at first vague and variable, become increasingly consistent, differentiated, and realistic representations of the self and object world.

Since the findings of infant research are couched in the language of interactive action patterns, an integration of infant research with the concerns of psychoanalysis will be facilitated if we broaden the concepts of self and object representations to encompass the definition of representation as originally derived from action patterns and their interactive regulation. This definition of representation also shifts the focus from the traditional psychoanalytic concern with representing oneself as clearly delineated from the other, to a concern with a representation of the relationship, that is, a representation of self-with-other, of how the self and other are interrelated in a constant dynamic experience. A different view of the nature of representation is also implicit here. In the older view, representations were understood to be built in a laborious piecemeal process, taking inside what was outside (Stern, 1983). The contrasting view that emerges from infant research is that, from birth, the infant has the necessary capacities to construct representation: memory, expectancies, the capacity to engage in mutually regulated interactive patterns, and the capacity to organize these dyadic experiences. Some specific examples of mutual influence structures will clarify how they operate and their implications for the organization of infant experience.

INTERACTION STRUCTURES OF MATCHING: HOW DO THEY WORK?

Various kinds of sharing, matching, "tuning in," and "being on the same wavelength" exist in the mutual influence structures of the first six months of life and can be considered to constitute the precursors of empathy.

"Normal" middle-class mothers and their three- to four-month-old infants were studied. By this age there is a flowering of the infant's social capacity, which is best observed and studied in the face-to-face play situation (Tronick, Als, and Adamson, 1979). Three- to four-month infants can see approximately as well as adults (Stern, 1974, 1977), and they show an extensive range of interpersonal affective displays (Beebe, 1973; Beebe and Stern, 1977; Beebe and Gerstman, 1980; Tronick, Als, and Brazelton, 1980).

To study this play, mother and infant are seated face-to-face in a comfortable laboratory room. Two videotape cameras, one on each partner, gives a split-screen view, so that the behaviors of each can be observed, moment by moment. Mothers are instructed simply to play with their infants as they would at home, and that anything they do is fine. Thus, the only agenda is mutual interest and delight (Stern, 1977).

In order to study the moment-by-moment interaction, a scale has been developed (Beebe and Stern 1977; Beebe and Gerstman, 1980) to chart the ways infants combine their orientation, visual attention, and subtle facial expressiveness to their mothers. It is a scale of increasing and decreasing affective "engagement." The scale quantifies a continuum from high positive engagement, through a midpoint of looking with neutral face at the partner, to a low point of a limp, motionless, nonreactive state. For example, going up the scale in the direction of increasing engagement, the infant would change from not oriented to oriented toward mother but still not looking; to looking at mother, but with a sober face; to looking with slight positive expressiveness and slight mouth openings and purses; to increasing degrees of positive and smiling; to a wide, open-mouth "gape-smile"

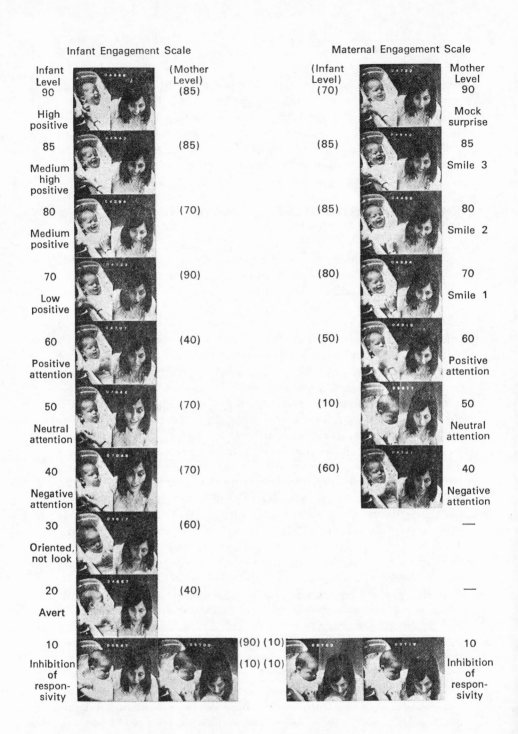

FIGURE 1.   Photographic Illustrations of Infant and Maternal Engagement Scales

at the top of the scale. Figure 1 illustrates the infant's engagement scale, and a similar scale for the mother. Thus, moment-by-moment each partner can be assigned a level on the scale and a direction on the scale, increasing or decreasing.

The videotapes were turned into 16mm films and examined with a movie editor. The film was rocked back and forth as slowly as necessary, to identify the beginning and ending of every action of each partner, precise to one-twelfth of a second. Each action was assigned a level and a direction on the scale, for each partner separately.

Facial Mirroring: Matching the Direction of Affective Change

Numerous psychoanalytic writers have referred to the concept of mirroring (Elkisch, 1957; Winnicott, 1974; Mahler, Pine and Bergman, 1975). For example, Winnicott (1974) has described mirroring: ". . . The precursor of the mirror is the mother's face; . . . what does the infant see when he looks at the mother's face? . . . He sees himself" (p. 131). This is the familiar concept that the mother matches, or reflects back, the infant's emotional state. It is conceptualized as a one-way influence phenomenon: it is the mother who reflects back. Various infant researchers have also described the mother–infant facial-visual exchange as "mirroring," "echo," or "imitation." These studies have also emphasized maternal responsivity to the infant, rather than examining whether and how the exchange is mutually regulated. For example, Schaffer (1979) has suggested that the mother chimes in to support, repeat, comment on, and elaborate the infant's responses.

Papousek and Papousek (1977, 1979) have suggested that the mother offers herself as a "biological mirror" from the beginning of life, imitating the infant's movements of mouth, nose, and eyes. Trevarthen (1979) has described the mother's imitative playful exaggeration of the infant's signals as an "echo," suggesting that "the infant invites the mother to share a dance of expressions and excitements" (p. 239).

In an examination of the facial-visual exchange using the scale just described (Kronen, 1982; Beebe and Crown, in preparation; Beebe and Kronen, in preparation), the level and direction of affective engagement of each partner was charted moment by moment. Two questions were addressed: what is matched in this exchange, and who influences whom to match. Although the metaphors of mirror, echo, and imitation all suggest some rather literal match, the results show that mothers and infants do not match the exact level of engage-

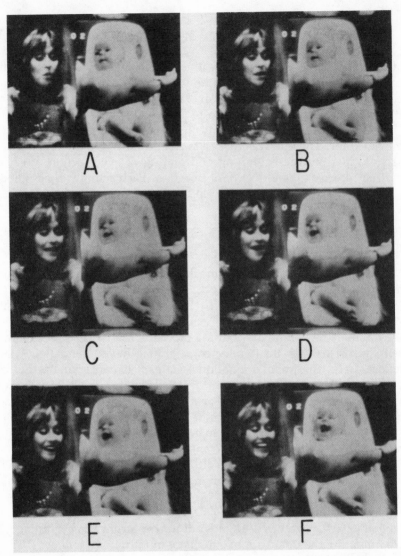

FIGURE 2. Photographic illustrations of a "mirroring" sequence. Mother and infant are seated face to face, and are looking at each other. At point A, mother shows a "kiss-face," and infant's lips are partially drawn in, resulting in a tight, sober-faced expression. At point B, .54 seconds later, mother's mouth has widened into a slightly positive expression, and infant's face has relaxed with a hint of widening in the mouth, also a slightly positive expression. At point C, .79 seconds later, both mother and infant show a slight smile. At point D, .46 seconds later, both mother and infant further widen and open their smiles. Again at points E, .46 seconds later, and F, .58 seconds later, both mother and infant further increase the smile display. Points E and F illustrate the infant's "gape-smile." At point F the infant has shifted the orientation of his head further to his left, and upward, which heightens the evocativeness of the gape-smile.

ment. Instead, they match the direction of engagement change, both increasing or both decreasing. That is, mother and infant match where the other is going, tracking the process of change as it is happening, moment by moment.

In addressing the question of whether any actual influence is occurring, and if so, who is influencing whom, a sophisticated statistical tool, time-series regression, was used. It is designed to address precisely these questions of influence, in two series of behaviors of two participants interacting over time (Gottman, 1981). Strong mutual influence findings are documented, in that each partner influences the other to follow his or her own direction of affective change. Not only is each partner sensitive to the fleeting affective engagement changes of the other (lasting less than a second), and to the affective direction in which the other is tending, but this sensitivity is continuously used in a mutual influence process regulating the moment-by-moment affective involvement. The photographs in Figure 2 illustrate this process.

Interpersonal Timing: Matching of Temporal Patterns

The analyses of "mirroring" examined the content of mother and infant behavior, that is, the level and direction of affective engagement. The *purely* temporal organization of these same behaviors was also examined. Microanalysis of film has revealed that mother and infant live in a split-second world where the behaviors last for less than half a second (Stern, 1971, 1977; Beebe and Stern, 1977; Peery, 1980; Beebe, 1982). Each partner responds to the other extremely rapidly in "latencies" ranging from simultaneous to one-half-second (Stern, 1971; Beebe, Stern, and Jaffe, 1979; Peery, 1980; Kronen, 1982). This rapidity suggests that, at least for the mother, these split-second adjustments occur partially or fully out of conscious control. In this interlocking responsivity, various temporal patterns are matched.

The examination of temporal patterns was suggested by studies of adults. Adults in conversation were found to match the purely temporal rhythms of dialogue (omitting the content of the speech) (Jaffe and Feldstein, 1970). Of special relevance was the finding of a relationship between matching rhythms of dialogue, and empathy and affect. When adult strangers match rhythms, they like each other more and perceive each other as warmer and more similar than when their rhythms do not match. In psychopathology, by contrast, matching of temporal patterns of dialogue is deficient. (See Feldstein and Welkowitz, 1978, for a review).

The experience of matching rhythms may be best illustrated by instances where matching goes awry. For instance, in walking down the street, if each partner does not try to match the other's pace, one ends up ahead of the other. Or, in a conversation, if one partner talks and never pauses, or waits a long time before responding, the other partner may "tune out."

In adult conversation we depend on the matching of temporal patterns to know that the other is "tuned in" and to take turns smoothly. Aspects of this same matching are in evidence in mother–infant vocal and facial-visual communication as early as three to four months and again at nine months. Through the use of time-series regression to analyze influence, mutual influence to match various temporal patterns of behavior between mother and infant has been documented (Alson, 1982; Jasnow, 1983; Mays, 1984; Beebe et al., 1985). They match each other's pauses, each other's "turns," and even the durations of actions (such as orienting to look or facial expression changes). One of the findings indicates that the more mother and infant match pauses between vocalizations, the more positive the infant's affect.

Thus each partner is extremely sensitive to the durations of the other's behavior, and each influences the other to track and match these durations, on a moment-to-moment basis. In this interlocking temporal responsivity, the infant acquires a basic microstructure of "being with" another person.

WHAT ARE THE IMPLICATIONS OF AFFECTIVE AND TEMPORAL MATCHING FOR THE ORGANIZATION OF INFANT EXPERIENCE?

As mother and infant influence each other to match both the timing and affective direction of behavior, this matching provides each partner with a behavioral basis for knowing and entering into the other's perception, temporal world, and feeling state. The implication is that similarity in behavior is associated with a congruence of feeling states; that there is a relationship between matching and empathy. How does this work?

First we have to acknowledge that the translation back and forth between the empirical findings and subjective experience is very difficult. Can we assume that the dimensions of behavior documented by the researcher are the same dimensions relevant for the infant's subjective experience? This is an unsolved problem. We can assume that what infants do, and what they experience, are roughly synonomous (as they probably will never again be as development proceeds).

For these matching studies, an experiment by Ekman (1983) offers a bridge between matching behavior and subjective states. This experiment suggests a mechanism of empathy, that is, how the sharing of subjective states can occur.

In the Ekman experiment, professional actors and scientists who study the face were taught an exact set of muscle movements (for example raising the outer corners of the eyebrows) necessary to produce a series of emotional expressions. In a second task, they were taught to relive various emotions (similar to the Stanislawsky method of learning acting). Simultaneously, a series of autonomic indices was recorded. Ekman found that simply producing the facial-muscle action patterns resulted in more clear-cut autonomic changes than reliving these emotions. He concludes that contracting the facial muscles per se brings forth the associated autonomic activity.

The implication is that by contracting the same facial muscles as perceived on another's face, the onlooker can literally feel the same autonomic sensations as the other person. Reproducing the expression of another (for example, in mirroring) can produce in the onlooker a similar emotional state.

Ekman's work thus provides a conceivable mechanism for sharing affect and for empathy: matching the pattern of the partner's behavior evokes a similar proprioceptive experience that corresponds to the state of the partner. Thus as mother and infant match each other's temporal and affective patterns, they create in themselves a psychophysiological state similar to that of the partner, so that each can be said to be participating in the subjective state of the other.

These matching experiences affect the ways in which self and object are represented. Not only the matching of affect and timing, but matching experiences of many kinds are assumed to be a ubiquitous aspect of daily social interaction for most infants and mothers. As these recur, the infant develops an expectation of being matched (see Stern, Hofer, Haft, and Dore, 1985). As representation begins to develop toward the end of the first year, the infant will represent the expectation of being matched by, and being able to match, the partner as well as the associated experience of participating in the state of the other. The very interactive process, of what it is like both to match and be matched or not, on a moment-to-moment basis, will be represented. These matching experiences and their representation presumably contribute to an expectation of being "attuned," "known," "tracked," "on the same wavelength," and understood. They may serve as precursors of the later experiences of being esteemed and approved.

INTERACTION STRUCTURES OF DERAILMENT

Every mother at times undershoots or overshoots an optimal level of stimulation. The infant has a virtuoso range of behaviors for responding to nonoptimal stimulation. This range can be conceptualized as a continuum from coping maneuvers to early "protodefensive" capacities. Beebe and Stern (1977) have illustrated part of this range: maternal overstimulation and infant withdrawal maneuvers. This relatively aversive encounter nevertheless reveals intricate interactive sequences, where each partner shows exquisite sensitivity to the other's behavior, each "reacting" to the other on a quasi-simultaneous basis, with latencies under one-half second. A mutual influence structure is again documented, where the behaviors of each partner influence the behaviors of the other. (See Stern, 1971, for another report of a similar interaction.)

In this study (Beebe and Stern, 1977), a four-month-old infant was observed with his mother in a standard face-to-face play paradigm, followed by an interaction between the infant and a stranger. Whereas the normative gaze pattern is a cyclical one with infant gazing at mother and gazing away, this infant briefly glanced at the mother only a few times at the beginning of the six-minute interaction; and the characteristic periods of long mutual gaze accompanied by positive affect were strikingly absent.

Instead, a pervasive quality of struggle, with mother "chasing" and infant "dodging," characterized much of the interaction. Repeated sequences were observed, in which, to every overture by the mother, the infant ducked, moved back, turned away, or pulled his hand out of her grasp. The infant appeared to exercise near "veto" power over his mother's efforts to engage him. He also systematically affected the mother's behavior: his avoidance maneuvers elicited further maternal "chase" movements, such as looming toward him, following the direction of his movement with her head and body, or pulling him toward her. The photographs in Figure 3 illustrate the "chase and dodge" sequence.

Associated with the infant's many avoidance maneuvers were fleeting but marked signs of negative affect by the mother. She grimaced, frowned, bit her lip, and thrust out her jaw. Toward the end of the interaction, the struggle was punctuated with brief periods of sudden total cessation of the infant's movement, when he went utter-

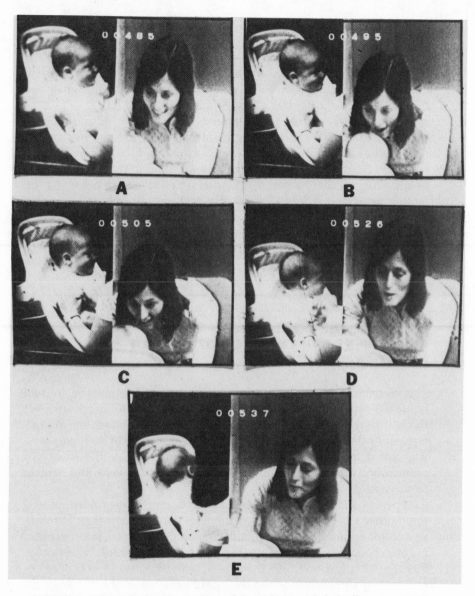

FIGURE 3. Photographic illustrations of the "chase and dodge" sequence. Numbers at the top of the photographs indicate frames (24 frames equal one second). Mother and infant are seated face to face. At point A, the infant is looking just slightly to the left of mother's face, and mother is smiling. At point B, .42 seconds later, mother "looms" in close to the infant's face, and she has a "mock surprise" expression. At point C, .42 seconds later, the infant has begun turning further away to his left, as mother completes the loom, with a smile. At point D, .87 seconds later, the infant moves still further away to his left, as mother begins to draw back, sobering. At point E, .46 seconds later, the infant completes a full 90° head turn away, while mother draws still further back, with a hint of a grimace.

ly limp (see Figure 1, "Inhibition of Responsivity.") Only at these moments could the mother lower her level of stimulation, when she briefly joined her infant in a limp, motionless head-hang.

Although the tenor of this interaction was one of mutual approach–withdrawal, or seemingly intrusive on the mother's part, nevertheless the mutual regulations documented that a sensitive relatedness continued. Each partner was sensitive to the other's movements, from moment to moment, with split-second latencies. As the mother approached and the infant withdrew, an ongoing complex compromise between engagement and disengagement was created. This interaction illustrates not an infant who "tunes out," but rather an aspect of the infant's range of "protodefensive" activity that could be characterized as continued responsivity and vigilance in the face of overstimulation.

WHAT ARE THE IMPLICATIONS OF DERAILMENT FOR THE ORGANIZATION OF INFANT EXPERIENCE?

This detailed interaction illustrates the possibility that the mutual influence aspect of the interaction may remain quite intact, and yet the pair may be "misattuned," or in an aversive interaction. *Relatedness* per se, that is, the sensitive mutual responsivity of both partners, was not disrupted in this interaction; rather it was the quality or attunement of the relatedness that was compromised and largely unsuccessful.

Whereas the infant's dodges and head aversions still influenced the mother's behavior, it was in the direction of *increasing* the intensity of her stimulation. The infant presumably learned to expect that his own behaviors "produced" the contingent maternal chase behaviors. Eventually he inhibited his own activity. Usually mothers decrease their stimulation when the infant looks away (Brazelton et al., 1974). Generally, infant gaze aversion decreases infant arousal (Field, 1981). In the "chase-and-dodge" pair, the infant used increasingly extreme and exaggerated aversions to accomplish a re-regulation. If infants characteristically must resort to increasingly severe and prolonged withdrawal states to regulate arousal, their attention and information-processing may be compromised. For example, extensive use of inhibition of responsivity may alter responsiveness to the environment, with consequences for later choice of defenses.

The range of infant responsivity documented in this interaction can be considered to be an aspect of the entire spectrum of interpersonal experiences available to the infant at this age, and the entire spectrum is presumably used in every relationship, with varying emphases (see Beebe and Stern, 1977). This spectrum ranges from encounters with sustained gaze and high positive affect, to milder positive affect and intermittant gaze, to negative expressiveness both gazing and gazing away, to increasingly extreme withdrawal maneuvers, to ultimately inhibition of responsivity, or a total breakdown of the interaction with severe infant crying (Beebe and Gerstman, 1980; Hirschfeld, 1985).

However, if the interaction structures documented in this interaction can be shown to be relatively characteristic of this pair's mode of interacting, they can provide us with a model of atypical and potentially pathological development. The infant's experience would then be organized by expectancies of misregulation. The easy balance between moments of engagement and moments of disengagement will be disturbed. The management of "being away from" will compromise the management of "being with." The infant's behavior continues to influence maternal behavior, but in the direction of increasing the intensity of stimulation, thus interfering with the infant's capacity to re-regulate arousal when he turns away. The infant comes to expect that he cannot benefit from his mother's participation in the management of his affect-arousal states.

If the interaction structures of derailment are characteristic, and hence expected, predictable, and generalized, they will organize infant experience and contribute to representations of self and object. We propose that what is represented is then the *interactive process* of mother "chasing" and infant "dodging" (see Beebe, 1985). The representations may include experiences of "self-as-moving-away-as-object moves in," or "I have to move so far away from you to calm down that I lose you." However conceptualized, these are representations of a delicately responsive interactive process.

DISCUSSION

"Dynamic interplay" and mutually influenced regulations as the substance of the representations are not usually underlined in discussions of self- and object-representations from a psychoanalytic point of view (see Fast, in preparation, as an exception). Rather than a self per se or an object per se, it may be more accurate to conceptualize representations in the purely social domain as interactive—actions-of-self-in-relation-to-actions-of-objects—in the precursors of representations (see Beebe and Stern, 1977; Stern, 1977; Beebe, 1985).

The implication of this interactive process model of representations is that the experiences of self and other are structured simultaneously. The origins of the representation of the self are inextricably linked to the representation of the other (see also Sullivan, 1953; Sander, 1977, 1983a,b; Stern, 1983; Atwood and Stolorow, 1984, who have expressed similar views).

The model of psychic structure formation underlying this discussion is that characteristic patterns of interactive regulation organize experience. Various infant researchers have proposed similar models (e.g., Sander, 1977, 1983a,b; Stern, 1977, 1983; Emde, 1981; Demos, 1984). For example, Sander (1976), using a biological systems model, proposed that the strategies which first characterize regulatory relationships with the interpersonal surround will come to function as features of the infant's regulation and will eventually characterize individual variations in the structure of the self.

A second model of structure formation is more prevalent in work on self psychology and is also used by some infant researchers. In this model, structure is accrued through efforts to resolve disruptions or breaches of expectancy in the interaction.

Although Kohut (1984) also noted the importance of successful mutual influence in self-regulation and psychic structure, he emphasized the second model of structure formation, that is, "disruption of regulation and repair." In his view, the infant gradually internalizes the psychic functions of the mother on those occasions when small, inevitable, phase-appropriate frustrations occur. He defines frustrations as empathic breaks and optimal frustration as inevitable minute fractions of empathic failures. That is, ". . . psychological structure is laid down (a) via optimal frustrations and (b) in consequences of optimal frustration, via transmuting internalization." (Kohut, 1984, pp. 98–99). Psychic structure is thus created when disruptions occur and the infant is able momentarily to take over functions of the parents.

Infant researchers Stechler and Kaplan (1980) also view self-development as a series of syntheses, active resolutions of crises that occur when expectancies about the relationship are violated. In this model of structure formation, the child's efforts to resolve "breaches" or "violations" by taking on aspects of the caretakers's functions result in the development of self-regulatory functions.

These two models both postulate that structure is acquired when a set of organizing principles become represented as the predictable "rules" of the relationship. However, they differ in that the first model emphasizes the *predictable* ways in which the dyad confirm expected interactions, whereas the second emphasizes the dyad's and the child's efforts to resolve mismatches and breaches of expectancy.

A combination of the two models yields a fuller picture of the complexity of the early organization of experience. Ruptures must be detected and evaluated within the context of ongoing expectable patterns of regulation. Any interactive system is never perfectly regulated, so that violations of expected patterns are inevitable. Thus, while structure can originate in the problematic moments of rupture, ongoing characteristic regulatory patterns must also be seen as powerful influences in structuring experience.

SUMMARY

Mother and infant generate ways of experiencing each other that become organized and represented. The organization of experience in the purely social, face-to-face exchanges in the first few months of life is viewed not primarily as the property of the individual, but as the property of the dyadic system. Various mutual influence structures of interaction in these social exchanges are described. These mutual influence structures are defined as interactions in which each partner systematically affects the behavior of the other; they include actions, perception, cognition, affect, and an associated proprioceptive experience for each partner.

Early mutual influence structures organize infant experience through expectancies, so that the recurrent, characteristic patterns which the infant recognizes, expects, and predicts, become generalized structures. The mutual interplay between infant and caretaker contribute to constructing "interactive representations." Empirical studies describing mutual influences in the matching of affect and timing between infant and caretaker provide each partner with a behavioral basis for knowing and entering into each other's perception, temporal world, and feeling state. The infant will represent the expectation of matching and being matched by the partner on a moment-to-moment basis. These matching experiences and their representation contribute to the experience of being attuned, known, tracked, or "on the same wavelength." An empirical study describing an interactive derailment illustrates that even in aversive interactions, mutual influence prevails. What the infant represents is a delicately responsive interactive process: actions-of-self-in-relation-to-actions-of-other. The implication of this interactive process model of representation is that the experiences of self and other in the purely social domain are structured simultaneously, and are inextricably linked.

This model of psychic structure formation—that characteristic patterns of interactive regulation organize experience—should be combined with the model that structure accrues through disruptions of regulation and their repair, in order to yield a fuller picture of the complexity of the early organization of experience.

REFERENCES

Alson, D. (1982). *Maternal Empathy in Relation to Infant Affective Engagement as Four Months*. Unpublished doctoral dissertation, Yeshiva University.

Anderson, B., Vietze, P., & Dokecki, P. (1977). Reciprocity in vocal interactions of mothers and infant. *Child Development*, 48:1676–1681.

Atwood, G. & Stolorow, R. (1984). *Structures of Subjectivity*. Hillsdale, NJ: The Analytic Press.

Basch, M. F. (1977). Developmental psychology and explanatory theory in psychoanalysis. *The Annual of Psychoanalysis*, 5:238–250.

Beebe, B. (1973). Ontogeny of positive affect in the third and fourth months of the life of one infant. Doctoral of Dissertation, Columbia University. *Dissertation Abstracts International*, 35(2), 1014B.

——— (1985). Mother-infant mutual influence and precursors of self and object representations. In J. Masling, ed., *Empirical Studies of Psychoanalytic Theories*. Vol. II. Hillsdale, NJ: Lawrence Erlbaum Associates.

——— & Crown, C. (in preparation), *Mutual Regulation of Engagement in Mother-Infant Face-to-Face Play*.

——— & Gerstman, L. (1980). The "packaging" of maternal stimulation in relation to infant facial-visual engagement. A case study at four months. *Merrill-Palmer Quarterly*, 26:321–339.

———, Jaffe, J., Feldstein, S., Mays, K., & Alson, D. (1985). Interpersonal timing: The application of an adult dialogue model to mother-infant vocal and kinesic interactions. In T. Field & N. Fox, eds., *Social Perception in Infants*. Norwood, NJ: Ablex.

——— & Kronen, J. (in preparation) *Mutual Regulation of Matching in Mother-Infant Face-to Face Play*.

——— & Stern, D. (1977). Engagement-disengagement and early object experiences. In N. Freedman & S. Grand, eds., *Communicative Structures and Psychic Structures*. New York: Plenum Press.

——— Stern, D. & Jaffe, J. (1979). The kinesic rhythm of mother-infant interactions. In A. W. Siegman & S. Felstein, eds., *Of Speech and Time: Temporal Patterns in Interpersonal Contexts*. Hillsdale, N.J.: Lawrence Erlbaum Associates.

Bell, R. Q. (1971). Stimulus control of parent or caretaker behavior by offspring. *Developmental Psychology*, 4:63–72.

Brazelton, T. B., Kowlowski, B., & Main, M. (1974). The origins of reciprocity. In M. Lewis & L. Rosenblum, eds., *The Effect of the Infant on Its Caregiver*. New York: Wiley-Interscience.

———, Tronick, E., Adamson, L., Als, H., & Wise, S. (1975). Early mother-infant reciprocity. In M. A. Hofer, ed., *The Parent-Infant Relationship*. New York: Elsevier.

Cappella, J. N. (1981). Mutual influence in expressive behavior: Adult and infant-adult dyadic interaction. *Psychological Bulletin*, 89:101–132.

Chappell, P. F., & Sander, L. W. (1979). Mutual regulation of the neonatal-maternal interactive process. In M. Bullova, ed., *Before Speech—The Beginning of Interpersonal Communication*. Cambridge: Cambridge University Press.

Church, J. (1961). *Language and the Discovery of Reality*. New York: Vintage Books.

DeCasper, A. & Carstens, A. (1980). Contingencies of stimulation: Effects on learning and emotion in neonates. *Infant Behavior and Development*, 4:19–36.

———— & Fifer, W. (1980). Of human bonding: Newborns prefer their mothers' voices. *Science*, 208:1174.

Demos, V. (1984). Empathy and affect: Reflections on infant experience. In J. Lichtenberg, M. Bonnstein, & D. Silver, eds., *Empathy*, Vol. II. Hillsdale, NJ: The Analytic Press.

Ekman, P. (1983). Autonomic nervous system activity distinguishes among emotions. *Science*, 221:1208–1210.

Elkisch, P. (1957). The psychological significance of the mirror. *Journal of the American Psychoanalytic Association*, 5:235–244.

Emde, R. (1981). The prerepresentational self and its affective core. *The Psychoanalytic Study of the Child*, 36, New Haven: Yale University Press, 165–192.

Erikson, E. (1950). *Childhood and Society*. New York: Norton.

Fast, I. (in preparation). *Body Image: An Alternative Perspective*. University of Michigan.

Feldstein, S., & Welkowitz, J. (1978). A chronography of conversation: In defense of an objective approach. In A. W. Siegman & S. Feldstein, eds., *Nonverbal Behavior and Communication*. Hillsdale, NJ: Lawrence Erlbaum Associates.

Field, T. (1981). Infant gaze aversion and heart rate during face-to-face interactions. *Infant Behavior and Development*, 4:307–315.

Gottman, J. (1981). *Time Series Analysis*. Cambridge: Cambridge University Press.

Hartmann, H. (1939). *Ego Psychology and the Problem of Adaptation*. New York: International Universities Press.

Hirschfeld, N. (1985). *Maternal intensity and infant disengagement in face-to-face play*. Unpublished doctoral dissertation, Yeshiva University.

Jacobson, E. (1964). *The Self and the Object World*. New York: International Universities Press.

Jaffe, J., & Feldstein, S. (1970). *Rhythms in Dialogue*. New York: Academic Press.

Jasnow, M. (1983). *Temporal Accommodation in Vocal Behavior in Mother-Infant Dyads*. Unpublished doctoral dissertation, George Washington University.

Kaye, K. (1977). Toward the origin of diaglogue. In H. R. Schaffer, ed., *Studies in Mother-Infant Interaction*, New York: Academic Press.

Kohut, H. (1984). *How Does Analysis Cure?* Chicago: University of Chicago Press.

Kronen, J. (1982). *Maternal Facial Mirroring at Four Months*. Unpublished doctoral dissertation, Yeshiva University.

Langhorst, B. & Fogel, A. (1982). Cross-validation of microanalytic approaches to face-to-face interaction. *International Conference on Infant Studies*, Austin, TX.

Lewis, M., & Brooks, J. (1975). Infant's social perception: A constructivist view. In L. Cohen & P. Salapatek, eds., *Infant Perception: From Sensation to Cognition* Vol. 2. New York: Academic Press.

————, & Goldberg, S. (1979). Perceptual-cognitive development in infancy: A generalized expectancy model as a function of the mother-infant interaction. *Merrill-Palmer Quarterly*, 15:81–100.

———— & Lee-Painter, S. (1974). An interactional approach to the mother-infant dyad. In M. Lewis & L. Rosenblum, eds., *The Effect of the Infant on Its Caregiver*. New York: Wiley.

Lichtenberg, J. D. (1983). *Psychoanalysis and Infant Research*. Hillsdale, NJ: The Analytic Press.

Mahler, M., Pine, F., & Bergman, A. (1975). *The Psychological Birth of the Human Infant*. New York: Basic Books.

Mays, K. (1984). *Temporal accommodation in mother-infant and stranger-infant kinesic interactions at four months*. Unpublished doctoral dissertation, Yeshiva University.

Papousek, H., & Papousek, M. (1979). Early ontogeny of human social interaction. In M. Von Cranach, K. Koppa, W. Lepenies, & P. Ploog, eds. *Human Ethology: Claims and Limits of a New Discipline*. Cambridge: Cambridge University Press.

Papousek, H., & Papousek, M. (1977). Mother and the cognitive head start. In H. R. Schaffer, ed., *Studies in Mother-Infant Interaction*. New York: Academic Press.

Peery, J. C. (1980). Neonate adult head movement. *Developmental Psychology*, 16(4):254–250.

Piaget, J. (1954). *The construction of reality in the child*. New York: Basic Books, 1937.

Rapaport, D. (1960). The structure of psychoanalytic theory. *Psychological Issues*, Monogr. 6. New York: International Universities Press.

Sander, L. W. (1983a). Polarity paradox, and the organizing process in development. In J. D. Call, E. Galenson, & R. Tyson, eds., *Frontiers of Infant Psychiatry*. New York: Basic Books.

———— (1983b). To begin with: Reflections on ontogeny. In J. Lichtenberg & S. Kaplan, eds., *Reflections on Self-Psychology*. Hillsdale, NJ: Analytic Press.

———— (1977). The regulation of exchange in the infant-caretaker system and some aspects of the context-content relationship. In M. Lewis & L. Rosenblum, Eds., *Interaction, Conversation, and the Development of Language*. New York: Wiley.

———— (1985). *Toward a logic of organization in psychological development*. In H. Klar & L. J. Siever, eds., *Biological Response Styles: Clinical Implications*. Washington, DC: American Psychiatric Press.

Schaffer, H. R., ed. (1977). *Studies in Mother-Infant Interaction*. New York: Academic Press.

Schaffer, H. R. (1979). Acquiring the concept of the dialogue. In M. Bornstein & W. Kessen, eds., *Psychological Development from Infancy*, New York: Wiley.

Schilder, P. (1964). *Contributions to Developmental Neuropsychiatry*, New York: International Universities Press.

Silverman, D. K. (1985). Som proposed modification of psychoanalytic theories of early childhood development. In J. Masling, Ed., *Empirical Studies of Psychoanalytic Theories*. Vol. II., Hillsdale, NJ: Lawrence Erlbaum Associates.

Spitz, R. (1959). *A Genetic Field Theory of Ego Formation: Its Implications for Pathology*. New York: International Universities Press.

Stechler, G., & Kaplan, S. (1980). The development of the self. *The Psychoanalytic Study of the Child*, 35. New Haven: Yale University Press.

Stern, D. (1971). A microanalysis of the mother-infant interaction. *Journal of the American Academy of Child Psychiatry*, 10:501–507.

———— (1977). *The First Relationship*. Cambridge, MA.: Harvard University Press.

———— (1983). The early development of schemas of self, of other, and of "self with other." In J. Lichtenberg & S. Kaplan, eds., *Reflections on Self Psychology*, Hillsdale, NJ: The Analytic Press.

———— (1974). Mother and infant at play: The dyadic interaction involving facial, vocal, and gaze behaviors. In M. Lewis & L. Rosemblum, eds., *The Effect of the Infant on Its Caregiver*. New York: Wiley.

————, Jaffe, J., Beebe, B., & Bennett, S. (1975). Vocalizing in unison and in alternation: Two modes of communication within the mother–infant dyad. *Annals of the New York Academy of Sciences*, 263:89–100.

————, Hofer, L., Haft, W., & Dore, J. (1985). Affect attunement: The sharing of feeling states between mother and infant by means of inter-modal fluency. In T. Field & N. Fox, eds., *Social Perception in Infants*. Norwood, NJ: Ablex.

Sullivan, H. S. (1953). *The Interpersonal Theory of Psychiatry*. New York: Norton.

Trevarthen, C. (1979). Communication and cooperation in early infancy. In M. Bullowa, ed., *Before Speech*. Cambridge: Cambridge University Press.

Tronick, E. (1982). Affectivity and sharing. In E. Tronick, ed., *Social Interchange in Infancy*. Baltimore: University Park Press.

————, Als, H., & Adamson, L. (1979). The communicative structure of early face-to-face interactions. In M. Bullowa, ed., *Before Speech*. Cambridge: Cambridge University Press.

————, Als, H., & Brazelton, T. (1980). Monadic phases: A structural descriptive analysis of infant-mother face-to-face interaction. *Merrill Palmer Quarterly*, 26:3–24.

Watson, J. (1985). Contingency perception in early social development. In T. Field & N. Fox, eds., *Social Perception in Infants*. Norwood, NJ: Ablex.

Werner, H. (1948). *Comparative Psychology of Mental Development*. New York: International Universities Press.

White, R. (1959). Motivation reconsidered: The concept of competence. *Psychological Review*, 66:297–333.

Winnicott, D. W. (1974). The mirror role of the mother and family in child development. *Playing and Reality*. Middlesex, Eng.: Penguin Books.

Chapter 2

Affect and the Development of the Self: A New Frontier

E. Virginia Demos

The central role of affect in development has increasingly captured the attention of researchers, theoreticians, and clinicians alike. Affect is thought to play an essential part in empathic exchanges, to be the primary medium of communication between infants and caregivers, and to remain an important nonverbal element in all communication throughout life. But what information is communicated by affects? Affective information is thought to be important because we assume it contains motivational information about the other person or about oneself. Thus, if we know what a person is feeling, we have information about the quality of his or her inner experience, whether it is intrinsically rewarding or punishing: the kinds of thoughts, intentions, fantasies, and memories likely to be associated with it; the kinds of behaviors likely to occur; and the kinds of defensive maneuvers likely to be adopted in order to avoid or to escape the experience. Affect, then, has both a communicative and a motivational function within the organism.

Much of the work on affect in infancy thus far has concentrated on the communicative importance of affective expressions. Attachment theorists, such as Bowlby (1969) and Ainsworth and Bell (1970), have emphasized the role of infant crying and smiling as built-in signals that promote physical closeness and bonding between infant and caregiver. Other researchers, who analyse the complex face-to-face exchanges between infants and mothers, have stressed the importance of the infant's affective signals in regulating the mother's behavior (Stern, 1974; Brazelton, Koslowski, and Main, 1974; Tronick, Als, and Brazelton, 1980; Fogel, 1982). My focus is primarily on the motivational function of affect for the developing infant. This focus neither ignores nor denies the importance of the interpersonal context in which the infant develops. Nor does it discount the importance of the communicative value of the infant's affective expressions for the caregiver, since these expressions provide information about the infant's state. But to focus on the motivational function of affect for the infant means to focus on the infant's experience of affective states, when alone and when in interaction with a caregiver, and to ask: How does the infant organize these experiences? What kinds of learning occur in relation to these states? And how does this learning gradually shape the infant's motivational stance toward the self, toward others, and toward the world?

I have called this focus on affect a new frontier because only in the last two decades have we possessed the conceptual and methodological tools to explore, analyze, and study affective phenomena in a systematic way. I refer here to the seminal work of Tomkins (1962, 1963). Building on Darwin's (1872) earlier work, Tomkins conceptualized affects as biologically inherited programs controlling facial muscle responses, autonomic, bloodflow, respiratory, and vocal responses. These correlated sets of responses define the number and specific types of primary affects. Tomkins presented evidence for nine primary affects and described the inherited set of patterned responses for each. Because the facial muscles in humans are more finely articulated and can change more rapidly than the correlated autonomic responses (three-tenths of a second versus one to two seconds), Tomkins argued that the face is the primary site of affect and takes the lead in establishing and creating an awareness of an affective state, with the other correlated responses coming into play more slowly. This theory is in opposition to the James-Lange (1890) theory of emotion adopted by many current cognitive theorists of emotion, who argue that one first becomes aware of a global visceral response, which, when given a cognitive interpretation or label, is then experienced as an affective state. Tomkins's theory has recently received some confirmation from neurological studies reported by Pribrim (1980), who states that the evidence from his laboratory indicates that the autonomic nervous system is involved in stabilizing emotional states, already set in motion. "James-Lange were correct in suggesting that visceral imput is important to emotion, but erroneous in the specific role they assigned it in the emotional process," (p. 225).

Tomkins's emphasis on the face was followed up by Ekman (1972, 1977) and Izard (1968, 1971) who independently explored the validity of the facial expression patterns described by Tomkins. Their work demonstrated that these expressions were produced, recognized, and given similar meanings in a wide range of Western and Non-Western cultures. This cross-cultural consensus supports the proposition that affects are biologically inherited responses, universally shared by all humans. Evidence from infant expressions, although still scanty, also supports this thesis. A number of infant researchers, such as Oster (1978), Izard, Huebner, Risser, McGinness, and Dougherty (1980), Field (1982), and Gaensbauer (1982), each using different experimental designs, have demonstrated that infant facial expressions are not random, but occur in the organized patterns designated by Tomkins, and that the specific affective expression displayed on the face is appropriate to the situation. For example, Gaensbauer reports that a fifteen-week-old girl, who had been physically abused by her father three weeks earlier, produced the facial expression of fear when approached by a male stranger, but not when approached by a female stranger. And Oster, examining the expressions of two infants from three to four weeks of life, reports organized, nonrandom sequences of smiling preceded by brow-knitting and prolonged gazing at the mother's face.

Both Ekman and Izard have produced detailed anatomically based, coding systems for analyzing facial muscle movements, which allow researchers to objectively and reliably score facial expressions. The procedure customarily involves coding the muscle movements in the three regions of the face separately—the upper face, with forehead and brows; the eyes, cheeks and nose; and the lower face, the mouth and chin—and then combining the codes into a composite score. This enables the researcher to distinguish between pure expressions and blends, for instance, anger components in the upper face, and distress components in the lower face, or vice versa. When the expressions are recorded on videotape or film, as opposed to still photographs, the coding is done in slow motion, and the onset time, duration at apex, and offset time of each movement is also noted. The availability of such a precise measuring tool, combined with the advances in video technology, opens the door to exploring the richness and complexities of affective expressions and by implication affective experience in a systematic way. The bulk of the work so far has focused on adult faces and the variety of ways that facial expressions are managed, controlled and falsified (Ekman and Friesen, 1969, 1974, 1975, 1978; Ekman, 1972, 1977). The work on infant faces has just begun, but it has already brought a new sophistication and precision in the handling of affective phenomena. For instance, the earlier studies of "fear of strangers" used global ratings and averaged responses over time. The presence or absence of fear was determined by whether or not the child cried at any time during the experimental procedure. By contrast, recent studies have recorded the sequence and details of the child's reactions, and report a variety of responses to strangers—ranging from smiling to crying and wariness, depending on a variety of contextual factors, such as the proximity of the mother, the speed of the stranger's approach, the child's familiarity with the room, previous experience with strangers, the age of the stranger, and so on. Indeed, there has been some questioning of the use of the word fear, since so little fear has actually been observed (see Lewis and Rosenblum, 1974, for a review of these studies). As this example illustrates, the more precise and sophisticated the methodology, the more complex our understanding of the phenomenon becomes.

The importance of the face for studying affect has always rested on the premise that the face was a valid indicator of an internal state, or as Tomkins has stated, was part of a set of correlated responses, including autonomic responses. Ekman, Levenson, and Friesen (1983) have recently reported evidence to confirm this part of Tomkins's theory. They demonstrated that by instructing subjects to contract their facial muscles in specific ways that replicated the universal emotion patterns, emotion-specific autonomic activity was produced, as measured by changes in heart rate, in right- and left-hand skin temperatures, and in skin resistance. Four negative emotions—disgust, anger, fear, and sadness—showed distinct autonomic patterns, which were different from the patterns of the positive emotions of happiness and surprise. These findings are of fundamental theoretical importance for they provide the first evidence for differential autonomic patterns among negative emotions, and for the correlation of these patterns, as well as the patterns for positive affects, with distinct facial expressions. The experiment also highlights the centrality of the face in this process as both Darwin and Tomkins have postulated. However, this leaves open the question of how these distinct correlated sets of responses relate to the subjective experience of emotion, or of what their function might be.

Darwin (1872), who focused on the expressive forms of emotion in animals and humans, argued that expressive components were selected for evolutionary survival because of their function as preparations for action. Thus, for example, the baring of teeth in primates, as an expression of anger, evolved becaused it prepared the animal to bite. Secondarily it came to serve a communicative function as a warning signal to an approaching animal. The facial expression of anger in humans is characterized by lowered and drawn-together brows, which creates vertical lines between the brows, by tensed upper and lower eyelids, so that the eyes have a hard stare and may take on a bulging appearance, and by open, tensed lips in a squarish shape, which bares the teeth, or by lips pressed tightly together with the corners straight or down, (Ekman and Friesen, 1975). This expression seems designed to focus the eyes intently on an object and to prepare the mouth for shouting or biting, or with lips pressed tightly together to contain the impulse to shout or bite. When we add the autonomic responses correlated with this expression, as reported by Ekman et al, and not known to Darwin, we find that when anger is on the face, the heart rate increases and the skin temperature rises. This correlated set of responses does indeed seem to prepare the organism to act!

Following Darwin's lead, Tomkins has asserted that the affect system is the primary motivational system in the personality, and has presented a model to explain how these inherited affect programs are activated, how the discrete affects relate to their activators, and how the correlated sets of responses, which are the affects, are experienced subjectively. His model is complex and densely argued, so I can present only a brief sketch of it here which may prove to be more confusing than clarifying. But the basic tenets of his theory are directly relevant to infant affect.

Tomkins postulates that affects function as abstract and general amplifiers of variants in the density of neural stimulation. There are three classes of variants: stimulation increases, that will activate surprise, fear, or interest depending on the suddenness of the increase; stimulation levels that remain at nonoptimally high levels, which will activate distress or anger depending on the level; and stimulation decreases, which will activate enjoyment. The affects evoked in this way act as amplifiers, generating by means of the correlated sets of facial muscle, autonomic, blood-flow, respiratory, and vocal responses an analogue of the gradient or intensity characteristics of the stimulus. Take anger, for instance, which is activated by any internal or external source of a continuing high, nonoptimal level of stimulation. The affect anger reproduces this nonoptimal level of stimulation by tensing the muscles in the brows, eyes, and mouth (as described earlier) and by increasing the heart rate, raising skin temperature, and forcing more air through the vocal cords. According to Tomkins (1980), the function of this simulation is to amplify, in a general and abstract way, the stimulus properties of the activator and to add a special analogic quality that is intensely punishing, as in anger, or intensely rewarding, as in positive affects. The biologic importance of this amplification through affect is to make the organism care about quite different kinds of events in different ways. Thus, "affect either makes good things better or bad things worse," (p. 148).

Affect, then, creates an urgency that is experienced as motivating and that primes the organism to act, but to act in a general, qualitative way, that is analogically similar to the triggering stimulus. In other words, there is a brief overlap in time so that the quality of the activator is imprinted onto the response. Thus "an excited response is accelerating in speed, whether in walking or talking," (Tomkins, 1981, p. 322). Or, to stay with the anger example, an angry response is intense and forceful. But this innate relationship between activator and response operates at an abstract and general level and has a very brief duration in time. Therefore, at the level of discrete behaviors or thought processes there are no innate responses to affect. One can learn a wide variety of discrete responses to a particular affective state. For example, when experiencing anger, one can learn to kick the nearest object, to yell, to count to ten or to bite one's knuckles, to plan revenge, or to never make contact again, to apologize or to make excuses, to condemn oneself or justify oneself, to minimize or deny the experience, or to maximize and dwell on it. Theoretically there is no limit to the kinds of behaviors, thoughts, and values that can be learned in response to a particular affect. Behaviors, however, that go against the innate analogic quality of the affect would be harder to learn, e.g., it would be harder to learn to relax the large striated muscles throughout the body as a response to anger.

Tomkins distinquishes between the affect per se and affect related information, such as the perceived activator of an affect, and the response to an affect, such as memories, plans, fantasies, perceptions and motor responses, that may or may not be co-assembled with the affect at any given moment. He refers to these co-assemblies as affect complexes or as ideoaffective organizations in which affect is seen as the core element in flexible and changing organizations of personality systems, for example, thinking, acting, and perceiving. Every affective complex, then, involves three components—first, the activator or triggering event; second, the affect per se, which consists of a correlated set of responses; and, third, the response to the affect, which includes both the recruitment in memory of past experiences and motor and cognitive responses. Each of these components has both innate and learned determinants, and thus each can be influenced and modified by experience. For example, the facial and vocal expressions of affect are managed and controlled according to social, cultural, and familial "display rules" that specify "who can show what emotion to whom, when," (Ekman and Friesen, 1969).

These various postulates have led Tomkins to conclude that discrete affects are present at birth, and that development consists of the gradual construction of affect complexes or of ideoaffective organizations. This view is in contrast to much current work on infant affect. Sroufe (1979) and Emde (1976, 1980), for example, both argue that affect expressions in early infancy represent precursors to affect, reflecting merely physiological tensions, and that only later, when the infant can become cognitively engaged with a stimulus, can one speak of psychophysiological tension and therefore of affect. And current psychoanalytic writers on affect, such as Brenner (1974, 1982) and Arlow (1977) argue that there are only global states of pleasure and unpleasure in the beginning, which gradually become differentiated into discrete affects as ideas become associated with experience. Tomkins is alone in asserting that affect and cognition can vary independently of each other, and that cognition need not be involved in activating or in prolonging an affective state. According to Tomkins, the cry of the hungry neonate and the smile of the cognitively engaged three-month-old are both manifestations of the same innate affect mechanism, which in the first instance is not coassembled with cognition and in the second instance is coassembled. The hungry, crying neonate, then, neither knows why she is crying nor that there is anything that can be done about it. The cry in this initial experience represents the innate affective response to distress that has been activated by a continuous level of nonoptimal stimulation, characteristic of hunger. The cry occurs in conjunction with a correlated set of facial muscle, bloodflow, autonomic, and respiratory responses, which, by acting together, will amplify the original stimulus characteristics and produce an inherently punishing experience for the infant. Over time, the neonate will gradually connect her experiences of this particular dysphoric state with a variety of causes and with a variety of consequences, and these ensuing affect complexes will gradually begin to guide her behavior.

What evidence do we have that the infant can perceive the general and abstract properties of stimuli, such as differing rates and intensities, that Tomkins has designated as the innate activators of affect? Recent work on infant perception seems to be converging on a relatively new view of the young infant's capacities—a view that contradicts earlier theories, such as Piaget's for example, which argued that the infant began with specific perceptions in each sensory modality and gradually built up schemas of the general properties of stimuli that cut across sensory modes. Bower (1982) has argued that the newborn lives in a world as close to pure perception as is possible. He describes the infant as responding to abstract forms of stimulation, such as rates of change, and not to patterns of stimulation, and as operating with high-order variables, such as intensities and rates that cut across sensory modalities and not with specific sensory variables. Spelke (1976, 1979), following Gibson's (1969) idea that perception is organized so as to detect invariants in stimulation, has demonstrated that infants can recognize the common temporal structure present in auditory and visual events, and will match a sound track to the appropriate film on the basis of temporal synchrony. And Stern (1983) has integrated research findings from a variety of infant studies that demonstrate the young infant's ability to match general characteristics of stimuli, such as shape, intensity levels, rhythms, and rising and falling contours, across sensory modalities. For example, infants can visually recognize the shape of an object that they have previously only explored with their mouth and tongue (Meltzoff and Borton, 1979), and they can match the intensity of a sound with the intensity of a light (Lewkowicz and Turkewitz, 1980). On the basis of these data Stern argues that the salient perceptual phenomena are largely prestructured, and thus do not have to be learned bit by bit.

These recent developments in infant perception are congruent with each other and present a picture of the young infant as a highly competent perceiver, able to operate across sensory modalities and to abstract from stimulus events their general properties. Such a view of the infant fits well with Tomkins's propositions concerning the innate activation of affect.

This convergence of the infant's perceptual capabilities with Tomkins's model of affect, as well as the evidence mentioned earlier regarding the organization of the infant's facial expressions, allows us to take neonatal affect seriously. We must, then, begin to accept the possibility that the young infant is capable of experiencing the full range of primary affects, and that this experience is real and meaningful, in the sense that the discrete affective quality of each negative affect will be experienced as uniquely punishing, and the distinctive qualities of each positive affect will be experienced as uniquely rewarding, and that each of these states will prime the infant to respond in a corresponding manner. For example, the interested baby will focus its eyes intently on a stimulus, holding its limbs relatively quiet, and will tend to scan the stimulus for novelty (Wolff, 1965; Stechler and Carpenter, 1967). The joyful baby will smile and tend to produce relaxed, relatively smooth movements of its limbs, savoring the familiar, (Tomkins, 1962; Brazelton et al., 1974). The angry baby will square its mouth, lower and pull its brows together, cry intensely, holding the cry for a long time, then pause for a long inspiration, and will tend to kick and thrash its limbs forcefully, perhaps even struggling against a caregiver, (Tomkins, 1962; Demos, 1986). By contrast, a distressed infant will produce a more rhythmical cry, with the corners of the mouth pulled down and the inner corners of the brows drawn up, and will tend to move its limbs and head around restlessly (Tomkins, 1962; Wolff, 1969). Thus the discrete characteristics of each affect are important aspects of the infant's early experience because they create discrete motivational dispositions in the infant and therefore become occasions for learning. With such a formulation, one can begin to explore the question of what kinds of learning become associated with each affect.

The intensity dimension of each affect is also an important aspect of the infant's early experience, for it also has a motivational impact on the infant and thus is likely to affect the kinds of learning that can occur. For example, an experience of distress or anger that combines intensity with duration, thereby producing a high density of negative affect, can cause the infant to retreat or to avoid similar experiences in the future, either by overcontrolling the expression of distress or anger in order to prevent another punishing escalation, or by constricting activities to avoid the eliciting stimulus or situation. In either case, the infant is unable to remain in the situation and develop adaptive skills or strategies for dealing with the causes of the distress or anger. At the other extreme, if the infant's experiences of affect are too mild or brief, then the infant's motivation to act will be diminished and opportunities to develop adaptive responses will not occur.

In a model such as Tomkins's, where affect is seen as an adaptive biological system, it is assumed that the occurrence of negative affect is inevitable and unavoidable. The task for the organism then becomes one of learning how to modulate, endure, and tolerate such experiences in order to benefit from the adaptive function of affect. This, in the case of negative affect, is to create a punishing, urgent state that will focus the organism to do something about the situation. Thus, the organism must learn how to keep negative affects within some optimal range of density that still contains sufficient information but allows the organism to remain in the situation and to develop or produce adaptive responses. Neonates possess some capacity to modulate their negative affective states at a low level of intensity, but as the intensity level rises they tend to continue to escalate, in a positive feedback loop that can lead from distress, to intense distress, to anger. Infants are therefore dependent on caregivers to modulate, soothe, and maintain them at more moderate or optimal density levels. I have focused here on the intensity of negative affects because the experience of intense positive affects is not innately punishing, although one can learn to feel distress, anxiety or shame, for instance, about one's excitement and joy.

Tomkins's model, then, focuses our attention on how the neonate experiences affective states, on what learning occurs at such times, on what capacities for self-regulation the infant possesses, and on what capacities the caregiving system possesses for helping the infant to maintain herself at optimal levels of affective intensity or for providing opportunities for the infant to maintain herself at such levels.

The centrality of state and state organization in early infancy has also been articulated by researchers, most notably by Sander (1969) and Wolff (1973), who have been interested in finding constructs that supercede the old nature-nurture dichotomy and that shed light on the complex connections between the biological level and the psychological level. In their formulations "state" is defined as any well-defined organizational coherence within the organism that can be recognized when it recurs. Most attention has been paid to the cyclical states along the sleep-awake continuum, which have been given descriptive labels—regular sleep, irregular sleep, drowsiness, alert inactivity, waking activity, alert activity, and crying. Wolff (1973) has emphasized that states are not merely behavior patterns in the usual sense, but represent organizational frameworks, or unities, that determine how the infant will respond. Thus, for example, a jar to the crib will evoke a massive startle during regular sleep, but has no effect during irregular sleep or waking.

Sander's (1969) data have demonstrated the recurrence of organized states within the infant in a context of recurrent interactions of regulative exchanges with the caregiver, and the sensitivity of the infant's regulation of sleep and wake states to even small changes in that context. Sander (1982) argues that the infant's experience of her own recurrent states represent the focal points around which the infant's inner awareness or consciousness consolidates. Sander goes on to say:

A capacity for inner experience exists at the outset of postnatal life—as an initial level in the organization of consciousness. This initial root of the sense of self does not await the organization of a body image or depend on production effects, or on visual or tactile experience, or the double-tactile experience that through touch begins the differentiation of self and other. The ego begins as a 'state' ego, rather than a body ego [p. 20].

It follows, then, that "the organization of state governs the quality of inner experience" (1985, p. 16).

This is a very important statement that forces us to reorient our thinking about early infancy. It is a proposition that I find both convincing and clarifying. But Sander is referring to recurring states along the sleep–awake continuum and differentiates between the initial interactive regulation of these states and emotions, which are thought to emerge gradually and then become included in a broader pattern of regulatory transactions involving states and emotions. In the light of Tomkins's theory, I would like to suggest a small modification of Sander's proposition to include the statement that the initial states of the neonate are affective states. I am claiming that there is no distinction between the awake states as described in the literature and affective states. Let us look closely at the descriptions of the awake states and compare them with descriptions of affective states, keeping in mind that the descriptions of awake states are somewhat global by current standards of precision used in describing facial expressions of affect.

In the state of alert inactivity the limbs and trunk are at rest, the face is relaxed, the eyes are open and have a "bright shining appearance." The eyes move together and are coordinated with head movements in order to maintain visual contact with an object. (Descriptions are taken from Wolff, 1973.) Please note the similarities between the relaxed face and open, bright, shining eyes of alert inactivity and Izard's (1979) description of the facial indicators of the affect interest: brows raised or knit, eyes widened and rounded, cheeks raised, mouth relaxed or may be opened. The absence of brow information in the Wolff description is probably due to the fact that the eyebrows of many Caucasian infants are very fair, making it difficult to see changes in brow position, unless one is alerted to their importance. Also, in low level interest, the brows may remain relaxed. The difference between "eyes widened and rounded" and bright shining eyes is the difference between using codes based on muscle actions that change the eyes, rather than using subjective discriptors. Langsdorf et al. (1983) report that for two- to eight-month-old infants the duration of facial indicators of interest was the most significant predictor of total fixation time on a stimulus. The restricted limb movement is not included in the facial description, but it is often reported along with an alert, focused expression by researchers of early infant attention (e.g., Stechler and Carpenter, 1967).

I would therefore maintain that what has been called alert inactivity or infant attention is in fact the affective state of interest, and that this state produces, at least in the early weeks of life, a quieting of the body and a visual fixation on a stimulus. Initially these states are brief and are easily disrupted by competing stimuli, such as motor activity. Nevertheless, they represent coherent, organized experiences, which can be extended by presenting the infant with interesting objects, and which, over time, increase in their duration (Wolff, 1969; Carpenter, Tecci, Stechler, & Friedman, 1969). Wolff (1973) reports that during the first month this state accounts for 50 percent of waking time.

Alert activity, a state not seen in the neonate but which occurs by the end of the second week, is similar to alert inactivity, except that the infant can now do two things at the same time. Thus the relaxed face and bright eyes, visually pursuing objects are now combined with controlled rhythmical motor actions, such as nutritive sucking. This waking state, then, is also a manifestation of the affect interest that is coordinated with other motor patterns.

Waking activity is characterized by frequent bursts of diffuse motor activity, involving limbs, trunk and head, of varying intensity and duration. There may be moans, grunts, whimpers, or brief cry vocalizations. The face may be relaxed or pinched in a "precry face." The eyes are open, but do not have a bright shining appearance. The skin may become flushed during motor activity, and respirations are grossly irregular. This description contains many different elements, including a variety of affect components. For example, the vocalizations are those generally associated with mild distress. And the pinched, precry face could be accounted for by a variety of facial movements associated with disgust, distress, or anger, such as a nose wrinkle and upper lip rise with brows drawn down and together, or loose trembling lips and brows drawn together with inner corners raised. And diffuse motor activity is often associated with either distress or anger depending on its intensity and duration. But this description is merely a list of behaviors and does not make clear whether or how these components are combined in recurrent, organized patterns. Thus this category may represent a lack of organization or coherence, and may not be experienced by the infant as a recurrent, recognizable state. Or, if behavioral elements were combined in particular patterns, it could represent several different states, such as a mild state of disgust, or of distress, or a blend of disgust and anger, or disgust and distress, or of distress and anger. Wolff (1973) reports that waking activity is highest in the first week of life and decreases sharply after that, becoming negligible by the sixth week.

The waking state of crying is defined by the presence of cry vocalizations. These are accompanied either by diffuse motor activity or by a rigid posture of the trunk in partial extension. The face is contracted into "the cry grimace" and is flushed red. The eyes may be partially opened or tightly closed. Here again, we have a description that contains many affect elements that are characteristic of more than one affective state. For example, diffuse motor activity is most associated with distress, whereas a rigid posture with an extended trunk, for example, arching the back, is associated with anger. And crying, as a defining term, is much too global, since there is more than one kind of crying.

The few studies that have focused on normal infant crying have reported two distinct patterns of crying produced by the neonate (Wolff, 1969; Wasz-Hockert, Lind, Vuorenkoski, Partanen, and Valanne, 1968). There is a rhythmical cry, with a modal unit consisting of a cry, .62 seconds; a rest, .09 seconds; an inspiration, .04 seconds; and a rest, .19 seconds. It has a rise–fall tonal pattern with frequencies ranging from 350 to 470 Hz. This cry has been given several labels—a hunger cry, a basic cry, and, at higher intensities, a mad cry. The other distinct pattern of crying consists of a long initial cry, which lasts from 2.6 to 4.2 seconds. This cry has a sudden onset and is followed by seven seconds of breath holding, then a brief respiration and rest. This has been called a pain cry; a variant on this pattern that includes the long cry but no breath holding has been called a "protest" cry. In a recent attempt to come to some overall classification of crying, Lester and Zeskind (1982) suggested that since some differences in the structure of the cry seem to be related to the intensity of the stimulus, perhaps the different patterns could be ordered along a single dimension of intensity. As I stated earlier, Tomkins too argues that different intensities of nonoptimal stimulation will evoke different patterns of response, but for Tomkins these differences represent a discontinuous change from distress-anguish at the lower levels to anger-rage at the higher levels. This differentiation should be evident on the face, as well as in the structure of the cry, but none of the studies of crying attended to the facial expressions of the infants.

I have reported elsewhere (Demos, 1986) on the expressive behavior of a nine-day-old infant during her bath. Both the vocal and facial expressions were recorded and examined. During a seven-minute episode, the infant's crying alternated between bouts of intense rhythmical crying and bouts of loud, long cries followed by three to five seconds of breath holding. Her facial expressions also alternated between a distress face, with oblique brows and the corners of the mouth turned down, which was correlated with the rhythmical crying, and an anger expression, with the brows pulled down and together, the mouth tensed and square-shaped, and a flushed face, which was correlated with the long cry and breath holding. Her eyes were closed throughout both patterns of expression. This is data on only one baby, and clearly we need more data on neonatal crying where both the cry and the face are recorded. Nevertheless, these correlated patterns of responses indicate a qualitative shift in affective state between distress and anger. The waking state that has been categorized as crying then probably contains at least two distinct states of distress and anger, as well as various blends of the two. The description of the face as contracted into "the cry grimace" is not precise enough to help us sort out whether this change in the face is an indication of distress or anger or a blend of the two.

This detailed comparison of the descriptions of waking states with current facial descriptions of affect and other indicators of affect has been instructive on several counts. First of all, it has highlighted the differences in the level of precision between the two descriptions. And these differences make it difficult to achieve an exact match between the waking states and affect states. Yet if we are going to take seriously the proposition that the ego begins as a state ego, then we must be able to demonstrate that these early states are in fact coherent, organized unities, around which inner awareness can begin to consolidate. And in order to do that, we need precise measures of the infant's behaviors and combinations of behaviors. When we attempted to apply the most precise measures we currently have of facial behaviors, vocal behaviors, and motor behaviors, we discovered that two of the waking states, namely, alert inactivity and alert activity, appeared to be organized unities that fit current descriptions of the affective state of interest. But the categories of "waking activity" and "crying" did not appear to be coherent unities and seemed to contain components of two or more affective states. More precise data are needed to determine what and how many waking states there are. For instance, none of the waking-state descriptions included infant smiling. Yet Wolff (1963) reports both spontaneous and elicited smiling in the first week of life. And examiners trained to use Brazelton's neonatal scale, which is designed to assess the infant's organizational capacities by determining the degree of facilitation necessary to produce an optimal performance from the infant, report that smiling can be elicited from some neonates when alert and held in an *en face* position (Madansky, 1981 personal communication).

Second, I would like to underscore the observation that most of the behaviors included in the descriptions of these early states are behavioral components of affect expressions. Descriptions of facial and vocal behaviors, although imprecise, were always included, as well as motor behaviors commonly associated with affective states in older infants. The details of these affective patterns in early infancy are therefore not trivial; their presence strongly suggests the presence of affective states. The ultimate validity of such a claim awaits evidence that would include detailed data, simultaneously recorded, on the neonate's facial movements, vocalizations, motor behaviors, heart rate, skin temperature, and respiration. This would allow us to determine the presence or absence of coherent unities. In the absence of these ideal data, the incomplete data we have so far are highly compatible with the descriptions of the correlated sets of responses related to affect. The facial components of interest, combined with a cessation of limb movements and the visual pursuit of objects, have been reported by several researchers already mentioned. The correlation between two distinct crying patterns and two distinct facial expressions that indicate a state of distress alternating with a state of anger has been observed for at least one infant. And we have a growing body of data on early infant facial expressions that are consistent and confirm that all the facial components of affect are present on the young infant's face and that these components are structured into the innate affect patterns (e.g., Ekman, 1982; Oster and Ekman, 1978; Field, 1982). Not only is this evidence compatible with the assumption that neonates are experiencing affective states, but to the best of my knowledge, there is no evidence from early infancy studies that is incompatible with such an assumption.

The third point: Even though these waking state descriptions are comprised primarily of affect components, none of the researchers utilizing these categories has made an affective interpretation of their meaning. We are willing to grant that an older child's or an adult's facial expressions and vocalizations are indications of an internal affective state. And since Ekman et al.'s recent experiment correlating specific facial expressions with specific autonomic patterns, we now have scientific justification for doing so. But when a young infant displays an identical set of behaviors (for instance, cries intensely with a flushed face and a tensed, extended torso), we are reluctant to call it affect. The infant is certainly experiencing something at such moments, and it is not a big inferential leap to assume that the experience is negative and punishing. These behaviors are labeled simply "crying." What prevents us from calling this state anger or distress?

I believe we are dealing here with a strong cognitive bias. It seems extremely difficult to acknowledge there can be affective experience independent of any learning or interpretive activity, in other words, independent of any cognitive imput. Here it is useful to remember Tomkins's distinction between affect per se and affect-related information, such as information about the causes and consequences, which may or may not be coassembled with the affect at any given moment. The newborn infant does not have any affect-related information to draw on—no memories of prior experiences, no expectations of what is likely to happen next. But the young infant does have organized patterns of facial expressions, and structured vocal expressions, and perhaps correlated autonomic patterns as well. The young infant's experience of affect, therefore, is as close to a pure experience as is possible. The neonate can neither know why he or she is experiencing this correlated set of responses that is affect, nor anticipate what will happen because of it. This initial period of purity and innocence is probably relatively brief. For, if the infant's affective states are sufficiently intense and coherent to enter the infant's awareness, and if they recur frequently, the infant will quickly begin to make connections between the affective state and its antecedents and consequences. How quickly the infant does this, and how many repeated experiences it will take, at what intensities, and with what causes and consequences are all questions to be explored. It is interesting to note in this context that DeCasper and Carstens (1981) have demonstrated that three-day-old infants perceived the contingent relationship between their behavior and the experimental stimulus and learned to space their sucking bursts in order to turn on the singing of a female voice. Thus the young infant's capacity to make connections between events on the basis of contingency is probably operating much earlier than has previously been imagined.

Here I would like to assume at least a provisional acceptance of the idea of neonatal affect, so that I can begin to discuss the implications for self-development. We must return to Sander's (1982) proposition that the ego begins as a state ego. That proposition now contains the amendment that these initial states involving awareness are affect states, and we now follow Sander's reasoning about the laws of organization that govern the infant and the infant–mother systems. For I believe that if we can combine what we know about affect with Sander's propositions about system organizations, we will have the ingredients of a new formulation regarding the early beginnings of psychological organization.

Sander's (1982) second proposition maintains "that the infant's own states, where coherent, recurrent, desired, or essential to key regulatory coordinations that become established with the caregiver, become the primary target or *goals* for behavior" (p. 16). This proposition fits remarkably well with Tomkins's (1981) statements regarding affect dynamics.

> In the case of the human being, the fact that he is innately endowed with positive and negative affects which are inherently rewarding or punishing, and the fact that he is innately endowed with a mechanism

which automatically registers all his conscious experience in memory, and the fact that he is innately endowed with receptor, motor, and analyzer mechanisms organized as a feedback circuit, together make it all but inevitable that he will develop the following General Images: (1) Positive affect should be maximized; (2) Negative affect should be minimized; (3) Affect inhibition should be minimized; (4) Power to maximize positive affect, to minimize negative affect, to minimize affect inhibition should be maximized [p. 328].

Thus the infant quickly becomes engaged in trying to bring about and prolong interesting and enjoyable states and in trying to modulate or avoid negative states, such as distress, anger, fear, or disgust. These early efforts are difficult to observe because the young infant has relatively few instrumental behaviors on which to draw. Gazing, head turning, and sucking are a few behaviors that can be regulated and used instrumentally by the young infant. For example, Kaplan and I (1987) have reported elsewhere on two infant girls whom we videotaped in their family settings every two weeks during the first year. At roughly five and a half weeks of age, each baby when left alone briefly was observed to regulate her gazing behavior in order to modulate mild fussiness. The following sequence occurred. As fussy vocalizations began and as arms and legs began to cycle, each baby began to move her head from side to side and started to scan the environment. They each found an object, visually focused on it, became motorically and vocally quiet, and continued to gaze for several minutes. Then they would look away, the fussiness would begin to build up again, and they would return their gaze to the object, once again becoming focused and quiet. This cycle was repeated several times before the mothers returned and intervened.

We are assuming that although the initial scanning may have been unmotivated and part of the fussy movements and thus the first encounter with the object may have been accidental, the subsequent refocusing on the same object looked like an active attempt by each infant to repeat a successful organizing experience. In other words, the infants were motivated to recapture the affective experience of interest with its organizing potential, which felt more rewarding than the unfocused fussy state. This formulation is similar to Piaget's (1952) description of a primary circular reaction, whereby an accidental action leads to a consequence and the infant then repeats the action in order to repeat the consequence. In this formulation, however, the goal or consequence the infant is trying to achieve involves the repetition of an internal affective state, rather than of an external event.

One of the infant girls developed two new instrumental behaviors at roughly three to three and a half months of age; the other one did not. This brings us to Sander's (1982) third proposition, which focuses on the role of the caregiver environment in fostering the infant's self-regulatory capacities.

> The third proposition, then, is that infant competence in initiating and organizing self-regulatory behaviors to achieve desired states as goals represents a *systems* competence, i.e., dependent on facilitation of goal realization as well as providing conditions for the infant's initiation of goal-organized behavior. Such systems competence insures a sense of agency in the infant. The emergence of infant-as-agent must be *granted by the system* because it means a reorganization of the system to admit the newcomer. If the system is such that it can permit the entrance of a new agent within it, it provides the conditions which establish not only the capacity for self-awareness, but conditions which insure the *use* of such inner awareness by the infant as a frame of reference in organizing his own adaptive behavior, i.e., being in a position that permits him to appreciate what behaviors lead to what states. The valence of this inner experience under these conditions of self-initiated goal realization will be felt as the infant's "own" [Sander, 1982, p. 17].

The dynamic implications of this proposition can be illustrated by drawing on the affective experiences of these two infant girls. We have called them Cathy and Donna (Demos and Kaplan, 1987). Both were born to professional parents and into families who had looked forward to their coming and were ready to care for them. Let us begin with the positive affects of interest and enjoyment and compare the experiences of these two infants.

By our second visit, when Cathy was 3½ weeks of age, her mother exhibited two behaviors that were to form a standard part of her interactive style throughout the first year. Whenever Cathy would gaze intently at her mother's face, without smiling, the mother would interpret this quiet, focused interest as boredom. She would then pull her own face back, out of Cathy's visual range, and jiggle a toy in front of Cathy's eyes. Also, whenever Cathy's older brother was around, the mother would turn away from Cathy and focus her attention on him, even though this often meant interrupting or foreshortening an exchange with Cathy. Cathy would begin each new exchange with her mother in a moderately intense state of interest and enjoyment. Then, as her mother turned away either to substitute a toy for her face or to attend to her son the animation on Cathy's face would fade as she looked at the toy with only mild interest, or looked away with a somewhat blank expression.

Cathy is learning several things in these exchanges. First, she is learning that her own states of interest and enjoyment do not last long. Second, she is learning that she has no control over initiating, prolonging, or ending such experiences; thus she cannot experience her self as an active agent. Third, she is learning that she is not the source of interesting and enjoyable events, that is, that she is not an interesting or enjoyable partner or that her self is not interesting and enjoyable. By two and a half months, she seemed to have developed the expectation that positive affect does not last long, and she made her own contribution to the interactive pattern by initiating the turning away in face-to-face exchanges with her mother. Initially this pattern of brief, low intensity exchanges occurred only between Cathy and her mother, and Cathy could enjoy more extended social exchanges with her father, brother, and visitors. But mother was the most frequent partner, and gradually, over time, the foreshortened, low-intensity exchange became characteristic of Cathy across many settings.

By three and a half months and continuing well into her seventh month, Cathy was relatively immobile, with only brief moments of enjoyment interspersed with longer periods of staring into space. Her play with toys was characteristically languid, suggesting only mild to moderate interest, and her explorations were dominated by sucking, with little elaboration of other behaviors. We view the prominence of sucking behavior at this stage of development not as a response to an oral drive, but as an indication of a failure of the caregiving system to facilitate both the acquisition of a repertoire of exploratory behaviors and Cathy's capacity to sustain her interest in people and toys. Cathy remained responsive to the social initiatives of others, but she rarely initiated such exchanges and did not protest their cessation. She had become a passive observer of events around her, a stance sometimes modeled by her mother, who would manifest a palms up, shoulder shrug, a "What can you do?" response, or she would say, "We've been left again," when Cathy's brother or father left the room. Thus the lessons of the early months continued to be reiterated, and Cathy continued to experience only brief, low-intensity states of interest and enjoyment, and continued to experience herself as not an effective agent in initiating or prolonging interesting events, and as not the source of such events. She required the active, vigorous stimulation provided by father, brother, or visitors as the necessary prelude to the mobilization of her interest and enjoyment.

An advance in Cathy's gross motor capabilities in her eighth and ninth months had a moderately invigorating impact on her capacity to pursue interests in the world around her. As she began to experience herself as an effective agent in this realm, she became somewhat

more active and took more initiative in seeking out toys to interest her
and "problems" to solve. These new behaviors engaged the mother's
interest and responsivity, and she showed her most consistent efforts
to engage Cathy. However, little sustained reciprocal interaction occurred, as if mother were now trying hard but Cathy was relatively
unavailable. Cathy remained more absorbed in her toys. George
Klein (1976) has described the "I" and "we" aspects of the self, and
here we see Cathy preferring "I" activities, where she had some
control over events, to "we" experiences, which placed her in a passive position.

Let's shift our focus now to Donna, who was not a particularly
"smiley" baby in the beginning, but who displayed a capacity for
long periods of focused, intent gazing at her mother's face. Her mother consistently facilitated this display of interest as she maintained
and prolonged *en face* interactions by providing Donna with an ever-
changing array of facial, vocal, and cutaneous stimulation, and allowed Donna to terminate these exchanges. The mother's capacity to
allow her daughter to be the active agent made it possible for Donna
to learn that, first, her states of interest and enjoyment could be
prolonged and intensified and thus she could become aware of their
intrinsically rewarding quality. Second, she was learning that her
own behaviors were effective in bringing these experiences about.
Third, she was learning that she could be the source of interesting
and enjoyable events.

Throughout the first year, the mother continued to facilitate Donna's efforts to pursue and sustain her interests and enjoyments, and
thus the lessons of the early months were continually reiterated. Donna was active and intensely involved in whatever she was doing. By
three and a half months, Donna and her mother enjoyed prolonged
social exchanges and had developed a rich variety of ways of being
together that involve a range of intensities of interest and enjoyment.
Her mother also facilitated Donna's engagement with toys by participating in the play, elaborating the possibilities inherent in the
toys, and contributing her own enthusiasm to these activities. In this
context, Donna's play with toys was characterized by sustained, intense interest and enjoyment, and by a variety of actions, e.g., bang-
ing, moving back and forth, dropping, picking up, shaking, and so
on. It is noteworthy that during this same period, and in contrast to
Cathy, Donna showed a paucity of sucking and mouthing behaviors.
Also in contrast to Cathy, Donna showed a more balanced engagement in both "I" and "we" activities, and because of her high affective investment in these activities, she was able to persist in her
efforts and to protest when her efforts failed. We witnessed an explo-

sion of riches in a positive feedback loop as Donna's manifest ability to succeed at a variety of tasks served to maintain her interest and enjoyment at a high level of intensity and to provide her with the significant message that she can make things happen.

In the later months we saw more evidence of Donna's taking the initiative to do just that; she was indeed making life more interesting and enjoyable. Between ten and half and twelve months Donna showed intense excitement and joy in the outdoor baby pool, as she was able to generate novelty and play for as long as fifteen minutes. At twelve and a half months Donna persisted in trying to climb up the steps of a small ladder chair. Once she succeeded, she repeated the climb over and over again, and each time she reached the top, she paused and sang a song of joy. There was no exhibitionistic quality in her behavior or her posture; she did not look around at her mother or the camera person for acknowledgment or approval. She appeared to be totally absorbed in her own activity and sang in order to prolong and magnify the joy of it all. Tomkins (1983, personal communication) referred to this phenomenon as "a celebration of positive affect," a phrase that aptly captures the spirit of Donna's singing.

A comparison of these two babies reveals striking differences in their experiences of themselves as active agents, and as the sources of interest and enjoyment, as well as in their experiences of all three components of the affect complexes involving interest and enjoyment. Because of Donna's greater sense of agency and her greater embodiment or ownership of rewarding experiences, many more objects and events were interesting and enjoyable for Donna than for Cathy. Donna's experience of these positive affects was more varied, more intense, and more prolonged than was Cathy's, and Donna developed a larger repertoire of behaviors and more elaborate strategies than did Cathy for prolonging and creating interesting, enjoyable experiences. Donna's experience of "I" and "we" activities was also more balanced than was Cathy's. Thus Donna was continually able to expand her experience of her self as competent and effective in prolonging rewarding experiences and in developing instrumental skills.

Let us turn briefly now to the experiences of distress, anger, and fear for these two infants. (See Demos, 1986, and Demos and Kaplan, 1987, for a more detailed presentation of the negative affects.) From the very beginning Cathy was not allowed to build up to even a mild level of distress or anger. At the first sign of restlessness or mild vocal fussing, the mother would pick Cathy up and nurse her. During the first five and a half months of our observations of this family, we never saw or heard Cathy cry. This absence of observed crying was not an artifact of our visits. At a two-and-a-half month visit, when the mother joined the observers in watching Cathy sleep, the mother expressed surprise in seeing Cathy wake with mild fussing, look around, and eventually fall back to sleep. She commented then that perhaps she had never given Cathy an opportunity to engage in this kind of self-regulation. This moment of self-reflection offers a plausable summary of the mother's basic stance toward her baby—she saw herself primarily as a soother and comforter.

Because of her mother's early interventions, there were very few experiences of even moderate distress or anger for Cathy. Thus her capacity to become aware of her internal states of distress and anger and to use their punishing quality as a guide for behavior, in terms of experiencing the need to do something about them, was being short-circuited. This left Cathy with little motivation and few opportunities to make a connection between a felt need and the remedy offered and few moments to experience herself as an active agent in bringing about the remedy. And the mother's continued interventions also prevented Cathy from developing any instrumental behaviors for soothing herself.

Throughout the first year, Cathy was unable to sleep through the night and from roughly eight months on was unable to fall asleep without being nursed. We interpret this as a failure in the caregiving system to encourage and allow opportunities for self-regulation. The mother acknowledged that she could not give up these middle-of-the-night feedings. "These are the loveliest moments we have together. I just adore it when we are in bed together and I am nursing her. It is idyllic." The mother felt most attuned to Cathy and most confident of her own caregiving abilities while nursing or soothing her baby. She had few strategies that fell outside these behaviors. Thus in the latter part of the first year, as Cathy began to experience fear in relation to strangers, and anger, as she became more invested in her plans, her mother could only hold Cathy or ignore her but was unable to help her develop instrumental behaviors for coping with these intensely negative experiences. At such times, we saw Cathy begin to retreat and to fall back on repetitive play, as a way to block out the stranger, or simply to scream in anger until the mother eventually responded.

Donna's mother presented a striking contrast. She saw herself primarily as a facilitator of Donna's efforts to be an active agent in her own regulation of these states. Thus, from the beginning Donna was allowed to experience a range of intensities of distress, going from mild fussiness to moderately intense crying, and occasionally even to intense, angry crying. The mother was able to respond to each situation with flexibility and confidence in her judgment as to what the baby could tolerate and manage. For instance, if Donna was fussing during a transition between sleep and wakefulness, the mother would tend not to intervene, thereby giving Donna the opportunity to regulate these transitions on her own, which Donna learned to do with relative ease. However, when Donna cried because she was tired of being in one position or of looking at the same thing for so long, or when she was hungry, the mother would respond quickly and appropriately by changing her position or providing her with a more interesting environment, or nursing her. And when she could not respond quickly with a solution, either because she was temporarily busy or wanted to stretch the feeding intervals out a little, she would offer a variety of supports or distractions to help Donna tolerate the delay. In general, then, the mother's reactions tended to provide the minimal responsivity needed to help the baby achieve and maintain an organized state.

Donna's experience of dysphoric affects was of sufficient intensity and duration so that she could become aware of the distinctive punishing qualities of the affects and of the need to do something about them, but they were not so intense and long-lasting that she was overwhelmed by them. These distinct experiences of distress and anger almost always resulted in Donna's own successful modulation of the negative experience or in bringing the mother, who successfully helped Donna to modulate the experience as she provided a remedy for the cause of the negative affect. This entire complex, consisting of a particular trigger, a distinct experience of a particular affect, and a successful management and remedy, was repeated many times during the first few months. And this enabled Donna to connect her awareness of each affect with a number of specific causes and consequences.

By three and a half months of age, Donna was able to produce a signal cry of distress and a protest cry of anger. Thus in this brief period, Donna's crying had gone from the expressive crying of early infancy that conveys neither a sense of the cause nor an expectation of relief to a signal or protest cry that conveys both the intent to communicate one's state and the expectation that the mother will respond quickly and appropriately. These changes represent an important advance in affective competence, for they require that the infant be able to modulate the cries in order to use them instrumentally, as a signal. This ability to modulate crying does not indicate that the cry has become "fake" or manipulative, but rather that the infant has learned, through her experiences of distress and anger, that they can be managed. At about this same time, Donna also developed the ability to get her thumb into her mouth voluntarily. This represented a gain in her control over her own states of fussiness and distress, since rhythmical sucking enables a baby to overcome the random movements of thrashing. We understood Donna's use of her thumb to be motivated by a wish to control the level of nonoptimal stimulation, rather than by the presence of an oral drive. These new instrumental behaviors enabled Donna to experience her self as competent, and thus enabled her to respond to the challenges of potentially distressing and frustrating situations with confidence, flexibility, and persistence.

Donna's experience of negative affect in response to strangers began at about five months of age and showed the full range of reactions from friendliness, to wariness, to a few episodes of intense fear and anger—depending on the closeness of the stranger, the suddenness of events, and the familiarity of the surroundings. Throughout this process the mother remained consistently available as she actively promoted and facilitated Donna's efforts both to cope with the distress, fear, and anger evoked by strangers and to develop adaptive ways of being with newcomers. By eleven months Donna was able to remain comfortably in the room with the stranger, and two weeks later she joyfully climbed into the arms of one of the observers.

SUMMARY

These data illustrate Sander's proposition that the emergence of the infant as agent represents a systems competence, which provides the conditions whereby the infant can become aware of her affective states and use this awareness as a frame of reference for organizing her own adaptive behaviors. Thus, we saw Donna flourish in such a competent system and continue to expand her areas of competence. And we saw Cathy become relatively passive, yet still trying to develop her agency in one realm, in a less competent system.

The data also highlight the role of affect in this process and stress its importance from the moment of birth. Placing affect at the core of the neonate's capacity for inner awareness is an attempt to allow the human infant full membership into the human species by acknowledging the infant's full biological heritage. It is also an attempt to provide an experientially based approach to the psychoanalytic understanding of the infant's psychological development. The implications of this approach for later development and for clinical theory and practice constitute exciting opportunities for ongoing research.

REFERENCES

Ainsworth, M. D. S., & Bell, S. M. (1970). Attachment, exploration and separation: Illustrated by the behavior of one-year-olds in a strange situation. *Child Development*, 41:49–67.

Arlow, J. A. (1977). Affects and the psychoanalytic situation. *Journal of Psychoanalysis*, 58:157–170.

Bower, T. G. R. (1982). The origins of perception and cognition. Paper presented at the International Conference on Infant Studies, March, Austin, TX.

Bowlby, J. (1969). *Attachment and Loss, Vol. I: Attachment*. New York: Basic Books.

Brazelton, T. B., Koslowski, B., & Main, M. (1974). The origins of reciprocity: The early mother–infant interaction. In M. Lewis & L. Rosenblum, ed., *The Effect of the Infant on its Caregiver*. New York: Wiley.

Brenner, C. (1974). On the nature and development of affects: A unified theory. *Psychoanalytic Quarterly*, 43:532–566.

———— (1982). The drives. In *The Mind in Conflict*. New York: International Universities Press.

Carpenter, G., Tecci, J., Stechler, G., & Friedman, S. (1969). Differential visual behavior to human and humanoid faces in early infancy. *Merrill-Palmer Quarterly*, 15:91–108.

Darwin, C. (1872). *The Expression of the Emotions in Man and Animals*. Chicago: University of Chicago Press (1965).

Demos, E. V. (1986). Crying in early infancy: An illustration of the motivational function of affect. In T. B. Brazelton & M. Yogman, ed., *Affective Development in Early Infancy*. Norwood, NJ: Ablex.

———— & Kaplan, S. (1987). Motivation and affect reconsidered: Affect biographies of two infants. *Psychoanalysis and Contemporary Thought*, 10:147–221.

DeCasper, A. J., & Carstens, A. A. (1981). Contingencies of stimulation: Effects on learning and emotion in neonates. *Infant Behavior and Development*, 4:19–35.

Ekman, P. (1972). Universal and cultural differences in facial expression of emotion. *Nebraska Symposium on Motivation*, 19:207–283.

———— (1977). Biological and cultural contributions to body and facial movement. In J. Blacking, ed., *Anthropology of the Body*. New York: Academic Press.

———— (1982). Personal communication, as reported in "Affect in early infancy," E. V. Demos, *Psychoanalytic Inquiry*, 1(4):533–574.

———— & Freisen, W. (1969). The repertoire of nonverbal behavior: Categories, origins, usage, and coding. *Semiotica*, I:49–98.

———— (1974). Detecting deception from the body or face. *Journal of Personality and Social Psychology*, 29:288–298.

———— (1975). *Unmasking the Face*. Englewood Cliffs, NJ: Prentice-Hall.

———— (1978). *Manual for the Facial Affect Coding System*. Palo Alto, CA: Consulting Psychologists Press.

———— & Levanson, R. W. (1983). Autonomic nervous system activity distinguishes among emotions. *Science*, 221:1208–1210.

Emde, R. N. (1980). Toward a psychoanalytic theory of affect: II. Emerging models of emotional development in infancy. In S. I. Greenspan & G. Pollock, ed., *The Course of Life: Psychoanalytic Contributions Toward Understanding Personality Development, Vol. I: Infancy and Early Childhood*. Washington, DC: National Institutes of Mental Health.

———— Gaensbauer, T., & Harmon, R. (1976). Emotional expression in infancy: A biobehavioral Study. *Psychological Issues*, Monograph 37. New York: International Universities Press.

Field, T. (1982). Discrimination and imitation of facial expressions by neonates. *Science* 218:179–181.

Fogel, A. (1982). Affect dynamics in early infancy: Affective tolerance. In T. Field & A. Fogel, eds., *Emotion and Early Interaction*. Hillsdale, NJ: Lawrence Erlbaum Associates.

Gaensbauer, T. (1982). The differentiation of discrete affects. *The Psychoanalytic Study of the Child*, 37:29–66. New Haven: Yale University Press.

Gibson, E. J. (1969). *Principles of Perceptual Learning and Development*. New York: Appleton-Century-Crofts.

Izard, C. E. (1968). The emotions and emotion constructs in personality and cultural research. In *Handbook of Modern Personality Theory*. Chicago: Aldine.

——— (1971). *The Face of Emotion*. New York: Appleton-Century Crofts.

——— (1979). *The Maximally Discriminative Facial Movement Coding System (Max)*. New York: Plenum Press.

——— Huebner, R. R., Risser, D., McGinnes, G. C., & Dougherty, L. M. (1980). The young infant's ability to produce discrete emotion expressions. *Developmental Psychology*, 16:132–140.

James, W. (1890). *Principles of Psychology*. New York: Dover.

Klein, G. (1976). *Psychoanalytic Theory: An Explorations of Essentials*. New York: Interantional Universities Press.

Langsdorf, P., Izard, C. E., Rayias, M., & Hembree, E. A. (1983). Interest expression, visual fixation and heart rate changes in 2- to 8-month-old infants. *Developmental Psychology*, 19:375–386.

Lester, B. M. & Zesking, P. S. (1982). A biobehavioral perspective on crying in early infancy. In G. Fitsgerald, B. M. Lester, & M. Yogman, ed., *Theory and Research in Behavioral Pediatrics*. New York: Plenum Press.

Lewis, M. & Rosenblum, L. (1974). *The Origins of Fear*. New York: Wiley.

Lewkowicz, D. J., & Turkewitz, G. (1981). Intersensory interaction in newborns. *Child Development*, 52:872–832.

Meltzoff, A. N., & Borton, W. (1979). Intermodal matching by human neonates. *Nature*, 282:403–404.

Oster, H. (1978). Facial expression and affect development. In M. Lewis & L. A. Rosenblum, ed., *The Development of Affect*. New York: Plenum Press.

——— & Ekman, P. (1978). Facial behavior in child development. *Minnesota Symposia on Child Psychology*. Vol. II. Hillsdale, NJ: Lawrence Erlbaum Associates.

Pribrim, K. (1980). The biology of emotions and other feelings. In R. Plutchik & H. Kerrerman, eds., *Emotion: Theory, Research and Experience*. New York: Academic Press.

Sander, L. (1969). Comments on regulation and organization in the early infant-care-taker system. In R. J. Robinson, ed., *Brain and Early Behavior*. New York: Academic Press.

——— (1982). Toward a logic of organization in psychobiologic development. Paper presented at the 13th Margaret S. Mahler Symposium in Philadelphia.

——— (1985). Toward a logic of organization in psychobiological development. *A.P.A. Monograph*, January.

Spelke, E. (1976). Infants' intermodal perception of events. *Cognitive Psychology*, 8:553–560.

——— (1979). Perceiving bimodally specified events in infancy. *Developmental Psychology*, 15:626–636.

Sroufe, L. A. (1979). The ontogenesis of emotion in infancy. In J. Osofsky, ed., *Handbook of Infant Development*. New York: Wiley.

Stechler, G. & Carpenter, G. (1974). A viewpoint on early affective development. In J. Hellmuth, ed., *The Exceptional Infant, Vol. I: The Normal Infant.* Seattle, WA: Special Child Publications.

Stern, D. (1983). The early development of schemas of self, other, and "self with other." In J. Lichtenberg & S. Kaplan, ed. *Reflections on Self Psychology.* Hillsdale, NJ: The Analytic Press.

Tomkins, S. (1962). *Affect, Imagery, Consciousness, Vol. I: The Positive Affects.* New York: Springer.

———— (1963). *Affect, Imagery, Consciousness, Vol. II: The Negative Affects.* New York: Springer.

———— (1980). Affect as amplification: Some modifications in theory. In R. Plutchik & H. Kerrerman, ed., *Emotion: Theory, Research and Experience, Vol. I: Theories of Emotion.* New York: Academic Press.

———— (1981). The quest for primary motives: Biography and autobiography of an idea. *Journal of Personality and Social Psychology,* 41:306–329.

Tronick, E., Als, H., & Brazelton, T. B. (1980). Monadic phases: A structural descriptive analysis of infant-mother, face-to-face interaction. *Merrill-Palmer Quarterly,* 26:3–24.

Wasz-Hockert, O., Lind, J., Vuorenkoski, V., Partanen, T., & Valanne, E. (1968). *The Infant Cry.* London: Heinemann Medical Books.

Wolff, P. (1963). Observations on the early development of smiling. In B. M. Foss, ed., *Determinants of Infant Behavior.* London: Methuen.

———— (1965). The development of attention in young infants. *Annals of the New York Academy of Sciences,* 118:815–830.

———— (1969). The natural history of crying and other vocalizations in early infancy. In B. M. Foss, ed., *Determinants of Infant Behavior, Vol. 2.* London: Methuen.

———— (1973). Organization of behavior in the first three months of life. *Early Development,* 51:132–153.

Chapter 3

Reflections on Self Psychology and Infancy

EMPATHY AND THEORY
Michael Franz Basch

We call ourselves self psychologists, but none of us treats a self, any more than ego psychologists treat or see egos, or id psychologists deal with the id. What we really do is best illustrated by the paradigm case of self psychology, Miss F, described by Kohut in *The Analysis of the Self* (1971).

Kohut tells us that, after repeated efforts to help Miss F to understand the meaning of what she was saying in terms of the theoretical framework that he brought to the analytic situation, and failing as often to overcome the patient's resistance, he one day realized that the patient was speaking two languages simultaneously. Behind Miss F's nagging, complaining, insistent, demanding whine, which is so typical of certain patients with narcissistic personality disorders, he heard the voice of a misunderstood child desperately trying to hold herself together. And when he taught himself how to speak to that child, he started to feel much better and eventually so did the patient—the rest is history.

In this sense Freud was the first self psychologist. He was able to hear behind the bizarre complaints, the irrational fears, and the senseless obsessions of neurotic patients the struggle between the sexually excited child demanding direct gratification and the adult who rejected these temptations as destructive to the integrity of his self-concept, or ego as the self was then called.

Freud learned that the way to cure this conflict is gradually to introduce the adult to the child he once was and that this is possible only when the patient is encouraged and permitted to relive the problematic aspects of his early development with the analyst, in derivative form. This process, interpretation in the transference, remains the basis of psychoanalysis and dynamic psychotherapy.

Freud found that all people demonstrate evidence in their adulthood that they are no strangers to incestuous sexual fantasies, nor to remnants of the childhood form of thought organization that he called the primary process. He then, however, came to the erroneous conclusion that this meant that the neurotic's unconscious struggle with incestuous sexuality and primitive aggression was childhood development writ large.

One can only speculate what might have happened if Mrs. Freud instead of Wilhelm Fliess had been Freud's muse, critic, and confidant; she might have suggested to him that he observe his offspring in the nursery to check on his hypothesis. I have no doubt, given Freud's penchant and ability for scientific observation, that he would have quickly seen that, though his reconstructions regarding childhood sexuality were borne out, there was more to development than could be explained by a study of neurotic symptom formation. However, this was not to be and, as we know, the so-called psychoanalytic theory of development, which has been passed on from one generation of analysts to the next, had for its shibboleths the centrality of the oedipal phase and the resolution of the oedipal conflict.

What happened then might seem ludicrous if it were not so tragic for both the therapists and the patients involved. Psychoanalysis became a ritual in which analysts, except when they were treating symptom or character neuroses, introduced their patients to—and insisted they must accept as representative of their past—the child they never were, because theory dictated that it must have been so. Fortunately, most analysts, at least some of the time, made what Glover (1931) calls "inexact interpretations," that is, they became empathic with their patients and responded accordingly. In this way patients and analysts at least benefited enough from the exercise to keep psychoanalysis alive. The worst case scenario of what the instinct theory of development can lead to is illustrated in Malcolm (1981), where the pseudonymous Dr. Aaron Green lays out for us, without any insight into what happened to him, the destructive effect a doctrinaire, so-called classic analysis has on the capacity for love and work in an individual who seems to suffer from a typical narcissistic personality disorder. This analyst, left chronically, unconsciously, narcissistically enraged by his own analysis, could not help but visit on his patients the damage done to himself.

Without taking away from the many analysts who already during Freud's time and down to the present day have recognized that we were not serving our patients adequately and tried to do something about it, I think it is fair to say that it was Kohut (1971) who was able to set back the clock to the point where Freud was still true to his own method—his findings dictated by empathy and introspection. In doing this, Kohut gave analysis what we all want and seldom get, a second chance; in this case a second chance to build a psychoanalytic theory, a guiding framework for our practice and for our research that will be scientifically viable and let us grow.

Just because we have had such a bad experience with it, do not underestimate the importance of theory for practice. Beginning with Freud, and echoed in every psychoanalytic institute since then, is the canard that theory is window dressing and that real scientists collect the data of observation. All philosophers of science, including Einstein, hold the contrary and tell us that it is theory that determines what it is we can observe.

In years past I often made the experiment of picking out one of the female candidates in my class at the analytic institute who was wearing a wedding ring and asking her to describe the psychological life of the infant. Invariably she would dutifully and solemnly recite the *tabula rasa* theory of the egoless baby, who is blindly motivated only by hunger and thirst, avoids stimulation whenever possible, and wants nothing more than to be left alone to sleep. I then ask if she has had a baby of her own and if so to describe her experience with it. Now the face and voice of the candidate become animated, and we hear about a small but very human person who, from birth on, displays a wide range of affect, engages and is very much aware of her surroundings, solves all sorts of problems for herself, and, above all, is very much affected by the nuances of the interpersonal transaction with and around her. Here is a classic demonstration of the power of theory over observation and practice. Here is a woman who has obviously experienced the joys and intimacies of motherhood but is nevertheless able to mouth with a straight face the fantasy of the driven, egoless, newborn, which until recently passed—and may in some quarters still pass—for a theory of infant development because it is associated with Freud and carries the stamp of his authority. Can allegiance to such a patently incorrect notion of development fail to have an effect on how one thinks about what patients tell us? And if an obviously involved, intelligent mother can be so misled, how about the rest of us?

The reader may now say that we self psychologists gather our data empathically and that we neither subscribe to nor need these avowedly incorrect and misguided ideas. Well and good. However, empathic listening, the ability to be attuned to our patients' communications in such a way that affective undertones and overtones are not lost or neglected, is only half the task Kohut assigned the analyst. He said that we *explain* to the patient what it is we have first understood. Empathic understanding tells us what it is patients are experiencing, though they may not be able to tell us directly about it. Indeed, some patients may not even know themselves what affective currents are motivating their behavior. Now that we have gathered this data through empathy, what are we going to do with it? How are we going to explain to ourselves and, when it is appropriate, to our patients, why they respond the way they do? In other words, on what basis will we make the genetic interpretation that in the context of the transference will lead to the transmuting internalization, that increment of change in the self system and its relationship that we consider curative?

We were taught that a patient's reactions are basically always related to the attempt to express in disguised form derivatives of unconscious sexual or aggressive drives. Biologists long ago rejected this explanation, and Kohut showed that it has no clinical universality in psychoanalysis, even metaphorically. But we must be careful not to substitute "empathic failure" for "dammed-up drive" as a genetic explanation for our patients' problems. "Empathic failure" is a descriptive term, not an explanation, for it does not tell us what constitutes empathic failure at various stages of development. In order to explain, for example, why a patient has been hurt, why some action or inaction on our part is experienced by the patient as an empathic failure, especially when the transference is an archaic one and we are dealing with preverbal, possibly even presymbolic material, we have to have more than an impressionistic knowledge of how that hierarchy of goal directed, deviation correcting, and deviation enhancing feedback cycles that we call the self or self system takes form. This is what we can and must learn from our colleagues in the field of infant and child development. "Normality" is defined as functioning according to design (King, 1945), and only developmental psychology can provide the template that we can use to evaluate our patients' development and its problems.

References

Glover, E. (1931). *The Technique of Psychoanalysis*. New York: International Universities Press, 1955.

King, C. D. (1945). The meaning of normal. *Yale Journal of Biology and Medicine*, 17:493–501.

Kohut, H. (1971). *The Analysis of the Self*. New York: International Universities Press.

Malcolm, J. (1981). *Psychoanalysis: The Impossible Profession*. New York: International Universities Press.

INFANT RESEARCH AND SELF PSYCHOLOGY
Joseph Lichtenberg

Beebe and Lachman emphasize "mutual influence structures as the prime candidates for structuring the infant's experience." Demos places "affect at the core of the neonate's capacity for inner awareness." Self psychology refers to the self as an independent center of initiative and attributes primary organizing significance to self-selfobject experience. How can these formulations be integrated?

Beebe and Lachman draw their inferences about mutual influence structures primarily from the microanalysis of face-to-face contacts. Demos draws her inferences from the remarkably perceptive theory of Tomkins, tested by careful analysis of facial expressions and autonomic nervous system responses in babies and adults. Self psychology has drawn its formulation first from observations made on narcissistic personality disorder patients. The self of these patients ceased to operate as an independent center of initiative when deprived of the opportunity for mirroring, twinship or idealizing experiences. Their motivational centering was restored as a result of the self-selfobject experience that ensued from empathic understanding of this regulatory deficit. Later, less dramatic but similar alterations in self-cohesion were observed as a broadly human phenomenon. How are we to go from the microanalyses of the faces of mothers and infants in social exchanges and the microanalyses of affect expressions and ANS (autonomic nervous system) responses to the micropsychoanalysis of empathic immersion in the changing of self-states?

I shall approach the task of integration through a discussion of motivation and then apply the conceptions I offer to the observations of infants presented by Demos and Beebe and Lachman. The evidence does not support the traditional psychoanalytic assumption of a dual drive theory or, before eighteen months, the existence of symbolic representation. We are called on, therefore, to seek a means to conceptualize motivations that fits both the psychic life of the infant in the phase before symbolic representation and the psychic life of the older toddler, child, and adult who employ symbolic representation.

I suggest that five motivational systems priming self-regulation in a mutual regulatory interaction are present at birth and remain throughout life: the need to fulfill physiological requirements, the need for attachment and affiliation, the need for assertion and exploration, the need to react aversively through antagonism and/or withdrawal, and the need for sensual and sexual satisfaction. At each period of life the hierarchy of needs, wishes, desires, aims, and goals that derive from the motivational systems may be rearranged in different hierarchies indicated by different conscious and unconscious preferences, choices, and proclivities. Nonetheless, I suggest, these five motivational systems are fundamental and continuities exist between infant and adult. It is necessary to be tentative at this point in suggesting these continuities.

My main assumption is that infants are motivated to do whatever they do with observable consistency. Infants are observed to take nourishment at regular intervals—implying they are motivated to do so. Since they can be observed using facial expressions and whole body responses to display interest at the sight of the breast or bottle and pleasure with the milk intake, it can be inferred that feeding involves perception and affect and that both perceiving stimuli and experiencing affect are components of a motivational system in operation. That infants cry when not fed implies that they are motivated to indicate their aversion to a dystonic state. Further, moving from crying before feeding to interest and joy with feeding indicates that infants are motivated to make the *transition* from the hunger state to the feeding state and that affect amplification provides a compelling push to their motivational trigger. That mothers adjust their feeding procedures to the infants' signals of readiness and infants alter their timing and rate of sucking to cues from their mother indicates that mothers and infants are motivated to engage in self-regulations that conform to the mutual regulatory requirements of an interactional system. Even so mundane an example as the feeding experience indicates that human beings, from the beginning, have motivational systems by which they are primed to perceive, feel, act, learn, and engage through self-regulation in a mutually regulatory interactional system.

I have chosen these five systems because each fulfills a paramount requirement for a motivational system—the recruitment of affect throughout life. At first, the affect recruitment occurs by virtue of the relatively active stimulus-potential inherent in the activation of the system. Following Tomkins and Demos, whatever this stimulation may be—hunger, the face-to-face interactions described by Beebe, the assertive, exploratory behavior of a neonate with a toy in its nine-inch gaze range, the aversion activity of the baby with the looming mother, or the sucking stimulation of the sensitive mucosa, the resulting variants in the density, direction, and duration of neural stimulation will be abstracted into one of a group of about nine basic effects. The affects evoked in this way act as amplifiers to the triggering need—turning what would otherwise be a weak call into a more powerful determinant of future expectancies and scanning for the possibility of repetition. Once activated, each motivational system leads to the formation of characteristic perceptual-affective-action patterns. Each can assist with or substitute for regulation in another.

Each of the five motivational systems is recognizable at any point in the life cycle but is not by itself the determinant of the mode of overall organization that characterizes any life epoch. Each motivational system at each period is influenced by biological-neurophysiological maturation, development, or senescence, which sets the organizational potential for the period. The organization of infancy lies in a continuum of sleep–awake states (non-REM sleep, REM sleep, drowsy, awake active, awake quiet, fussing and crying). Behaviors indicative of each motivational system are recognizable if the 24-hour cycle of infant life is scanned for them but the dominant *mode* of organization is change in state and its relation to the caregiver-infant mutual regulatory system.

I believe that the self as the "container" best fits with this way of viewing motivation. I define the self as did Kohut, as an independent center of initiative, but I add of organizing and integrating. Self in the infant refers not to symbolic representations or to an awareness of self, but to the experience of a *totality in space* in the course of the infant's activities, a concept well documented in Stern's (1985) work. "Self," as I define it, emphasizes motivation (initiative) and its function with respect to experience (organizing and integrating). The overarching concept that conveys the mutual relationship of self-regulation and regulation between self and environment is of a "selfobject experience." This experience is a particular affective state characterized by a sense of cohesion, safety, and competence. My hypothesis is that for each of the five basic motivational systems at each period of life, there are specific needs and that when these needs are met the result is a selfobject experience. When these needs are not met, the person experiences a sense of disturbed cohesion ranging from an acute alarm, signaling, for example, the need for air, to the sense of disquietude that occurs if a distracted friend fails to mirror one's greeting. I distinguish between needs and wishes. Need satisfaction is fundamental to the establishment and maintenance of self-cohesion and is the source of selfobject experience. Wishes are manifold conscious and unconscious motivations derived from each system, often competing one with another. Wishes and needs may coincide, as in the wish and need of toddlers to have their caregiver put them off to sleep with a reassuring word, or wishes and needs may not coincide, as in the wish of toddlers to follow a lost ball into the street and their need for protective restraint. Using these distinctions, we can refine the concept of empathic failure by specifying in response to what need the failure occurred, which motivational system was primarily affected, and which developmental organization was placed under brief or lasting stress. Traditionally, psychoanalysts have been extremely adept explorers of wishes—ferreting out secret desires in the "unconscious" as a topographic locale. The traditional emphasis on conflict and compromise in symptom formation has also placed analysts in the forefront of studying wishes construed as derived from sexual and aggressive instinctual drives, executive functions and morals, ethics and ideals. Historically, we have concentrated less on the discernment of needs; thus our ability to distinguish between need and wish remains preliminary in many instances.

With this mind-boggling summary of definitions and propositions about motivation behind us, I shall apply this way of conceptualizing to the infant Cathy. In the area of physiological requirements Demos tells us that Cathy's mother derived so much of her pleasure (probably both competence and vicariously sensual) from feeding that whatever selfobject experience Cathy derived from this meeting of physiological need must be weighed against the disturbed regulation of sleep. Cathy's motivation for attachment experiences was severely thwarted by the mother's own gaze aversion and preferential attention to Cathy's brother. The mother tried to shift Cathy's interest from attachment as a motive to exploration activities with the jiggling toy. Here the deprivation in the attachment motivational system outweighed the opportunity offered on the assertion-exploratory system. Later Cathy had some opportunities for selfobject experiences associated with affiliative motives when she was offered active vigorous stimulation by father, brother, and visitors. Cathy began actively to exercise aversion by turning away from her unresponsive, avoidant mother—but even in the expression of aversion she was sharply curtailed. Direct anger and antagonism was short-circuited by immediate feeding and soothing. Cathy was left with only one way to express aversive motivation: withdrawal into a languid, immobile state, or what sounds like Mahler's (Mahler, Pine, and Bergman, 1975) concept of low-keyedness. Sensual pleasure seeking was for Cathy the motivation promoted by her mother through activation, one might even say seduction. It is not surprising, then, that "her explorations were dominated by sucking, with little exploration of other behaviors." Sucking was, as Demos states, not a manifestation of oral drive in the conventional sense but the activation of one motivational system into dominance to compensate for deficits in others. Through sucking Cathy could regulate her states, stirring herself up as do sexually promiscuous or perverse narcissistic disorder patients when faced with failing cohesion, or calming down and soothing herself probably from states of antagonism for which she had no other means of expression. Later, her lack of support from a base of secure attachment and the absence of maternal guidance signals kept her from welcoming strangers as friends. Cathy experienced fear, not anger, after unsuccessful attempts to employ withdrawal as her means of aversion. Overall, Cathy's self was an independent center of initiative in only a few areas, mostly in respect to physiological requirements. Much of her initiative went into aversion patterns of withdrawal from attachment and from exploratory-assertive possibilities. Some initiative remained for the pursuit of mouth sensual pleasure. What selfobject experience could she have had to organize and integrate her self-cohesion around? Certainly interaction with a caregiver as feeder, soother and calmer, and participant in joint searching for exclusive merger with shared sensual pleasure, and, with or without a partner, competence in frustrating through avoidance, withdrawal, and diminished vitality. It may seem odd to speak of selfobject experience of need satisfaction in competence in frustration, but observation and clinical experience tells us that interest and competence can take many aversive forms.

When it is structured, as it was with Cathy, and with Beebe's infant attached through chase and dodge interactions, the resulting perceptual-affective-action patterns follow Sander's (1985) thought provoking suggestion that if maintenance of continuity is a task of self-regulation, the individual will attempt to recreate conditions which allow him to experience familiar states by which he recognizes himself. That is, an affectively experienced self-state of aversion becomes sought after for the security of the familiarity that continuity produces. I have tried here to illustrate the possibilities in a broadened view of motivation in which affect plays a significant role in each of five motivational systems and to place these two superb observational studies into a larger context offered by self psychology. In turn, self psychology by its open minded nondoctrinaire interest in exploring research findings offers psychoanalysis the opportunity to view babies as they are, not as reconstructive theories would construe them to be.

References

Mahler, M., Pine, F., & Bergman, A. (1975). *The Psychological Birth of the Human Infant.* New York: Basic Books.

Sander, L. (1985). The inner experiences of the infant: A framework for inferences relevant to development of the sense of self. Unpublished.

Stern, D. (1985). *The Interpersonal World of the Infant.* New York: Basic Books.

THE EVENT-STRUCTURE OF REGULATION IN THE NEONATE-CAREGIVER SYSTEM AS A BIOLOGICAL BACKGROUND FOR EARLY ORGANIZATION OF PSYCHIC STRUCTURE
Louis W. Sander

To have the chance to reflect on the papers of Drs. Beebe and Demos is an enriching experience. Each of their papers has been developed from sets of data that are as close to the empirical beginnings from which the self is organized in postnatal life as can possibly be studied. Each grapples with the four fundamental questions that grip all of us: (1) On what basis do we describe precursors of a phenomenon as elusive and complex as the self? (2) In terms of observable behaviors, can we correctly infer inner experience? (3) How is inner experience welded into the psychic structure we call the self? (4) What are the changes in organization and representation that both inner experience and the self as a psychic structure undergo over the longer term spans of development?

Both presenters couched their work and their thinking within the systems perspective, each particularizing dimensions of inner experience that belong in different time domains and involve different functional and regulatory subsystems of the human organism. At this point, most of us who are dealing with the complexities of early development anchor our thinking in the systems perspective. It must be realized that one of the drawbacks of taking a systems viewpoint of organization is that the living system ultimately includes everything—particularly the entire range of *time dimensions* within which interactive structures of mutual influence can be organized. In regard to this more inclusive system we can ask, What are the *larger regularities*, and the more extensive time spans within which Beebe's interactive structures of microsecond mutual influence fit, and within which Demos's affect systems are organized?

I propose here that this longer temporal dimension is occupied by the basic requirement for biological regulation of infant states along the arousal-quiescent continuum, i.e., initially the sleep–awake continuum. It is essential in gaining a wider perspective on infant and caregiver, as an example of a living "system," to recognize that we are dealing with the fundamental property of self-regulation that characterizes all living organisms from single cell upward. The function of self-regulation characterizes the infant and it characterizes the caregivers. What we are seeing in this earliest example of regulation in the living infant-caregiver system is the interaction of two uniquely self-regulatory subsystems, that of the new born and that of the caregivers. Solutions to their interaction that allow infant and caregiver to reach the harmonious and enduring coordination required for "regulation" of each will be individually unique in its temporal organization, and its perceptual, motor, and sensory configurations. (Note: The course of special features of character organization and of pathogenesis can be seen to begin immediately in early derailments of coordination and regulation. We consider in this paper only the usual course in which reasonably stable regulation is achieved over the first three months of life.)

The neonate's distribution of states on the sleep-awake continuum that the caregiver can observe from birth onward is endogenously determined. The daily, around-the-clock distribution of a newborn's states on this continuum varies from individual to individual as do the characteristics of the events that can modify this temporal organization of states as infant and caregiver move toward their achievement of an initial regulatory equilibrium in the system.

My comments on this earliest context within which we observe affect and interactional structure are based on data of continuous, around-the-clock, noninvasive bassinet monitoring of infant and infant-caregiver interaction. From these data has emerged a background picture we have termed the "event-structure" of the infant-caregiver system. This event-structure becomes a characteristic background configuration of events that emerges from the recurrent patterning of interactions that are needed to establish and maintain the infant's self-regulation of state. Within this framework, microsecond interactions are occurring and affects are experienced, both of which are coming via mutual modifications to gain their meaning for the regulation of the system.

The event-structure of an infant-caregiver system stems from the *recurrent* interactions between a mother with her agenda, a father with his agenda, a generational family system with its agenda within a social system with its agenda. Into the midst of this comes a new infant with its agenda. The individually unique features of each infant's state organization, with its own particular requirements for regulation, are basic to the agenda that the neonate introduces now into this already complex system. These features of state organization and state regulation influence the interactions that take place between the neonate and the caregiver as they move via mutual modifications toward a stable, harmonious, and enduring adapted coordination. When the configurations of state regulatory interaction settle down to a predictably recurrent pattern, a daily "event-structure," uniquely configured for each system, can be said to have become organized, becoming thereby part of the regularly recurring *configurations* of *expectancy* for both infant and caregiver. This forms the background of at least a 24-hour time frame, against which shorter term events in the foreground must be described. The actual *time* organization of this uniquely configured background event-structure becomes shared by both infant and caregiver in the harmoniously regulated system. This time background begins to serve as a reference structure for ascribing meaning to foreground events or events that perturbe the unique background structure.

To illustrate just how soon after birth the individually unique features of a particular caregiver become part of the event-structure of the regulatory interaction, we have included Figure 1.

Figure 1 illustrates the situation in the early infant-caregiver system when one highly experienced surrogate mother caregiver is replaced on the 11th day of life by another, equally experienced and able surrogate mother. In this study, the surrogate mothers provided the only caregiving around the clock for only one infant at a time, beginning at birth. In the sample of nine infants, only two surrogate mothers were used; the initial assignment of the infants to caregiver alternated between these two without bias. The crying and distress measures after day ten indicate the disruption of the adapted coordination that had already been established over the first ten days of life between the neonate and the initial caregiver.

It is helpful to review a bit further some of the biological features that govern neonatal state organization and underly the recurring structure of events the infant requires of the caregiving system. These features, as mentioned earlier, begin with the 24-hour time organization of the infant's states on the sleep–awake continuum. This organization is governed by the phenomena of biorhythmicity and their related rhythms: circadian, ultradian, and others. This represents a different biology than Freud began with. The facts are that a fundamental property of organization is given to living systems as a whole and to each of their living components by the cyclic oscillations that characterize them. The mechanisms by which a multiplicity of endog-

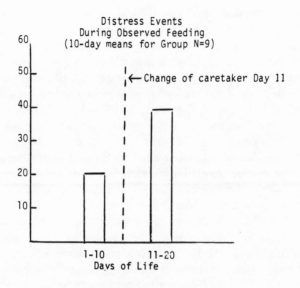

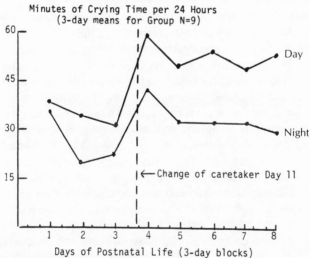

Change of Surrogate Mother on Day 11
a) Distress Events During Feeding (10-day group means, N=9)
b) Cumulations of Minutes of Actual Crying Time per 24 Hours
   (3-day group means, N=9).

FIGURE 1.

enously arising physiological rhythms can become harmoniously phase-synchronized within the individual generate an organism that has coherence as a whole. The empirical demonstration of "coherence" among the various oscillating physiological subsystems of the infant and the relation of this coherence to infant sleep organization and to later problems of caregiving was reported by Prechtl (1968, 1969) and Kalverboer, Touwen, and Prechtl (1973).

Our group has demonstrated the powerful influence played by individual differences in this 24-hour temporal organization and its relation to the regulation of both infant and of caregiving systems. We have demonstrated the way adaptation between the two then establishes a framework of recurrent events in which specific functions, behaviors, and strategies are carried out (Sander, 1969).

It is helpful to think of this event-structure of a system, and the affects that may or may not be associated, as each related to separate domains. Affects may, but do not necessarily, determine the event-structure of the system. Recurrent goal organization of both infant and caregiver and the motivations that promote the recurrent goal realization, which establishes the adapted coordinations on which enduring state regulation rests, may be amplified and shaped by affects but do not necessarily arise from affects.

Within the organization and regulation of the event-structure of the larger system, we can identify at least a half dozen features and/or constraints that this fundamental property of biorhythmicity imposes on the framework of recurrent events that characterize the infant-caregiver system. Among some of the properties that the elemental biorhythmic nature of living systems impose are: (1) the preeminent role given to timing, i.e., to the temporal organization of events in the regulation of the system; (2) the assurance that situations will be recurrent. When recurrence becomes dependable, it provides a condition essential for habituation and adaptation; (3) that within this recurrence, there will be a capacity for the reorganization needed to reach harmonious coordination. Phase-shifting and phase-synchrony of rhythms between functions of infant and caregiver that have different periodicities take place. This is a mutual modification that makes coordination achievable; (4) that there will be a patterned specificity of cues specifically timed and recurrent that provide the *entrainment* necessary for this coordination of rhythms. Entrainment by specific and regularly recurrent patterning of perceptual and sensorimotor cues within a specific temporal framework of events is the mechanism by which rhythms of one period length in one oscillating system can be phase linked to periodicities in another such system. Much attention is being given to this critical phenomenon now in premature nurseries and intensive care units to facilitate phase-synchrony and coherence in infants who are seriously impaired in the temporal organization of their sleep states and of their related physiological subsystems. At the same time, they are being exposed to an environment that provides few if any of the rhythmically recurrent events that are necessary for entrainment; and (5) that coherence and equilibrium in regulation of the system over longer time spans provides a temporal organization of events in the system that allows for what has been called loose-coupling (Glassman, 1973) or disjoin (Ashby, 1952). This is a temporary and partial *disengagement* of infant and caregiver when they are in a state of coordination and harmony of regulation. Such disengagement in a state of equilibrium in the system is a condition that favors the achievement of a sense of agency in the infant and the sense that its motivations and goals are its own.

I am suggesting, furthermore, that, in addition to underlying the event-structure of the system in adapted equilibrium, the property of biorhythmicity also sets the background for the regularities of the interactive situations in the system that are necessary for the infant's regularly recurrent *experience of its own inner states.* Successful regulation in the system on a 24-hour basis is an important condition for recurrence of this inner experience. We find that individual characteristics of sleep organization provide one of the most sensitive indicators of risk in the neonate. And, of course, this risk is a risk for the infant-caregiver system in its task of achieving a harmonious and enduring regulation. Consequently the qualities of infant's inner experience related to the recurrent states and the interactional context in which they are regularly reexperienced quickly become part of the infant's recurrent expectations and organization of his/her own self-regulatory behaviors.

The well-organized normal infant wakes up four to six times a day. Each awakening exhibits a sequence of clearly identifiable states until the infant falls back to sleep. These states are recognizable with a high level of interobserver reliability, and provide the first specific observational cues as to the infant's inner experience that the caregiver intuitively infers and reads from moment to moment. It is from these inferences that the caregiver regularly makes her decisions. This is a first link in the neonate between the observable and the inner experience. Around these decisions, a regularly repeated interactive context becomes established so that state, and thus inner experience, is experienced by the infant within a specific behavioral context. The time frame of each awakening has direction to it—a sequence that progresses in terms of both state and interaction. Within this directional context, affects acquire their meaning, and motivations their specific goals. As was pointed out earlier, in the competent system the recurrent sequence of states on the sleep-awake continuum can be seen as the first level of initiative that the infant introduces into the system.

I am in full agreement with Demos that there is evidence that affect systems are identifiable from the beginning—especially in the awake end of the continuum—that they become engaged from the outset in the interactive patterns with the caregiver. Almost at once affects of surprise and interest can be described in the awake infant. In a description of self regulation of earliest infant states coupled with the infant's inner experience of them, affects can be referred to as recognizable states that begin in the context of, or combined with, state position on the sleep-awake continuum. In this earliest time of state regulation, affects can be seen to be embedded within a recurrent sequence of sleep-awake state organization, a subsystem of its own, distinct from but interacting with affect systems that are brought into play as initial caregiving coordination is being achieved in the process of establishing harmonious and enduring state regulation. From the start, qualities of, sensitivity to, and regard for the endogenous determination of the timing and duration of sleep-awake states of the baby can be observed and assessed in the caregiver's decisions. Similarly, one caregiver's sense that the states of the baby should be contingent on her control, and their occurrence and timing should be her responsibility, contrasts with that of another, who perceives the timing and direction of state change in the baby as an endogenously arising primary property of the baby, with *her* proper response then being contingent to that state change.

What has become strikingly clear is the mutual influence at this initial level and how very *early* in the normal infant-caregiver pattern the system gains 24-hour temporal organization through this mutual influence of infant and caregiver. Day–night differentiation in the location of sleep and awake states (sleep predominating in the night time 12 hours, and awake states in the daytime 12 hours) becomes evident between the fourth and sixth day of life in such a system. This differentiation does not appear when such recurrent mutuality is lacking. This is illustrated in Figure 2, which illustrates the 24-hour distribution of sleep states in an infant experiencing the noncontingent caregiving of the neonatal nursery with multiple caregivers.

In the instance of the experienced natural mother/caregiver, there is regularly recurrent caregiving contingent to the endogenous rhythms of neonatal states. This sets the stage necessary in state regulation for both entrainment and the necessary adaptive modifications involving habituation, learning, and goal organization. Given

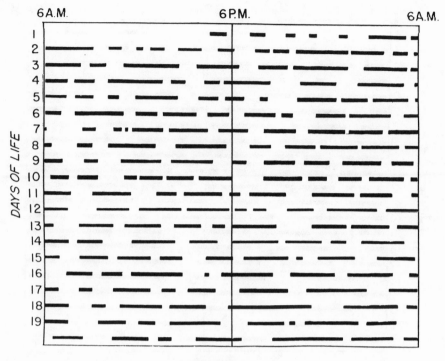

FIGURE 2.

these features, the entire 24 hours can become organized in a pattern of napping and waking periods by the seventh day of life. After some days of regularity, there are days of changing organization followed by the appearance of a new stability of nap organization. In Figure 3, the infant begins three daytime naps and a night nap on day 7. This continues through day 11. There is a reorganization between days 12 and 14, and we see two daytime naps and a still longer night sleep period, days 15 through 19. There is a second reorganization, days 20–21, and we find a shorter morning nap, a longer afternoon nap and the long night sleep. Although not shown in the figure, this latter pattern for the infant endures stably over the rest of the first two months of life.

We have demonstrated also the mutual interactive influence between caregiver behavior and the longer sleep–awake periodicities. In two samples of nine infants each, each infant was cared for around the clock, one at a time, over the first month of life by a single surrogate mother. There were two such mothers, each caring for a sample

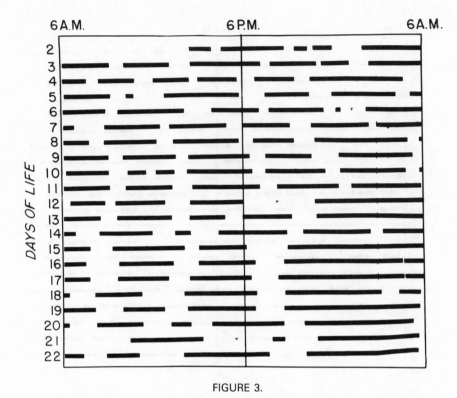

FIGURE 3.

of nine infants. The infants of one mother emerged with significantly longer longest-awake and significantly longer longest-sleep periods over 24 hours than did the infants cared for by the other surrogate caregiver. (See Figure 4.)

The interactive sequence over an awake period itself becomes part of episodic memory. In our experiment in which the natural mother's face is masked just before the first awakening on the *seventh day* of life, we showed infant reactions of notable surprise to this violation of expectancy. This reaction began at one specific moment in the feeding interaction, which had become by seven days a familiar sequence of caregiving events. The context for experience is being learned with the content. As Ashby (1952) first delineated in the early 1950s, state is a configuration of variables that recurs and can be recognized when it recurs again. This can be a highly complex configuration of variables, but a pattern, however, that can be recognized, often, as a single recurrent cue for the observer. This is, of course, the same model Demos has pointed out in thinking about the emotions, highly complex configurations of behavior and physiology that can be recognized when they recur by a single configuration of cues. The question has also been raised whether or not the neonate comes equipped to recognize recurrent states of the caregiver (Meltzoff, 1985; Stern, 1985).

In the caregiver system, where the states of the infant become the infant's first initiative in modifying the system to achieve regulation, the infant gains actual agency in self-regulation within that system. We can call a harmoniously regulated infant caregiving system that makes it possible for the infant to exercise agency in its own state regulation, a competent system. The extent to which an infant can be an agent in his/her own self-regulation differentiates one infant-care-giver system from another from the outset. Differences between systems and their relative competence can be traced from the earliest interactions. As time goes on, the harmony of regulation can persist, improve, or deteriorate. Systems differ in their resilience or rigidity to maintain or alter such organization.

In regard to regulation in the competent infant-caregiver system at this early point, we make three simple proposals: (1) That the *inner experience* of the infant first consolidates around this recurrent sequence of states on the sleep–awake continuum, *particularly those at the awake end,* i.e., transitional, drowsy, awake active, awake quiet or alert, fussing or crying. As just noted, state comes quickly to include affects (such as surprise or interest); (2) That because of this regular

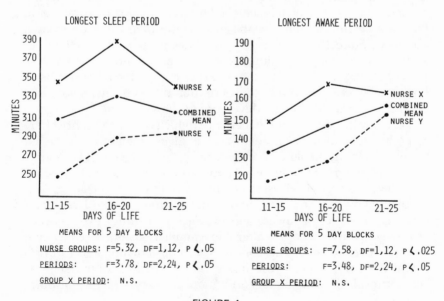

FIGURE 4.

daily recurrence in the competent system, these particular experiential states, as well as the state of sleep, *become goals* for the infant and begin to determine goal organized behavior within the familiar recurrent event-structure of the infant-caregiver system. The self-regulatory capabilities of the infant become activated and organize infant behavior to reconstruct *situations* associated with reexperiencing desired states and avoiding states not desired; and (3) That in the competent system which ensures infants as agents in their own self-regulation, such recurrent inner states as goals become the inner criteria, or set points, for generating increasingly varied and complex goal-organized behavioral schema. These bring about the situations in the competent system associated with the experience of the desired states. This is a sequence in which infants change the situations that then directly change their own states via their own initiative. Arrived at as part of the mutual influence of regulatory coordinations, such schemes become part of the organization of the system as well as of the infant. One's own states are indeed one's own when such competence is achieved.

In terms of this organization of coordinated behavior, which becomes characteristic for a system, the infant's sense of continuity over time can be considered to be carried by this recurrent conservative configuration of inner experiences associated with the regulatory strategies that have now become characteristics of the system. The importance of thinking in terms of the systems perspective is that the mutual adaptation, which is achieved between infant and caregiver in the "competent" system, establishes for the infant that one's own actions can directly effect one's own states in desired directions. In such a system, self-regulation becomes an active interpersonal skill. Hence, the role of the infant's inner experience in the organization of his/her adaptive behavior becomes central to the effectiveness of the interactive strategies he/she develops. At the same time, the organization of awareness of inner experience (which can be thought of here as an awareness of one's own state) is given a central role in self regulation. In the stable and competent system (which will be characterized by recurrent situations related to state regulation), these strategies become organized as structures of psychic organization, i.e., proceeding by goal organization of behavior from the regularly recurring experience of an awareness of one's own inner experience— awareness of own state—to alter it in a familiar, goal-ordered fashion to a more desired state. This contrasts with the situation in the incompetent system, in which the infant reexperiences its own state as being a result of or secondary to a more primary structure of outer events.

At this point in the discussion of the earliest development of psy-chic structures related to the sense of self, discussed here as aware-ness of own inner experience, we realize we must begin to address the question of ontogeny in the organization of awareness (i.e., con-sciousness). In the model presented here, such ontogeny would re-volve around the conditions that influence the unique way in the caregiving system that awareness of inner experience in the indi-vidual is allowed or is not allowed to organize the generation of that individual's adaptive behavior. It is here that derailment in the devel-opment of the sense of self can be seen to begin. This, however, is the subject for another paper, addressing the role within an infant's own particular system that infant awareness of own inner experience is allowed to play in that infant's organizing of his/her own self-reg-ulatory goals.

There is another point: How can the origins of the self as a psychic structure emerge from the mutuality of influence required to achieve enduring state regulation? With such a powerful mutual shaping of behavior and of biological responsivity going on, it is easy to envision the shaping effects of projective identification and the unconscious response to another's attribution. These conditions make it difficult, even impossible, for the individual to make any distinction between which experience is his/her own endogenously arising one, and which is part of this mutual interactive influence elicited by or in response to the other.

Elsewhere, based on the concepts of regulation, adaptation, and integration in living systems, we (Sander, 1983) have proposed the idea of a disengagement between infant and caregiver in terms of "open space," a first edition of Winnicott's (1958a) intermediate area. The idea in this is that in the competent system, in which regulation can be maintained at a well-balanced equilibrium, there is during an awake period often a time span of long enough *disengagement* be-tween infants and caregivers to allow the infants to proceed from clearly endogenously arising motivations and interests. These are quite clear, because the disengagement is quite clear at that point of regulatory equilibrium so that there is no preemption of action by regulatory needs that are imposed either from within or from with-out. This is only a span of time in the longer time frame of the awake sequence that I have been talking about, in which such disengage-ment is possible; but it is, I think, similar to what Winnicott has been describing in his suggestions about the origins of the capacity to be alone. This longer time frame of regulatory stability he speaks of in terms of "the mother holding the situation in time" (Winnicott, 1958b). He describes the disengagement in the following way:

The infant is able to become unintegrated, to flounder, to be in a state in which there is no orientation, to be alone to exist for a time without being either a reactor to an external impingement or an active person with a direction of interest or movement. The stage is set for an id experience. In the course of time there arrives a sensation or an impulse. In this setting the sensation or impulse will feel real and be truly a personal experience [p. 34].

I suggest, then, that it is in the system in regulatory equilibrium related to a longer time domain of regulation, namely, the 24-hour day, that such endogenously arising directions of infant initiative can be pursued repeatedly by the infant. Under these conditions the infant will experience inner experience, with its endogenously arising motivations and goals, as his/her own. This is associated with option as agent to act on this inner experience, in both reconstruction and new construction. This begins the possibility for the infant to experience an alternative to the indistinctness of agency in the experiences associated with mutuality. How one comes to regard one's own inner experience as anlage of sense of self emerges over the first two years in the context of the outcome to these initiatives that emerge within the "open space." Their success or failure biases the long-term trajectory, as do the regulatory conditions that permit or deny option to pursue them. We can see a model for formative influences on the quality of this regard as a systems property from the outset. What we have tried to do is to draw attention to the lawfulness that governs this very earliest edition of inner experience in the success or failure of self-regulation of one's own recurrent states. For example, one can see here the powerful role that the intrusive, controlling caregiver or the nonresponsive mother would play in compromising such a dyadic opportunity for allowing the infant a working role in the active organization of inner experience.

The capacity for psychic structuralization is indeed a systems characteristic, but all levels of temporal and goal organization need to be considered if we are to start from the beginning to understand the complexity and role of an inner frame of reference in the ontogeny of a sense of self.

References

Ashby, W. R. (1952). *Design for a Brain*, London: Chapman & Hall.

Glassman, R. B. (1973). Persistence and loose coupling in living systems. *Behavioral Science*, 18:83–98.

Kalverboer, A. F., Touwen, B. C. L., & Prechtl, H. F. R. (1973). Follow up of infants at risk of minor brain dysfunction. *Annals of the New York Academy of Sciences*, 205:172.

Metzoff, A. (1985). The roots of social and cognitive development: Models of man's original nature. In T. Field and N. Fox, ed., *Social Perception in Infants*. Norwood, NJ: Ablex.

Prechtl, H. F. R. (1968). Polygraphic studies of the fullterm newborn infant II: Computer analysis of recorded data. In M. Bax & R. Mackeith, ed., *Studies in Infancy*. London: Heinemann.

———— Weinman, H., & Akiyama, Y. (1969). Organization of physiological parameters in normal and neurologically abnormal infants: Comprehensive computer analysis of polygraphic data. *Neuropaediatric*, 1:101–129.

Sander, L. W. (1969). Regulation and organization in the early infant-caretaker system. In R. J. Robinson, ed., *Brain and Early Behavior*, London: Academic Press.

———— (1983). Polarity, paradox and the organizing process in development, In J. Call, E. Galenson, & R. Tyson, eds., *Frontiers of Infant Psychiatry*. New York: Basic Books.

———— (1985). Toward a logic of organization in psychobiological development. In H. Klar & L. Siever, ed., *Biologic Response Styles: Clinical Implications*. APA Monograph. (Note: This paper contains most of the ideas presented herein in summary form).

Stern, D. (1985). *The Interpersonal World of the Infant*. New York: Basic Books.

Winnicott, D. W. (1958a). Transitional objects and transitional phenomena. In *Collected Papers*. New York: Basic Books.

———— (1958b). The capacity to be alone. *The Maturational Processes and the Facilitating Environment*. New York: International Universities Press, 1965.

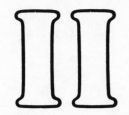

Self Psychology and the Psychoses

A Short History of the Psychoanalytic Approach to the Treatment of Psychotic Disorders

Arthur Malin

A psychoanalytic approach to the theory and treatment of psychosis has been discussed in the literature since Freud's early writings. In "Further Remarks on the Neuro-Psychosis of Defence" (1896) Freud reported a case of chronic paranoia. At that time, before the development of an instinct theory, he described paranoia as proceeding from the repression of distressing memories, and the symptoms were determined in their form by the content of what had been repressed. These ideas were later modified by Freud especially with the introduction of instinct theory.

Freud was basically pessimistic about the treatment of psychosis. He wrote in 1905: "Psychosis, states of confusion and deeply rooted depression therefore are not suited for psychoanalysis; at least not for the method as it has been practiced up to the present" (p. 264).

In 1916–17, he also advised against treatment of the psychosis. "The narcissistic neuroses can scarcely be attacked with a technique that has served us with the transference neurosis. . . . What always happens with them is that, after proceeding for a short distance, we come up against a wall which brings us to a stop. . . . In the narcissistic neuroses the resistance is unconquerable" (p. 423).

Later (1933, 1937, 1940), Freud continued to advise against psychoanalytic treatment in the narcissistic neuroses. He believed that with the decathexis of internal and external objects, a narcissistic neurosis would result with the inability to form a transference. The term "narcissistic neurosis" as used by Freud refers to psychosis, and since these patients cannot form transferences they cannot be treated by psychoanalysis.

The 1911 paper "Psycho-Analytic Notes on an Autobiographical Account of a Case of Paranoia" (The Schreber Case) was a discussion of a book published by a German judge that described in some detail a psychotic breakdown. Schreber's psychosis was that of paranoia, and it is in this paper that Freud made the connection between homosexuality and paranoia. Niederland (1974) described Freud's explanation of the mechanism of paranoia in this way:

> The exciting cause of the illness was the appearance of a feminine (that is, a passive homosexual) wishful fantasy, which took as its object the figure of his doctor. An intense resistance to this fantasy arose on the part of Schreber's personality, and the ensuing defensive struggle, took on that of a delusion of persecution. The person he longed for now became his persecutor, and the content of his wishful fantasy became the content of his persecution. The patient's struggle with Flechsig became revealed to him as a conflict with God. This is construed as an infantile conflict with a father whom he loved; the details of that conflict were what determined the content of his delusions. In the final stage of Schreber's delusion a magnificent victory was scored by the infantile sexual urge; for voluptuousness became God-fearing, and God himself (his father) never tired of demanding it of him. His father's most dreaded threat, castration, actually provided the material for his wishful fantasy of being transformed into a woman [pp. 24, 25].
>
> Freud explained that during the first stage of psychotic illness, the process of repression decathects the repressed mental representations of objects which, as a result, cease to exist. Hence, the psychotic patient's break with reality. The delusions and hallucinations which, in Freud's view, characterize the second or restitutive phase of the illness are attempts to recathect object representations [pp. 25–26].

This theory of paranoia requires instinct theory and the concepts of cathexis and decathexis of mental representation of objects (internal objects), as well as the cathexis and decathexis of real, external objects.

Abraham also discussed the treatment of psychosis by psychoanalysis. In contrast to Freud, Abraham (1911, 1916, 1924) reported the development of transference and successful psychoanalytic treatment of psychotic patients, including manic-depressives, through interpretation.

Starting in the 1930s, Melanie Klein (1935, 1946) and those influenced by her ideas, developed an approach to psychoanalysis that included working with psychotic patients. The developmental phases which they called the depressive position and the paranoid schizoid position were described as occurring in the first months of life. Rosenfeld (1965) has written extensively on psychosis and schizophrenic states. He has discussed the concepts of transference psychosis and of projective identification in the psychoses. Instinct theory, especially the death instinct, and internal object relations are very significant in his work. Bion (1959) was also influenced by Klein in the early part of his career and did make contributions to the treatment of schizophrenia, particularly with his concept of the attacks on linking.

Bullard, in the early 1940s, began a tradition of psychoanalytic dynamic psychotherapy of psychotic patients at Chesnut Lodge. Bullard was able to work with his very severely ill patients who manifested intense swings of transference, both positive and negative.

Sullivan (1947) made contributions to the dynamic therapy of severely ill psychotic patients. Freida Fromm-Reichmann (1939) worked under Sullivan and then continued treating schizophrenic patients at Chesnut Lodge. She was very sensitive to the severe problems of trust in psychotic patients. Therefore, she advocated an atmosphere of relatively complete acceptance toward the patient since any aggressive approach by the therapist would reactivate a very early traumatic situation in the patient's childhood. In her later papers (1948, 1952), Fromm-Reichmann revised her views and advocated less caution and a more vigorous analysis of the transference relationship. The doctor–patient relationship and its distortions should be a part of the psychodynamic treatment.

In 1951, Wexler, working at the Meninger Clinic, described his work with a psychotic patient in which he felt he could observe the effects of the decathexis of internal and external objects. For that reason he felt that he had to find a technique which would force the patient to take the therapist into account. Wexler took on a superego role with the patient and would actually agree with the patient's condemnation of herself for sexual interest and activity, and so on. His theoretical idea was that the severe ego defect would be filled in by the superego injunctions of the therapist, and when sufficient internal structure was built up through this means then further therapy could go on in a more traditional way. Wexler struggled with his patients to overcome the severity of the decathexis of objects. In later writings (1971), he emphasized both conflict and deficiency in schizophrenia.

Edith Jacobson (1967) described working with manic-depressive states and the analysis of the developing intense transference reactions. With ambulatory schizophrenic patients she would let the patient "borrow" the analyst's superego and ego and to "project his guilt, his faults, and weaknesses onto me; or turn me into the ideal of saintliness he needed." (p. 57).

Searles (1965) made a number of contributions to the understanding of psychodynamic psychotherapy of schizophrenia. He took up the term "transference psychosis," which had been introduced by Rosenfeld (1965) and discussed an approach to the patient that included what he called symbiotic relatedness. He stated that "the therapist must become able to function as a part of the patient" (p. 661). The therapist has to interpret the patient's transference psychosis that was dominated by projective identification and, finally, to interpret the patient's whole object relations. The idea was to develop a transference neurosis from the transference psychosis. Searles made a number of contributions concerning countertransference. He suggested that the analyst had to be aware of countertransference and make it a part of the therapeutic relationship.

It appears that a number of contributors were describing transference relationships that could now be called selfobject transferences.

Arlow and Brenner (1969) pointed out that the psychoses were never described by Freud from the structural point of view, only the topographic. They stated that, therefore, the concepts which Freud applied so fruitfully to the neuroses can be applied with great advantage to the psychoses and will prove a more useful frame of reference than the earlier concepts of decathexis, hypercathexis and recathexis (p. 12). They therefore advocated that "Interpretations of conflict, motivation, danger and defense can be given to patients in a manner which, if not identical, is at least analogous to the approach used in the treatment of the neurotic" (p. 12). They went on to state that as compared to the neuroses, "In the psychoses, instinctual regression tends to be more severe . . . , conflicts over aggressive impulses are more intense and more frequent . . . , [and] disturbances of ego and superego functioning are much more severe . . ." (p. 10). Arlow and Brenner used the structural point of view and ego psychology as a way of revising earlier concepts of psychopathology in the psychoses, and they advocated a new approach to therapy that was similar to working with the neuroses.

Boyer and Giovacchini (1967) have advocated a basically classical psychoanalytic approach to working with psychotics with very little use of parameters.

Over the years many psychoanalysts have been concerned with

the treatment of the psychotic patient. But the injunction of Freud that psychoanalysis would not be applicable in psychotic states has always remained in the background. In recent years the advent of psychotropic medication has offered a promise of a new, more effective, and very medical approach to the treatment of the psychotic. The psychopharmacological approach has been around long enough for studies that might put that approach in perspective. In a recent book by Karon and Vandenbos (1981), there is a well-designed study demonstrating that over both a twenty-month period, and a four-year period psychotherapy without use of medication was more effective in the treatment of schizophrenia than medication alone or medication and psychotherapy. The patients were all from the black inner-city subculture. The evaluation of results included cost effectiveness, which turned out to be very much in favor of the psychotherapy approach. Has the psychopharmacological approach been available long enough for disappointment in the promise of a fast cure? Have we come around again, or perhaps even increased our awareness, to the possibility of psychoanalytic, psychodynamic psychotherapy of schizophrenia?

REFERENCES

Abraham, K. (1911). Notes on the psycho-analytic investigation and treatment of manic-depressive insanity and allied conditions. In *Selected Papers*. New York: Basic Books, 1953.
———. (1916). The first pregenital stage of the libido. In *Selected Papers*. New York: Basic Books, 1953.
———. (1924). A Short Study of the Development of the Libido. In *Selected Papers*. New York: Basic Books, 1953.
Arlow, J., & Brenner, C. (1969). The psychopathology of the psychosis: A proposed revision. *International Journal of Psychoanalysis*, 50:5–15.
Bion, W. (1959). Attacks on linking. *International Journal of Psychoanalysis*, 40:308–315.
Boyer, B., & Giovacchini, P. (1967). *Psychoanalytic Treatment of Schizophrenia and Characterological Disorders*. New York: Science House.
Bullard, D. (1940). Experiences in the psycho-analytic treatment of psychotics. *Psychoanalytic Quarterly*. 9:493–504.
Freud, S. (1896). Further remarks on the neuro-psychosis of defence. *Standard Edition*, 3:162–185. London: Hogarth Press, 1962.
———. (1905). On psychotherapy. *Standard Edition*. 7:257–268. London: Hogarth Press, 1953.
———. (1911). Psycho-analytic notes on an autobiographical account of a case of paranoia. *Standard Edition*, 12:9–82. London: Hogarth Press, 1958.
———. (1916–17). Introductory lectures on psycho-analysis. *Standard Edition*, 15–16. London: Hogarth Press, 1963.
———. (1933). New introductory lectures on psycho-analysis. *Standard Edition*, 22:5–182. London: Hogarth Press, 1964.

————. (1937). Analysis terminable and interminable. *Standard Edition,* 23:216–253. London: Hogarth Press, 1964.

————. (1940). An outline of psycho-analysis. *Standard Edition.* 23:144–207. London: Hogarth Press, 1964.

Fromm-Reichmann, F. (1939). Transference problems in schizophrenics. *Psychoanalytic Quarterly.* 8:412–426.

————. (1948). Notes on the development of treatment of schizophrenics by psychoanalytic therapy In D. M. Bullard, ed., *Psychoanalysis and Psychotherapy.* Chicago: University of Chicago Press, 1959.

————. (1952). Some aspects of psychoanalytic psychotherapy with schizophrenics. In D. M. Bullard, ed., *Psychoanalysis and Psychotherapy.* Chicago: University of Chicago Press, 1959.

Jacobson, E. (1967). *Psychotic Conflict and Reality.* New York: International Universities Press.

Karon, B., & Vandenbos, G. (1981). *Psychotherapy of Schizophrenia. The Treatment of Choice.* New York: Aronson.

Klein, M. (1935). A contribution to the psychogenesis of manic-depressive states. *International Journal of Psycho-Analysis.* 16:145–174.

————. (1946). Notes on some schizoid mechanisms. *International Journal of Psycho-Analysis,* 27:99–110.

Niederland, W. (1974). *The Schreber Case.* New York: Quadrangle.

Rosenfeld, H. (1965). *Psychotic States.* New York: International Universities Press.

Searles, H. (1965). *Collected Papers on Schizophrenia and Related Subjects.* New York: International Universities Press.

Sullivan, H. S. (1947). Therapeutic investigations in schizophrenia. *Psychiatry.* 10:121–125.

Wexler, M. (1951). The structural problem in schizophrenia: Therapeutic implications. *International Journal of Psychoanalysis.* 32:157–167.

————. (1971). Schizophrenia: Conflict and deficiency. *Psychoanalytic Quarterly.* 40:83–100.

Chapter 5

Manic–Depressive Illness: Analytic Experience and a Hypothesis*

Robert M. Galatzer-Levy

The fascinating phenomena of manic-depressive illness are not well understood psychoanalytically for two reasons. First, conflict psychology and libido theory seem particularly forced when applied to this illness. Freud's few pages on mania are perhaps the most obscure of his writings. Later analytic contributions, though evocative, have not led to the development of theories accepted widely even within the analytic community. More important, analytic experience with manic–depressives is very limited. Analysts have rarely used their most powerful research tool, the psychoanalytic setup, to explore bipolar affective disorders. This lack of experience reflects not only the analyst's appropriate caution but also character defenses common in this disorder that make the patient particularly reluctant to enter analysis. Deprived of systematic exploration of transference configurations, sustained empathic immersion in a patient's psychological life, and the opportunity to study in depth the operations and genetics of character structures, analysts have made little headway in understanding this illness. In the presence of extensive evidence for

*This paper is dedicated to the memory of Heinz Kohut, who was my consultant in the analysis of the patient described here. His enthusiasm for psychoanalysis as a method of research and his support for new ideas, even when they disagreed with his own, were invaluable in pursuing this work.

biological determinants of manic–depressive illness, the false dichotomy between organic and psychological pathology has further discouraged analytic exploration.

Lithium makes management of the illness easier and so increases patients' capacity for analytic work by reducing the likelihood of catastrophic reactions that require nonanalytic interventions and that disrupt the analysis. Of course, pharmacological interventions complicate psychological investigation, modifying the illness itself and, like all parameters that have psychological significance to the patient, they may be inadequately explored and resolved. Even so, manic–depressive patients on lithium provide the best opportunity we have for analytic exploration of this condition.

I have worked analytically with three such patients. At the outset the patients were told that psychoanalysis was not a standard treatment for their condition—that our work was research. The first patient terminated a seven-year analysis two years ago; the other two are in analysis at present, one for five years, the other for three and a half years.

All three patients were on lithium, which I managed. The first patient discontinued the lithium during the fifth year of analysis. I anticipated that the medication would be an important issue in these analyses and carefully watched for this possibility. Although the medication served several functions, including as a defense against psychological insight ("If you believe that my condition is treatable with lithium, a chemical, how can it be psychologically meaningful?"), transitional object, an indicator of failures of empathy, and a symbol of the patients' enslavement to the analysis, it never emerged in any of the analyses as a sustained central issue.[1]

The patients were seen four times a week, on the couch, using standard analytic techniques. In this paper I describe some major themes in the analysis of the first patient, indicate some commonalities among the patients, and offer a hypothesis about the psychology of the illness.

THE CASE OF MR. L

At the age of nineteen, Mr. L was working in an artists' commune which he had helped organize. After a successful high school career, he was disappointed and enraged when his college teachers did not

---

[1]This finding leads me to doubt the central role of orality and regression to the oral phase discussed by analytic investigators, starting with Abraham. What a lovely opportunity being given medication by the analyst would be for expression of oral fantasies. Yet such fantasies did not emerge as significant themes in these analyses.

appreciate his creativity; he quit college during his freshman year. The commune was intended to both provide an opportunity for creativity and a livelihood. After a brief financial success, business slowed and the commune faced dissolution. Mr. L grew agitated—sleepless and rapid thinking. He felt full of energy, spoke rapidly, and worked incredible hours. He was convinced that if people would only follow him, if "they got it all together, everything would be fine." This grew into a full-blown manic state. Mr. L was brought back to Chicago, and hospitalized. In retrospect, he recognized two other times during adolescence when he was almost as manic, but because these states were socially syntonic he was not seen psychiatrically. I saw him first after his discharge and offered to manage his lithium and to try to help him make sense of the episode. Initially he disliked me and went to another psychiatrist.

Waiting in the reception room for his initial appointment with the second psychiatrist, Mr. L realized that he disliked him in the same way as he disliked me. He decided that since he had never met the second psychiatrist, his dislike must reflect something about himself, and he returned to me to try to figure it out.[2] Psychoanalysis was offered as an experimental procedure, and the patient accepted this suggestion.

In the first six months of the analysis, Mr. L complained bitterly of his former colleagues' foolishness in not following his advice. Later, he complained of employers' not appreciating or letting him actualize his abilities, insisting instead that he fit their mold. He never said in any specific way, either in the analysis or to the offending party, what they should do better. When I asked him to clarify what he wanted, he grew angry. I was demanding that he behave socially acceptably by articulating what he desired. At the same time it became apparent that both now and in the past Mr. L's parents responded to his visions of greatness and creativity with worried urgings that he be "reasonable" and act conventionally.

To learn from someone else was to be untrue to himself. In his first job, Mr. L used a multicolor photographic process. The details of the process were peripheral to his work, but he insisted on experimenting with the process to see for himself that if different procedures were followed, the difficulties the manufacturer described would actually occur.

[2]As this episode illustrates, Mr. L, a man of exceptional talent and with a profound commitment to truth, was in many ways an extraordinary analytic patient. Lest the reader think that such qualities are essential to analysis of manic-depressive patients, I mention that neither of the two other patients treated analytically had an unusual commitment to understanding, and neither, I think, would have acted like Mr. L in this situation. Rather, they entered analysis because other treatments had in one way or another proved inadequate.

Mr. L and his parents struggled about his clothing. His careful dress, superficially sloven, in truth suggested considerable creativity. For example, one day he wore old, baggy, khaki pants. Well into the session, I noticed several three-inch-long alligator pins of the same color arranged to look as if they were crawling up his leg. The trousers had been carefully selected to create the desired visual effect, although superficial observation suggested indifference to appearance.

Mr. L spoke only of concrete realities. There were no fantasies or dreams. He masturbated in response to feelings of genital tension without conscious fantasies and ejaculated quickly. Affects were not described in words. That someone could feel different from him in a given situation was incomprehensible to him.

Most of the time Mr. L felt I understood him reasonably well. Being understood made it easier to tolerate frustrations. When employers' criticisms felt like failure to appreciate his abilities, he usually considered resigning jobs. As with many grandiose people, indications that I understood how he felt and was not interested in "correcting" him helped him tolerate these frustrations more easily and respond to them more adaptively.

For much of the analysis there was little, if any, "as if" playful quality to this transference. I simply fulfilled or failed to fulfill functions. By playfulness, I mean the state of mind, often unavowed, in which patients, even at the height of the transference, know that something different from ordinary living is going on; they can get up at the end of an hour, albeit reluctantly, leave the transference situation and go on with their lives—much as a six-year-old superman can relinquish his superherohood at suppertime.

A few days before the start of the first long break in the analysis, Mr. L became tense. Despite close attention, I detected no change in the content of his associations. In the last hour before the vacation, Mr. L spoke very rapidly. His body was extremely tense. Suddenly he sat up, put his face six inches from mine, and told me with complete conviction that he controlled my mind.

I said that it was essential to him to control me since my continued attention and understanding were vital and he would lose that during the vacation. Mr. L became calmer. He continued to assert that if I would only let myself, I would know he controlled me; but the absoluteness of this belief lessened. He reported later that during the vacation a tense, manicky state had persisted for several days, followed by depression and a conscious sense of missing the analysis.

After the summer break, complaints continued both about employers and parents. Gradually, longstanding patterns of relationship between parents and child emerged. What at first seemed the simple concern of his parents that he get along in the world slowly emerged as a pattern of anxiety that they and their child might behave in a way that would lead to social rejection. For example, the father had worked for the same liberal-minded employer for twenty-five years but chronically worried that his son's unconventional dress would be so offensive that he would lose his job. Both parents encouraged their son to limit his creativity so as not to upset his own employer. Confronted with these attitudes, Mr. L became enraged but remained silent. As a child he had complied with his parents' wishes. His mother, observing that he was a good swimmer when he was ten, encouraged him to swim competitively in school, which he did—never telling her that he hated every minute of it, but enraged that she did not know he hated it.

These difficulties arose partly because he had no words to describe his feelings. With his parents, in the analysis, and in his internal life, matters went on in a highly concrete and specific fashion in the sense that situations were not thought of as involving motives, fantasies, or emotional states. Affect and emotion were inseparable from the concrete situation in which they occurred. For example, when a supervisor vetoed a project that Mr. L had designed, Mr. L was unaware of being angry or sad and found it alien and unuseful when I described his state of mind in this way. Instead, he needed to make the supervisor change his mind. Similarly, the idea that a situation was distressing because it represented something or even was a typical instance of a type of occurrence that Mr. L disliked, seemed unhelpful and distant from his experience. This concreteness of thought got him into particular difficulty in managing grandiosity.

As I tried to clarify these matters with Mr. L, he worried that I was imposing my way of thinking on him. He discovered that there was one relatively successful mode of communication between him and his parents and, as we came to realize, also between him and himself: At times he developed a tremendously painful spastic colon that left him writhing in pain on the floor. This elicited sympathetic responses, especially from his father. When he was a child, "telling" his parents that he was afraid to be alone had resulted in lectures about his being old enough to take care of himself,[3] but telephone

---

[3] I do not think we were dealing here with a simple failure of ordinary parental empathy or disrespect for the child's affective states. Rather, I suspect that the same inarticulateness about feelings seen in the analysis was also present during Mr. L's childhood, so that it would have required extraordinary parental interest and perceptiveness to comprehend the boy's anxiety. However, in the absence of such comprehension, the parents had failed to assist him in developing effective language to communicate emotional states. A vicious circle then developed in which the child's inarticulateness strongly contributed to failures in parental comprehension, which in turn made them unuseful in assisting him to articulate his experience.

calls to them at a dinner party that he was having an attack brought their return and the father's massage of his abdomen.

Mr. L treated my interest in dreams and fantasies as an annoying intrusion of my own arcane interests into his analysis. It thus surprised me when, the day before the next major break in the analysis, he reported a dream, the first of the analysis. He was being chased by zombies. If they caught him, he would become one of them. They did catch him, and he dragged himself to a room with two doors with a layout like my waiting room. His mother came in and, looking down at him lying on the floor in agony, said "Oh! Are you still alive?"

The dream was understood as a response to the coldness with which Mr. L felt I was reacting to the agony the upcoming vacation was causing him. During the vacation he was depressed and irritable but far more able to get along than during the previous vacation. He had no hypomanic episode.

Much of the analysis of Mr. L was devoted to working through grandiose positions. Dreams and fantasies, though used by the patient, remained alien to him, although they grew in frequency and complexity as the analysis progressed. Most of the dreams were self-state dreams communicating in only slightly disguised fashion such states as overstimulation and fears of deadness. Mr. L's conscious fantasies were grossly exhibitionistic and were experienced largely as plans for action. The transference centered on the analyst as mirror of Mr. L's greatness and as alter ego—the companion who shared his world view. These transferences came to the fore in response to interferences with the fantasy caused, for instance, by my misunderstanding. Repeatedly, real or anticipated failures of the environment or the analyst to appreciate some aspect of Mr. L's actual or planned accomplishments led to states of rage, episodes of manicky excitement, and depression, which were ultimately comprehended in the analysis. As these episodes were repeatedly worked over, the intensity of the reaction lessened, the capacity to verbalize the experience increased, the episodes were related to other experiences (especially developmentally important ones), and the patient's capacity to find adaptive solutions to the problem—without feeling that he betrayed himself in the process—grew enormously. (I am terse in describing this material because it so clearly conforms to well-known descriptions of selfobject transferences and their working through.)

Although the patient's transferences were of a familiar kind, Mr. L's attitude toward the material was different from that observed in stable disorders of the self. For example, interpretations of the debilitating effect of being misunderstood were minimally soothing. The experience of being (accurately) understood did not have the obvious and immediate effect commonly seen in disorders of the self. Instead, such interpretations initially seemed to mean little to the patient and later often called forth straightforward demands that I, his psychoanalyst, do better. This last, of course, was a profound development in a man who had never previously articulated his needs.

In many ways the constraints of the analytic situation were even less tolerable to Mr. L than to other patients. The artificial analytic time schedule was hard on him. Though we both understood that emotional life does not go on in forty-five-minute segments, Mr. L was persistently unable to do the type of unconscious arranging that allows patients to entrain to the analytic setup, nor was he easily able to use my statements of understanding to soothe himself. I am not speaking here of the very ordinary phenomenon in which patients fully in tune with the schedule unconsciously arrange crises in the last minutes of the hour or postpone material until the hour is ended. Rather, this patient seemed repeatedly to be caught off guard by the session's end or to have finished what he had to do during the hour after 25 minutes. (Kohut [personal communication] observing a similar phenomenon in the manic-depressives he treated, scheduled some of their hours for the end of the day to last as long as they required. Aside from being an impractical arrangement, it was in my experience an unnecessary parameter.) Mr. L thought that if I understood how artificial and difficult the schedule was for him, I should change it.[4]

Mr. L had few friends when he began analysis. He hoped that a brief, intense, midadolescent friendship would revive. He also had few relations with women. When he found a woman attractive, the anticipated narcissistic injury of rejection was so great that the acquaintance seldom went beyond one date. An adolescent homosexual relationship, in which a man had essentially worshiped Mr. L's body, and a briefer similar relationship with a woman were grossly overstimulating.

As the analysis progressed, Mr. L's capacity for relations with other people grew. These relationships were based on the other person's enthusiastic appreciation of some quality of Mr. L and ended

---

[4]Mr. L's failure to learn to conform his needs to the timing of analytic hours serves to remind us what an important piece of work is done by the majority of patients in this regard. The infant's ability to achieve a similar but much larger scale entrainment to parental schedules (and the pathogenic consequences of failing to do so) has been discussed at length by Thomas, Chess and Birch (1968). The capacity that develops ordinarily in the first weeks of life, and infant–parent mismatching in this regard, is a major source of strain and empathic failure in the mother–infant dyad.

when he felt inadequately appreciated. This need gradually brooked more frustration, so that friendships stabilized and ended less often in angry disillusion.

In the fourth year of the analysis, Mr. L had his first relatively stable relationship with a woman. Each partner saw the other as brilliant. The couple's sexual athletics further supported Mr. L's image of them as an ideal pair. That image was marred by his premature ejaculations, which troubled him greatly. Although the theme was explored at length, no evidence emerged that this was a symptom of intrapsychic conflict. Rather, it reflected a state of enormous physiological excitement. The patient thought that this state, like others involving overexcitement, should be brought directly into the analysis. He thought that I should masturbate him so that he could learn to control himself better. Failing this, I should provide him with a sexual partner who would describe in detail what went on between them to help him master his symptom. The exhibitionism or homosexuality were not surprising. What was startling was the inability to bring the issue into the analysis in even a slightly disguised form or to find a symbolic expression for it.

Similarly, we talked of the decoration of his apartment in ways reflecting himself, he could not do in words. He said I should visit him at the apartment. My understanding of his need for the visit and his frustration in communicating with words, which was unnatural for him, somewhat lessened his distress. However, my not actually going to the apartment remained unsatisfactory to him.

This central feature of his personality—that things could not be fully worked out using language alone and that an area of serious play did not exist for him—arose repeatedly in numerous transference situations. At first I thought it reflected a basic, biologically determined disinclination toward verbal experience, perhaps involving some anomaly in hemispheric dominance. But as we worked over this material and examined his current interactions with his parents, an additional hypothesis emerged. Virtually any evidence of unconventionality in this extremely unconventional man rapidly evoked anxious cautions about its dangers. When Mr. L wore a narrow tie when wide ties were popular, his parents warned him of the dangers of improper dress. This fearful conventionality dominated their own lives, and evidence gradually emerged that it related to their own fear of psychosis. Needless to say, when it came to the areas of Mr. L's personality that were genuinely unconventional—in particular his artistic creativity—this worried conventionality precluded any appreciation or pleasure in Mr. L's startlingly unusual work and ideas.

In the transference, Mr. L assumed that his work would be entirely incomprehensible to me and that I would attend only to the external difficulties that might result from his unconventionality. This intense conviction went far beyond the common anxiety and pessimism about being appreciated that are felt by many creative people. As a result of his conviction, this most important part of his personality was brought into the analysis only after many years; his creative life was entirely private to Mr. L until he brought it into the analysis. He had believed with manic excitement that his work would be completely understood because he willed it to be; or he was convinced, despite such external approval, that the work was not genuinely understood at all.

It would be worthwhile for analysts to study the developmental line of the highly ambivalent relationship of the creative individual to his audience. It may be that the experience of being creative, like experiences of good bodily functioning, can sustain states of narcissistic equilibrium for relatively long periods of time even in the absence of adequate selfobject affirmation. Later developments increasingly include the selfobject as part of the creative process and are associated with the vicissitudes of selfobject failure. Particularly important in this regard is anxiety about being exploited or tricked by the selfobject—allowing oneself to be abused for the sake of being appreciated or accepting approbation only to realize later that one's real accomplishments remain unappreciated. Conflict psychological issues clearly become important here too. Mature creativity, as discussed by Kohut (1971), reflecting adequately transmuted internalization of selfobjects. Though it is again, from the point of view of the external observer, independent of social approbation, it is psychologically very different from the autistic type of creativity mentioned earlier. At the beginning of the analysis, Mr. L's creative work was, I think, motivated primarily by pleasure in functioning and the invigorating and stabilizing effect this had on his self. Other people were psychologically important only because they provided the instrument for his work. As the analysis progressed, the importance of selfobjects in his work increased, which was distressing because of their failures but also enriched the experience of creativity. For example, at one point he became interested in directing his work, which previously had been for a highly elite audience, to a mass market, even though this would limit some of the technical devices he could use. The idea was to find a more genuinely appreciative selfojbect. By the end of the analysis, Mr. L's creativity was highly integrated into an environment of carefully chosen and responsive selfobjects.

I hypothesized, and we could demonstrate in episodes going back at least to the patient's third year, that playful engagement with parents about all sorts of things, but especially about his artistic creativity, was chronically impossible because of the parents' anxiety. This developed into an incapacity for play, fantasy, dreaming, and the use of language in an affectively meaningful way.

The repeated examination of this process resulted in an increased capacity in the area and a concomitant development of some humor and sufficient empathy to understand that people had motives of their own. Even though the lack of ordinary playfulness remained an important aspect of Mr. L's character, this increased capacity made a major difference in his life.

Mr. L's capacity to verbalize and enter an area of playful fantasy allowed him to work with problems both within and outside the analysis in entirely new ways. States of tension and demand that could be put into words and discussed greatly reduced the frustration of the analysis and my own and his anxiety that global and over-whelming responses would endanger him. Manic episodes were re-placed by states of irritable tension—which Mr. L used first with my prodding, then on his own efforts, and finally spontaneously—as signals of distress that needed to be located and worked over.

Similarly, outside the analysis these capacities served him well. He often substituted fantasies of action for the enactment so charac-teristic of him early in treatment. He *imagined* how enraged an em-ployer would be if he did not show up one morning rather than failing to show up. Though it continued to anger him, the idea that his employer had business and psychological needs of his own be-came comprehensible and more tolerable. Being able to articulate his feelings led to many experiences of being satisfactorily understood by friends, and he no longer felt chronically isolated and alone. In the manner of many late adolescents who come to terms with the actu-ality of their parents, he was able, for the first time, to explore his parents' reluctance to support and understand his creativity. His par-ents appeared *not* to be tremendously ill—neither of them seemed latently psychotic nor even to be suffering from severe disorders of the self. Rather, they were neurotically inhibited. There was evidence that the father feared overwhelming affective states, which was not surprising since it became clear that both his own father's and his brother's lives were largely distroyed by undiagnosed bipolar affec-tive illness.

By the seventh year of the analysis, both Mr. L and I felt that termination was reasonable. But the idea of a defined termination phase seemed unreasonable and artificial to Mr. L. Here too he could not enter into the "as if" quality of termination knowing I was always available to him now. Setting a termination date was another example of externally imposed time on what should have been a spontaneous psychological process. He insisted we not set a date. Rather, he would inform me when we were stopping. Though there was much reworking of earlier material from the analysis, the mourning of the loss of the analyst and the analysis were definitely abbreviated. Since termination, the patient has used one reason or another to remain in contact with me, although with decreasing frequency. The termination process is incomplete at this point. Mr. L is doing well in his life and has had no manic episode in six years.

SOME CLINICAL GENERALIZATIONS

The most important conclusion that can be drawn from this and my two other clinical experiences in the analysis of manic–depressive patients is that some patients with this illness can successfully undergo analysis. They can do so not merely in the sense that they can conform their behavior to the analytic situation and do some analytic work, but, more important, they can engage their central psychopathology, in particular aspects of the manic state, in the transference situation. In this sense, these have been analyses of the manic–depressive illness and not simply analyses of people with the illness. The analyses have been therapeutic. The patients developed more flexible and firmer character structures through the repeated working through of characterological issues. They have had fewer and less severe manic episodes, at least while in analysis.

What is the theoretical yield of these experiences? Though psychoanalysts have always maintained that the biological and psychological factors play interacting roles in behavior, there is a strong tendency to regard the illnesses most appropriate to analytic investigation as psychogenic, and those with clear biological determinants as certainly inappropriate for psychoanalytic treatment. Thus it is argued that owing to the extensive evidence for a major biochemical basis for manic–depressive illness, psychoanalysis is not an appropriate treatment. In an informal discussion, for instance, I was told by a colleague that I will not alter defects in catacholamine metabolism by talk. The merits of this position deserve careful discussion.[5] But, in

---

[5]Obviously, if analysis has any effect at all there must be some physical change in the brain associated with analytic work. However, since the nature of the physical changes accompanying any form of learning in higher animals remains unknown, and since there is evidence for many distinct types of learning, it is premature to speculate about the physical basis of this treatment or any other analysis. Nevertheless, with regard to my colleague's remark, local changes in neurotransmitter metabolism are among the plausible candidates for the physical basis of learning in general and there-

addition, this idea should be recognized as important with manic–depressive patients because it is syntonic with the characterologically antipsychological position of many of them. My own patients have seen their difficulties almost exclusively in terms of forces external to themselves—whether those forces be the social milieu or the bio-chemistry of their own brains.

In any case, there is overwhelming evidence of a heritable biolog-ical factor in manic–depressive illness. Likewise, it is evident from analytic experiences such as those described here that the episodes of illness make psychological sense and, at least early in the course, respond to psychological intervention. The problem is to provide an idea which integrates these two observations as specifically as possible.

Let's begin with some clinical generalizations about the three pa-tients I have seen in analysis. These generalizations are consistent with less complete investigations of several other manic–depressive patients by myself and others. Manic–depressives seem to have much in common with patients with self-disorders. Selfobject fail-ures, both within and outside the analysis, threaten catastrophic ex-periences of loss of vitality, fragmentation, or both. At the same time they are unable to find adequate selfobjects. They may form relatively stable and sustaining selfobject relations by drastically constricting their needs. I suspect that the reluctance of these patients to enter psychotherapy and the (often conscious) care with which they select people to become involved with, reflects an acute awareness of the catastrophe that can ensue with selfobject failure. Mania and hypo-manic states in these patients appear as a defense against the dangers of the loss of the selfobject. These states are continuous with simple denial of the selfobject's importance; these difficulties come into par-ticular prominence with separations.

As I got to know my patients better, it seemed that a depleted depression was more or less a chronic state of being for them. Periods of supposedly good functioning were periods when denial worked adequately to manage the depression. The anticipation of further and overwhelming depletion precipitated manic episodes, and depres-

---

fore in analysis in particular. A more plausible hypothesis is that although the basic metabolic defect that manifests itself in manic–depressive illness is not changed through analysis, the further processing by the brain and psychological states arising as a result of this defect are profoundly influenced. The new, firmer, and more effective psychological structures developed in the course of the analysis result in an altered, more successful handling of these states.

sion was often more clearly manifest as the mania cleared. But generally these patients were constantly struggling with depression and attempting to keep it from becoming overwhelming.

There were striking differences in the three patients' character structures, but certain features prominently recurred. Although language was used competently, verbal description and experiences associated with important affective states were either entirely absent or severely limited. Emotions were experienced principally as bodily states or impulses to action. The patients had their own major interests or accomplishments or carried out their major intellectual work in a nonverbal area, which in some instances involved direct plastic expression and in others involved a type of translation into language. Parenthetically, I mention a group of patients who use language exceptionally well and may even appear to offer elegant descriptions of emotion, but whose language is deeply disconnected from their own emotional experience.

Another area of commonality was the patients' attitude toward play, fantasy, and dreaming. Whether in or outside the analysis, a special area of serious, yet not externally actual, reality was largely alien to them. Dreams were rare, and fantasies were almost always viewed as plans. Masturbation was often unaccompanied by conscious fantasies. Transferences were experienced as actual and urgent needs and wishes. The analytic setup, which assumes the patient's ability to treat the transference as serious play, was often very stressful for these patients. They avoided these modes of experience because of the dreadful content of some of the material that emerged and because of the feared overstimulation from the material. However, after prolonged work with these patients, it became evident to me that these capacities were simply very poorly developed in them. They had never learned to employ dreams, fantasy, and play to deal with psychological difficulty.

Though they differed sharply from one another in other ways, there were certain commonalities in these patients' backgrounds. None had parents who were overtly or as far us I could determine even latently psychotic. The parents all, however, tended to be deeply conventional people who suppressed psychological difficulties and urged their children to do the same. Whether in response to their own grander fantasies or their children's intense states of creativity, anger, or grandeur, they responded with early and intense reminders of the bad consequences of loss of control and unconventional behavior. Undue intensity was seen as dangerous and in need of prompt interruption lest it get out of hand. The parents responded to concrete physical distress in their children but not to their psychological distress, except by urging them to take up their own defenses of denial, suppression, and, in some cases, addiction.

It is, of course, only possible to reconstruct the childhood experiences of patients in analysis. From these reconstructions it is clear that, from early on, the patients felt (probably correctly) that their various intense affective states had been misunderstood; the limitations of their parents in understanding these states can be reasonably inferred from the parents' behavior both during the analyses and as recalled and reconstructed in the analysis. Studies of depression in childhood have consistently pushed the onset of the recognizable disorder to earlier ages (Anthony and Gilpin, 1976; Cantwell, 1983). Characteristically, these earlier manifestations of depressions—irritability, somatic symptoms, delinquency, "hyperactivity," and so on—are often difficult for even the clinician to recognize as depressive equivalents except in the most severe cases. It may well be that, in addition to the parental limitations demonstrated for these patients, it is generally difficult for adults to recognize and appreciate depressions in children.

A HYPOTHESIS ABOUT MANIC-DEPRESSIVE ILLNESS

I would like, then, to suggest a unifying hypothesis regarding these patients. They do indeed have a biological endowment that is manifest in an unusual intensity of affect in the area of grandeur and depression. Their parents, though somewhat constricted, probably would be capable of reasonable empathy with more ordinary affective states. Confronted, however, with the intensity of their offspring, their empathic capacity is strained beyond its limit, and instead of engaging the child in fantasies, working over this material through play or talk, they protect themselves and the child by introducing and advocating their own defenses against psychological intensity. Like the children who failed to learn to play because their parents were too anxious to play in important areas and who therefore failed to develop derivatives of play, such as fantasy (Greenspan, 1981), the manic–depressive fails to learn to use play, fantasy, and dreaming to deal with intense affective states. Hence, the not surprising emergence of grandiosity as a defense against depletion always carries with it the danger of getting entirely out of hand because it cannot be engaged in a playful fashion. Similarly, language, which like the capacity for play and fantasy develops prominently in the second year of life, is undeveloped in these patients because the parent cannot help the child employ language to deal with central aspects of the experiential self that the parent finds intolerable.

Thus, the parents' failure to empathize with child's unusual endowment results in a failure of the development of the structures involved in using language, play, and dreaming to deal with states of psychological distress, leaving to the patient only states of manic excitement to avoid feelings of overwhelming depletion. In addition, the parents' incapacity to respond to the unusual needs of these children leaves the children chronically vulnerable to such distressing states. Obviously, an absent selfobject cannot be internalized.

These patients have much in common with alexithymic patients, including particularly the tendency for difficulties to be manifest in nonverbal, nonsymbolic modes. Psychosomatic and somatoform problems are common. It is as though they are alexithymic when, more than others, they need the tools of language and fantasy to deal with intense unusual experiences, and precisely that intensity and unusualness of experience made it particularly difficult for their parents to bring these important experiences into the arena of language.

The therapeutic goal of analysis with manic–depressive patients is to overcome the arrest in development manifest in the absence of the capacity to dream, to fantasize, and to talk of their psychological situation through the reactivation of the processes that were interrupted by the unavailability of appropriate selfobjects in the second year of life. This is done by a combination of the experience of, insofar as possible, being accurately empathized with by the analyst and analyzing failures in the analyst's selfobject functions as described by Kohut (1971). Additionally, the specific anxieties and failed development associated with the use of fantasy must be addressed directly.

SUMMARY

I have described some of my experiences with manic-depressive patients in analysis and put forward a hypothesis about the genetics and dynamics of the illness. What do I want you to take away from this? Most important, manic-depressive illness *can* be explored analytically. Second, specific failures in the capacity to use fantasy, dreams, and play characterize the illness and result in the delusional intensity manifest in overt manic episodes. Finally, these developmental failures reflect the experience of patients of failure of their parental figures to support the development of such capacities in the young child because of the limitation of the parents' personalities in understanding biologically determined, unusually intense, experiences of their young children.

REFERENCES

Anthony, J., & Gilpin, D. (1976). *Three Clinical Faces of Childhood* New York: Spectrum.

Cantwell, D. (1983). Depression in childhood: Clinical picture and diagnostic criteria. In D. Cantwell & G. Carlson, ed., *Affective Disorders in Childhood and Adolescence: An Update.* New York: Spectrum.

Greenspan, S. (1981). *Psychopathology and Adaptation in Infancy and Early Childhood.* New York: International Universities Press.

Kohut, H. (1971). *The Analysis of the Self.* New York: International Universities Press.

Thomas, A., Chess, S., & Birch, H. (1968). *Temperament and Behavior Disorders in Children.* New York: New York University Press.

Chapter 6

Symbols of Subjective Truth in Psychotic States: Implications for Psychoanalytic Treatment

Robert D. Stolorow
George E. Atwood
Bernard Brandchaft

If there is one lesson that I have learned during my life as an analyst, it is the lesson that what my patients tell me is likely to be true—that many times when I believed that I was right and my patients were wrong, it turned out, though often only after a prolonged search, that *my* rightness was superficial whereas *their* rightness was profound.
—Heinz Kohut, *How Does Analysis Cure?* (pp. 93–94)

In our earlier efforts to formulate the basic theoretical constructs for a psychoanalytic science of human experience (Stolorow, Brandchaft, and Atwood, 1983; Atwood and Stolorow, 1984), two fundamental ideas gradually crystallized as central guiding principles. First, we found the concept of an *intersubjective field*—a system of differently organized, interacting subjective worlds—to be invaluable in illuminating both the vicissitudes of psychoanalytic therapy and the process of human psychological development. Second, the concept of *concretization*—the encapsulation of organizations of experience by concrete, sensorimotor symbols—was seen to illuminate a diverse array of psychological phenomena, including neurotic symptoms,

An earlier version of this chapter appeared in *Psychoanalytic Treatment: An Intersubjective Approach* (Hillsdale, NJ: The Analytic Press, 1987).

103

symbolic objects, sexual and other enactments, and dreams. We have come to believe that all forms of psychopathology must be understood psychoanalytically in terms of the specific intersubjective contexts in which they arise. A broad range of psychopathological symptoms are thereby recognized as concrete symbols of the psychological catastrophes and dilemmas that emerge in specific intersubjective fields.

Here we extend these two basic principles to the most severe reaches of psychological disorder. Our aim is to show how the concepts of intersubjectivity and concrete symbolization illuminate the origins, meanings, and functions of psychotic states and how, through this new understanding, psychotic patients can become accessible to psychoanalytic treatment.[1] We begin by presenting a schematic outline of our conceptualization of psychotic states and their treatment.

SCHEMATIC CONCEPTUALIZATION OF PSYCHOTIC STATES AND THEIR TREATMENT

(1) Essential to the structuralization of a sense of self is the acquisition of a firm belief in the validity of one's own subjective experiences. The early foundations of this belief are consolidated through the validating attunement of the caregiving surround to the child's perceptions and emotional reactions (Socarides and Stolorow, 1984–1985). When such early validating responsiveness has been consistently absent or grossly unreliable, the child's belief in his own subjective reality will remain unsteady and vulnerable to dissolution—a specific structural weakness that we regularly find as predisposing to psychotic states in later life.

(2) The *intersubjective context* in which psychotic states take form can be formulated in the following general terms: A person with the structural weakness just described encounters a triggering situation that evokes both a powerful emotional reaction and an urgent need for a response from an object that would validate the subjective reality of the experience. When this validating response is not present, replicating the faulty attunement of his childhood surround, then his belief in his own psychic reality cannot be sustained, his affective

---

[1]In earlier, valuable contributions, Magid (1984), Trop (1984), and Hall (1984–85) have shown that the use of a self-psychological approach can enhance the psychoanalytic treatability of psychotic patients. Josephs and Josephs (1986) have arrived independently at an approach to psychotic states that is similar in important respects to ours.

reaction cannot be integrated, and he is threatened with impending fragmentation.

(3) In a desperate attempt to maintain psychological integrity, the psychotic person elaborates delusional ideas that *symbolically concretize* the experience whose subjective reality has begun to crumble. The concrete delusional images serve to dramatize and reify his endangered psychic reality, casting it in a material and substantial form, thereby restoring his vanishing belief in its validity. Inchoate terror, for example, is transformed into a clear and tangible persecutory vision, damaging intrusions into poisoned food, disbelief into mocking voices. Psychotic delusion formation thus represents a concretizing effort to *substantialize* and *preserve* a reality that has begun to disintegrate, rather than a turning away from reality, as has been traditionally assumed (Freud, 1911, 1924).[2]

(4) Once set in motion, the concretizing process encompasses everwidening spheres of perception, as the psychotic person strives futilely to evoke the needed responsiveness from objects in the surround. The escalation and tenacity of the delusional elaborations are a measure of the urgency of the need for validation of the core of subjective truth that they symbolically encode. When the concretizing symbols are taken literally and dismissed as madness, this only intensifies the need for validation and further escalates the psychotic process.

(5) In our experience, such delusional ideas form the nucleus of psychotic states. Other symptoms represent either further, more extreme concretizations of the delusional ideas (e.g., sensory hallucinations) or defensive formations that protect against them and their accompanying affects (e.g., catatonic stupor).

(6) It follows, from the foregoing conceptualization, that it is essential to the psychoanalytic treatment of psychotic patients that the therapist strive to comprehend the core of subjective truth sym-

---

[2]Within our proposed phenomenological framework, the classical dichotomy between psychosis and neurosis is replaced by the idea of an *experiential continuum* involving differing degrees of subjective validity. At one end of this continuum lie the phenomena of psychosis, characterized by a crumbling of the subjective reality of the person's experience. At the other end, in the realm of neurosis and normality, the validity of experience is more firmly established. Intermediate between these poles, we suggest, lie a group of phenomena that object relations theorists have subsumed under the concept of the "introject." An introject, from our vantage point, is a region of invalidity in a person's experience that has been filled in by the perceptions and judgments of some emotionally significant other. This conceptualization helps us to understand why it is that in psychotic states a person's introjects so often undergo dramatic materializations in hallucinations and delusions. Such materializations serve to reify experiences of subjective usurpation, as the fragile validity of the person's experience comes under increasing attack.

bolically encoded in the patient's delusional ideas, and to communicate this understanding in a form that the patient can use. Consistent empathic decoding of the patient's subjective truth gradually establishes the therapeutic bond as an archaic intersubjective context in which his belief in his own personal reality can become more firmly consolidated. Concomitantly, we have found, the delusional concretizations become less necessary, recede, and eventually even disappear, only to return again if the therapeutic bond or its subjective validating function becomes seriously disrupted.[3]

This formulation extends our earlier work on so-called negative therapeutic reactions and borderline phenomena (Brandchaft, 1983; Stolorow, Brandchaft, and Atwood, 1983; Brandchaft and Stolorow, 1984), in which we demonstrated that it was essential for the progress of treatment for therapists to recognize that embedded in their patients' emotional storms, enactments, recalcitrance, and escalating symptomatology were kernels of subjective truth deriving from asynchronies and derailments occurring within the therapeutic system. Before turning to some detailed clinical illustrations of these principles, we wish to offer some reflections on why analysts have so often failed to recognize or even search for the subjective reality symbolized in psychotic productions.

OBSTRUCTIONS TO THE SEARCH FOR SUBJECTIVE TRUTH

One source of interference with the quest for subjective truth is a basic and largely unexamined philosophical assumption that has pervaded psychoanalytic thought since its inception—namely, the existence of an "objective reality" that can be known by the analyst and eventually by the patient. This assumption lies at the heart of the traditional view of transference, initially described by Breuer and Freud (1893–95) as a "false connection" made by the patient and later conceived as a "distortion" of the analyst's "real" qualities that analy-

---

[3]Subsequent to the writing of this paper it came to our attention that during an interview conducted on March 12, 1981, Kohut offered some remarks on the psychoanalytic treatment of psychotic states that closely parallel our views. He said, "The borderline, with the psychoses, is a relative one. It depends not only . . . on the patient and his pathology, but also on the ability of the therapist to extend his empathy to the patient. Insofar as you can truly build a bridge of empathy to a person, to that extent he is not psychotic . . . I am calmly treating people now who are delusional . . . The delusions are in response to things felt about me and the world. They become a psychologically meaningful way of expressing states" (quoted in Kohut, 1985, pp. 250–251).

sis seeks to correct (Stein, 1966). Schwaber (1983) has argued persuasively against this notion of transference as distortion because of its embeddedness in "a hierarchically ordered two-reality view" (p. 383)—one reality experienced by the patient and the other "known" by the analyst to be more objectively true (see also Gill, 1982; Stolorow and Lachmann, 1984–85).

A fundamental assumption that has guided our own work is that the only reality relevant and accessible to psychoanalytic inquiry (i.e., to empathy and introspection) is *subjective reality* (Kohut, 1959)—that of the patient, that of the analyst, and the psychological field created by the interplay between the two. From this perspective, the concept of an objective reality is another instance of the ubiquitous psychological process that we call concretization, that is, the symbolic transformation of configurations of subjective experience into events and entities that are believed to be objectively perceived and known. *Attributions of objective reality*, whether by an analyst or a delusional patient, *are concretizations of subjective truth.* When analysts invoke the concept of an objective reality along with its corollary concept of distortion, this tends to obscure the subjective reality encoded in the patient's productions, which is precisely what psychoanalytic investigation should seek to illuminate.

A good example of this obscuring effect can be found in the persisting controversy over the role of actual childhood seduction versus infantile fantasy in the genesis of hysteria. What proponents of *both* of the opposing positions on this issue fail to recognize is that the images of seduction, *regardless* of whether they derive from memories of actual events or from fantasy constructions, contain symbolic encapsulations of critical, pathogenic features of the patients' early subjective reality.

In general, we find that therapists are most likely to invoke the concepts of objective reality and distortion when the patient's experiences contradict perceptions and beliefs that the therapist requires for his own well-being (Stolorow and Lachmann, 1984–85). This can be seen especially clearly in the treatment of psychotic patients when the therapist reacts to the literal content of their delusional ideas (rather than their symbolic meaning) which, in turn, threatens to usurp the *therapist's* objectifying reifications of his own personal reality. The danger of psychological usurpation has been *reified* in the widely used theoretical concept of "projective identification," a mechanism through which patients are presumed to be able to translocate parts of themselves into the psyche and soma of their therapists.

Searles (1963), whose clinical accounts clearly demonstrate the role of intersubjective reality and concrete symbolization in the psychotic process, candidly describes his own experience of this threat to personal selfhood encountered in his work with two psychotic patients:

> One of my great difficulties in the work with this woman had to do with my susceptibility to being drawn into arguing with her delusional utterances. On innumerable occasions I could no longer sit silent while the *most basic tenets of my concept of reality were being assaulted,* not merely by the content of her words but by the tremendous forcefulness of her personality; on these occasions, the *preservation of my sanity* demanded that I speak [p. 679, italics added].

> I had come to experience . . . a deep confusion in myself in reaction to her forcefully and tenaciously expressed delusions, which I came eventually to feel as *seriously eroding all the underpinnings of my sense of identity,* all the things about myself of which I had felt most sure: namely, that I am a man, that I am a psychiatrist, that I am engaged in fundamentally decent rather than malevolent work, and so on. . . . [p. 692, italics added].

As Searles also points out, therapists who feel the mainstays of their sense of reality threatened may then be compelled to erect a defensive wall between their reality and their patients', dismissing the latter as madness, projective identification, or transference distortion. Therapists may also attempt to persuade their patients to admit they are mad, projecting, or distorting in order to fortify the therapist's own endangered psychological world. The resulting struggle between therapist and patient stems not from wishes to "drive each other crazy" (Searles, 1959), but from their efforts to preserve the integrity of their respective psychic realities. To the extent that the therapist is drawn into such a struggle, any inquiry into the patient's subjective truth becomes thereby precluded, further accelerating and entrenching the psychotic process.

An additional hindrance to the investigation of the subjective reality symbolized in psychotic states can be found in prevailing theoretical ideas that attribute such disorders to the operation of intrapsychic mechanisms located solely within the patient. A particularly clear example of this trend is Freud's (1911) interpretation of the Schreber case, in which he claimed that Schreber's persecutory delusions of being transformed (by his physician and later God) into a woman for the purpose of sexual abuse were a product of his defensive struggle against passive homosexual impulses. Subsequent studies (e.g., Schatzman, 1973; Niederland, 1974) have uncovered persuasive evidence that these delusions are best understood as symbolic transformations of Schreber's early experiences at the hands of his father, whose abusive and autocratic child-rearing practices were clearly aimed at crushing his son's will and coercing him into submission. These subjective dangers apparently were revived at the time of onset of Schreber's psychosis. For Freud, the path to this kernel of subjective truth was blocked by his commitment to a theory of instinctual determinism. The frequently observed correlation between conflictual homosexuality and paranoia does not warrant the conclusion that a projective transformation of homosexual wishes causes persecutory delusions. In the case of Schreber, *both* the homosexuality *and* the delusions can be understood as attempts, using different pathways, to symbolically reify a primary experience of victimization. The homosexuality that was interwoven with his paranoia can thus be seen as an eroticized depiction of a primary persecutory reality.

Not only can certain theoretical assumptions obstruct the quest for subjective truth, they can also contribute to an exacerbation of the psychotic process when they lead a therapist to make interpretations that are experienced by the patient as indicating a lack of comprehension or a consistent rejection of his psychic reality. In such instances, the interpretations themselves are experienced as inherently persecutory, and if the therapist fails to understand this, because of his belief in the correctness of his ideas or his conviction that he is acting in the patient's best interests, then a "persecutory spiral" (Meares, 1977) is set in motion, often resulting in a delusional transference psychosis.

We have previously reported one of our own cases in which the analyst's interpretive approach eventuated in such a persecutory spiral (Stolorow, Brandchaft, and Atwood, 1983; Atwood and Stolorow, 1984, Ch. 2). In this case, the analyst's interpretations of the patient's fears of women, which were well documented in the analytic material, repeatedly confirmed the patient's belief that the therapist's sole motivation in offering interpretations was to humiliate him, lord it over him, and ultimately destroy him. Interpretations of projective mechanisms only confirmed further and inflamed the patient's persecutory vision of the analyst, which eventually became entrenched in the form of a full-fledged transference psychosis. It was gradually understood that the patient had been desperately attempting to solidify his crumbling self-experience by establishing an archaic transference bond in which he longed for his brittle grandiosity to be affirmed and sustained by the therapist's admiring gleam (Kohut, 1971, 1977). In this specific transference context, the analyst's interpretations of the patient's fears of women were experienced by the patient as mortifying rejections of his yearning for the admiration that he felt was necessary for his psychological survival. What we wish to stress here is that it was *essential* for the progress of the treatment that the analyst was able to recognize the kernel of subjective truth encoded in the patient's persecutory transference delusions. In the context of the transference revival of the patient's archaic longing for unconditional admiration, the interpretations of his fears *were persecutory*, because they threatened him with self-obliteration. When the analyst, over the course of several sessions, was able to clarify how, in the context of the patient's desperate need to feel admired and esteemed by him, the interpretations of fears were experienced as deadly assaults on the patient's sense of psychological intactness, this made possible both a dissolution of the transference psychosis and a beginning consolidation of the archaic selfobject transference bond.

We believe that certain theoretical ideas and corresponding interpretive stances are especially well-suited to evoke persecutory feelings in the transference; namely, those that claim to discover the bedrock of patients' psychological disturbances in their inherent, unconscious instinctual viciousness.

In this connection, it was revealing to us to review the case material collected in Rosenfeld's *Psychotic States*[4] (1966). In nearly every case presented, the patients developed intense persecutory feelings in the transference, which Rosenfeld regarded as evidence supporting the Kleinian assumption of a primary paranoid position, at which these patients were presumably fixated because of their excessive aggression and pathological splitting and projection. This conclusion seems to us to be entirely unwarranted since it fails to take into account the contexts in which the patients' persecutory feelings crystallized in the analytic dialogue. In our reading of these cases, the persecutory transference feelings regularly arose from intersubjective situations in which Rosenfeld's interpretations of the patients' primary aggression and primitive projective mechanisms were experienced as destructive, disintegrative intrusions into their precariously structured psychological worlds, thereby replicating the invasiveness of the original childhood surround.

In a particularly vivid example, the patient's ability to sustain any activity seemed to be completely crushed by her mother's intrusions.

---

[4]We wish to acknowledge our respect for Dr. Rosenfeld's courage in his pioneering attempts to investigate and treat psychotic states psychoanalytically. In addition, we are aware that his case studies reflect early efforts in an uncharted field. Our purpose here is to illustrate our thesis concerning the part played by certain theoretical concepts, still widely in use, in codetermining the escalation of a delusional process within a therapeutic dialogue.

Her acute transference psychosis (that is, her delusional reactions to Rosenfeld's interpretations) was characterized as follows:

> Her greatest suspicion was that I was *making her think entirely in my way*, so that she no longer knew what she had thought of before, and that thus she would *lose her own self* [p. 22, italics added].

> The central anxiety was a fantasy of the persecuting analyst forcing himself into her to control her and rob her, not only of her inner possessions, for instance, her babies and her feelings, but her *very self* [p. 22, italics in original].

> She could not bear to hear me speak because, as she said, it hurt her, jarred on her, felt like an attack splitting her up into a thousand pieces, as if one were to take a hammer and hit a drop of quick-silver [p. 29].

In another context, Rosenfeld himself remarks on the possibility "that if many of the analyst's interpretations are in reality faulty and inexact, the patient's fantasy of the analyst as a persecutor may become *completely real* to him" (p. 61, italics added). We stress once again that from the perspective of the patients' archaic subjective frames of reference, such faulty interpretations *are persecutory.*

We believe that Rosenfeld's adherence to the Kleinian theories of innate primary aggression, splitting, and projective identification led to departures from the cardinal principle that he himself recognized as indispensable—namely, that if interpretations fail to meet with success, it is the understanding that is faulty and that must be revised. The insistence on the correctness of the theories in the face of continued and repetitive adverse reactions had its own impact on the psychotic transference manifestations that Rosenfeld sought to understand and explain. It precluded the investigation of these transference experiences from the perspective of the patients' own archaic frames of reference, which alone could disclose the core of subjective truth being concretely symbolized, elaborated, and communicated. When a therapist fails to recognize and clarify this kernel of subjective truth, the only options left to the patient are to accelerate the delusional process in the hope of evoking a validating response, to struggle angrily against or to withdraw defensively from the therapist's interpretations, or to subjugate his own subjective reality to the therapist's, leading only to pseudorecovery based on compliant identification with the therapist's psychological organization.

Following are some detailed clinical cases that illustrate the therapeutic action of successfully decoding the subjective truth concretely symbolized in psychotic delusions.

THE CASE OF MALCOLM[5]

Malcolm was twenty-three when he entered psychoanalytic treatment. He had been raised in a primitive area of Mexico by illiterate
and inexperienced caretakers. His father was portrayed as a swash-
buckling adventurer with a violent contempt for weakness, especially
in his son. His mother emerged in his memories as a childlike, inadequate, superficial woman, prone to hypochondriacal worrying. When
Malcolm was three, she went to New York with her husband to
undergo emergency medical treatment, leaving the boy with un-
supervised caretakers for two years. He had no recollection of being
told that his parents were leaving or when they would return. The
outstanding characteristic of Malcolm's experience of his mother that
gradually emerged in analysis was her absolute unawareness of or
concern for his boundaries. Most strikingly, she would regularly
barge into his room at any time and proceed to dress or undress as if
he were not present, often without a word to him, and never with
any acknowledgment that he might be reacting emotionally.

In consequence of the intrusiveness and disregard to which he was
chronically exposed, a rigid pattern of distancing from others developed as his principal mode of self-protection. In college he had not a
single friend nor any contact with women. His only reliable source of
comfort and stimulation came from immersion in books. At twenty-
two, with no professional skills or employment experience, he settled
near his parents, who had returned to the United States. His sole
ambition was to become a playwright.

His life, in the small town where he lived, was uneventful until he
became attracted to the daughter of a neighbor and, he believed, she
to him. Malcolm became preoccupied with the young woman and
wrote her a letter—intending to put a stop to the romance before it
could get started. The girl and her parents were startled by Malcolm's
assumptions and called the police. The officers treated him rudely
until they recognized that he needed psychiatric care. Thus began the
first of Malcolm's three psychotic episodes. He was hospitalized, diagnosed paranoid schizophrenic, treated with drugs and, after some
months, discharged. It was then that he sought analysis.

After several months of analysis, Malcolm completed a play. At a
social gathering he was introduced to a female theatrical agent, who
expressed interest in his play and, he again believed, in him. Again
he was both stimulated and frightened; he became enthralled. He
sent her the manuscript but her response was slow in arriving and

[5]We are grateful to Dr. Ernest Schreiber for providing us with the clinical material
for this case example.

her eventual rejection was curt and businesslike. In an attempt to quiet himself, Malcolm began to write to the agent, his letters becoming the vehicle for his escalating pleas and demands. The more urgent his letters, the stonier and more ominous seemed her silence. Malcolm began to hear noises. Neighbors said cruel things to him and laughed at him. Messages were coming through his radio and noises outside increased in volume to hound and torture him. Threatening figures followed him or peered at him through the window of his room. He was hospitalized for a second time, treated again with drugs, and, after three months, once again discharged. If he had doubted his sanity before, the certainty and authority of his analyst in diagnosing, hospitalizing, and medicating him had now all but convinced him that he was incurably mad.

After many unsuccessful attempts, Malcolm wrote a play that was accepted and produced. Though not an overwhelming success, it nonetheless enabled him to continue the only pursuit through which he could maintain a positive sense of self. Having learned from past experience, he steered a wide course from any contact with women for a long time. One day, however, he happened to encounter a volunteer at the theater where his play was being staged. She seemed as lonely and isolated as he and, he felt, as much of a misfit. After a prolonged period in which he observed her unfailing and childlike dedication to him and his play, her unqualified acceptance of him, and especially her willingness to ask nothing from him, he began, fearfully and tentatively, to seek a romantic involvement with her.

Fate, nevertheless, chose to deal him a third cruel blow. He was at the pool of his apartment house when a female tenant, ten to fifteen years older than he, appeared beside him. Dressed in a tunic covering a scanty bathing suit, she disrobed with what seemed to him an obvious flair. She attempted to engage him in conversation but he would not respond. She invited him to her apartment for a drink and he summarily refused. It was then that he could see the angry bolts flashing from her eyes.

Now began the familiar cycle of escalating persecutory malevolence: hirelings sent to kill him, mail not delivered, poisonous gases coming through air vents, food tampered with, and, eventually, deadly neurotoxins seeping into his brain. He could neither eat nor sleep, and he began losing weight. The more terrified he felt the more diabolical was the torture that he pictured to make sense of his terror. He talked of doing harm to the woman or to himself. He felt an irresistable urge to flee to some foreign shore, but he could not think of a place where he would feel safe.

Throughout this period, Malcolm appeared, mostly on time, for every analytic session, even though the analyst soon became drawn into the delusional system. Since the analyst seemed to do nothing to protect him from danger, and since the analyst had already shown, by hospitalizing him before, that Malcolm was not to be believed, Malcolm could only conclude that the analyst must be a silent partner in the plot against him. He believed the analyst's office was wired and every movement and facial mannerism became suspect. For long periods of time Malcolm remained silent except to state, under duress, his name, date of birth, and serial number.

The analyst's dilemma became ever clearer and more distasteful. He could not validate his patient's persecutory perceptions without, he believed, playing into and fueling the psychosis. Yet his failure to do so continually confirmed for Malcolm that he was incurably mad or that the analyst was part of the plot. When the analyst tried to reassure Malcolm that he was not in danger or to offer alternative explanations, and especially when Malcolm sensed that the analyst was thinking that he should again be hospitalized and treated with drugs, then Malcolm's delusions would grow markedly more florid and his insistence on his own perceptions more unyielding.

The crucial turning point in stemming this persecutory spiral occurred when, after considerable supervisory consultation, the analyst recognized the absolute necessity that he somehow decenter from his own structuring of Malcolm's reality and from his own fears of joining the patient in his "madness." When the analyst was able to desist from trying to persuade Malcolm to accept *his* reality, he could begin to understand what his patient had needed throughout his life—the presence of someone who could comprehend and affirm the validity of his perceptual reality. It was then that the analyst could grasp, and interpret, the kernel of subjective truth that had been symbolically elaborated in Malcolm's persecutory delusions: the sexual intrusiveness of the woman at poolside, which replicated critical pathogenic experiences with his mother, and his terrifying recognition of the woman's hurt and the vindictiveness in her eyes when he rejected her. Most importantly, the analyst was able to interpret Malcolm's urgent need for him to confirm, with conviction and without hesitation, the validity of that frightening poolside impression, irrespective of how it had subsequently become elaborated. Without this vitally needed confirmation, the analyst could now explain, Malcolm's belief in his own sense of reality, in his sanity, and, indeed, in his very existence had begun to dissolve, just as it had in countless early experiences with a mother who so often was oblivious to his presence and his emotional states. As Malcolm came to believe that these interpretations were not a new ploy to disarm him, his persecutory delusions subsided and then disappeared within a period of three weeks.

Threats to the sense of reality can be concretely symbolized in images of irreversible damage to the brain. This was the danger that Malcolm was trying to communicate in his delusion of the deadly neurotoxins—an archaic experience of damage that he was attempting to rework in analysis. During the months that followed the dissolution of his persecutory delusions, a memory gradually crystallized that seemed to encapsulate the most irradicable scars of his early formative years—a memory of himself as a child, believing that he was in mortal danger and crying out for help, only to draw the mocking, leering response, "How *could* you think anything like that? That's crazy!" It was this early experience, and countless others like it, that had been inadvertently revived by the analyst, codetermining the patient's accelerating transference psychosis. Now Malcolm had at last found in the analytic bond an intersubjective context in which archaic subjective truths could be recognized and affirmed and his brittle belief in his own personal reality could gradually become consolidated.

THE CASE OF JANE

Our next example concerns a twenty-seven-year-old hospitalized patient who, at the time she entered treatment, had been experiencing episodes of psychosis for several years. Jane's initial contact with her analyst followed shortly after a bitter argument between her and one of the hospital attendants. When asked why she had become so upset, she angrily replied that it was "all the fault of the Catholic Church," which, according to her, had never fully recognized "the human side of Jesus Christ." She argued that Jesus was human and real, and not just a deity, and furthermore that his "human realness" had been neglected in the teachings of Catholicism, which emphasized instead his perfect spiritual nature. She intended to bring this fact to the attention of the world and personally correct the historical cne-sidedness of Catholic theology. Jane's affirmations of the reality of Jesus Christ as a human being were associated with her conviction that she was the earthly embodiment of the Holy Spirit. As a member of the Holy Trinity, she pictured herself as a channel through which God's love was being miraculously transmitted to the strife-torn, suffering world. She also claimed to be personally acquainted with God the Father and God the Son, who she said were incarnated in two individuals living in her hometown. In addition, she frequently asserted that the Second Coming of Christ was at hand and looked forward to the end of the world. In the world's final hour, as she pictured it, she and the two persons just mentioned were to undergo a glorious ascension into the Holy Trinity and participate in eternal life.

In what follows, we first trace the course of certain events during Jane's childhood and adolescence, with the aim of reconstructing the meaning of her delusional preoccupations in the context of her life history. The specific incidents reviewed came to be understood in the long course of her treatment as pivotal in shaping her psychological development. In the second section we discuss how a decoding of the subjective truths symbolized in her religious delusions was essential in establishing a therapeutic bond with her.

Historical Background

The patient's immediate family circle included only her mother and two older brothers. Jane's father had killed himself when she was ten years old. Both of the parents were Irish Catholics who had met and married shortly after emigrating to America in the early 1930s. During the first period of her life, Jane was a sensitive and vulnerable child whose only relationships were with the members of her family. In the parochial school she attended she formed no other friendships, relying instead for companionship on her more outgoing brothers. She remembered her mother during her early and middle childhood as a distant and punitive figure. There were numerous memories of being scolded, told to go to bed on time, and do her schoolwork, but no recall of incidents involving positive interactions with her. Jane's mother, in a separate interview, confirmed that she had been emotionally unavailable during much of her daughter's early life because of feeling overwhelmed by family responsibilities and especially by the needs of her husband. Throughout Jane's first ten years her father was subject to severe recurrent depressions and outbursts of unprovoked physical violence. The mother summarized her own experience of Jane's childhood with the statement, "It was all I could do to tread water and keep from being drowned."

In contrast to the tie with her mother, Jane felt extremely close to her father. In spite of his emotional instability, she experienced him as a nurturing figure who loved her very deeply. There were many memories of him comforting her when she was frightened by bad dreams, intervening when her brothers teased or fought with her, encouraging her to help him in working around the house, and allowing her to sit on his lap in the evenings when he came home from his job. This situation of being her father's favorite provided the organizing context of central aspects of Jane's self-definition. The central importance of her early bond with her father was suggested by the quality of her reactions to his periodic outbursts of rage and violence. In describing such incidents, which were always incomprehensible to her, she said, "When he exploded I felt the world coming to an end."

When Jane was ten years old her father's depressions grew more severe and prolonged. They eventually reached the point that her mother often had to physically force him to get dressed in the morning and leave the house for work. On one such morning, following several weeks of his apathy and inactivity, Jane found her father sitting in the kitchen, smiling and laughing to himself in a silly manner. She recalled hoping that this apparent good mood was a sign that he at last might recover from his long illness. On the contrary, he disappeared from the house and a few hours later was discovered hanging by his belt from a tree, with both wrists slashed.

The suicide was a devastating shock to everyone concerned and a source of special agony to Jane's mother, who was obliged to arrange her husband's burial in an atmosphere of deep shame. Jane only learned of it in the newspapers. It was never discussed in the home and, according to Jane's account, it was several years before her father's name was even mentioned by anyone in the family.

Jane remembered crying to herself upon learning of her father's death, but there was no protracted period of mourning and absolutely no sharing of feelings about the death by anyone in or outside the home. She told of how after the suicide a "dark cloud" descended upon the family. Her mother became deeply depressed and spoke frequently of dying, warning her children that they should now learn to fend for themselves. Jane described her mother's condition at that time with the words, "My mother closed up like gates crashing shut." She also experienced desertion in her life at school. She recalled writing short stories for two of her favorite teachers concerning the plight of lost animals that could not find their way home. Hoping for personal reactions to the stories, she was terribly disappointed and crushed when her work was handed back with comments only about her many errors of grammar and spelling.

The absence of any new bond in which Jane could feel comforted and the meaning of her devastating loss understood left her without a foundation for surviving and continuing to grow as a person. At this point a shift occurred in which the focus on her father's life and death was gradually supplanted in her awareness as she constructed from sources deep within herself a preoccupying relationship with Jesus Christ. She began to experience as literal truth the idea that Jesus enters the hearts of those who need him; in nightly prayers she sought to bring the power of his love into the center of her shattered life. Included within the developing bond to Jesus was a sense that he expected and needed her to perform his work in the world, a project in return for which he promised her the gift of everlasting love.

When Jane was thirteen years old, the tie to Jesus led her to form a close relationship to a younger girl who was suffering from bone cancer. The course of this relationship was to foreshadow many of her later experiences. She visited this girl regularly, comforted her when she lost hope, helped her carry her books to and from school, and prayed nightly to Jesus for her recovery. A secret salvation fantasy crystallized in which Jane pictured herself as an intermediary between God and her friend, as a conduit through which the miraculous powers of Jesus could be transmitted. This young friend's illness thus presented an opportunity for the God to whom Jane prayed to show his love in a tangible way. In spite of these efforts, the condition of the girl worsened, and when she eventually died, Jane thought to herself: "Jesus Christ abandoned me." Her pain in this situation was enormous, for she had believed that Jesus, if she did what he wished of her, would surely never let her down.

During the next few months, Jane reassessed the meaning of her friend's death, entertaining the idea that perhaps her faith had not been sufficiently strong and pure for her prayers to be answered. She thereby restored her tie to Jesus by a familiar means: holding herself to blame for its demise. Carrying such thoughts to great extremes, she underwent a religious crisis profoundly affecting the subsequent direction of her life. Two great pathways seemed to open up before her, one leading to the satisfactions of earthly existence, and the other to spiritual development and ultimate union with Jesus Christ. Keeping her thoughts secret from her family, she chose the latter path and resolved to become "spiritually perfect," no matter what the cost. This project meant eradicating within herself all traces of self-interest and generally dissolving all the ties that ordinarily hold a person to the mundane world of human affairs. It meant obliterating her emerging sexuality, her need for human companionship, and her enjoyment of all the simple pleasures of life. Spiritual perfection, as she pictured it, also involved acquiring the Christlike qualities of kindness, compassion, and mercy. As a way of carrying through her resolve in action, she looked forward to becoming a nun and missionary, and to spending the remainder of her life helping unfortunate people around the world.

After graduating from high school, she made an effort to put these plans into effect. She entered a convent with the expectation of drawing closer to Jesus Christ and attaining inner peace and fulfillment. The rigorous training and instruction she encountered there, however, were utterly unlike the union with God she had anticipated, and instead of achieving perfection and tranquility, she came to feel deeply confused and depressed. At the end of her first year she found herself in chaos, and again felt abandoned by Jesus Christ. Her plans to become a nun and missionary were therefore relinquished and Jane returned home to live with her mother.

She remembered thinking that something disastrous was occurring in her life during the period after leaving the convent. Terrifying sensations that she described as "inner deadness" afflicted her, along with relentless depression and periodic outbursts of anger. Although she was now twenty years old, Jane was still unable to form relationships with anyone outside her family; and her anxiety kept her from becoming involved with any of the young men who occasionally expressed interest in her. She talked over some of these matters with her priest and, following his suggestion, entered on a brief but fateful course of treatment with a Catholic counselor who worked closely with the Church. This man consulted frequently at convents and seminaries and was himself a deeply religious person. Jane saw him on a weekly basis for eighteen months and, with his help, obtained a part-time job in a charity organization that was overseen by the bishop of her diocese.

Shortly after this therapy commenced, Jane developed great love and respect for her counselor. He seemed to her to be a very spiritual person and their weekly meetings quickly became the center of her life. So far as it was possible to determine, the major portion of their time together was spent in informal exchanges touching on Jane's everyday experiences and often also on various aspects of her counselor's work in the area of civil rights and other social causes. At no time did Jane disclose her secret relationship to God that had been the theme of her inner life, and the counselor apparently did not recognize the extent of her emotional disturbance. As time passed, she increasingly experienced him as a special person with qualities setting him apart from other human beings. She was particularly impressed with his ability to cope with the suffering of other persons, and imagined that he was taking on to himself the pain and misery of hundreds of people. Sometimes it seemed to her that his compassion was without limit and that the whole world was depending on him. In part because of such perceptions, Jane offered support and sympathy to him and listened patiently as he told her of his work for the Church. She also remembered experiencing a strong sexual attraction during this period, which confused and bewildered her. Jane's counselor now seemed to be a perfect and holy figure, and she was terrified to let him know about any of her secret ideas and feelings.

In a state of growing inner turmoil, exacerbated by losing her job with the charity organization, Jane one day suggested very tentatively that perhaps she should stop coming to the counseling sessions. She recalled her counselor replying, "Oh Jane, now what would I do without you?" This response added to her confusion and she then dramatically shouted the words: "Jesus Christ abandoned me!" As she recounted it, her counselor's jaw dropped in surprise. He mumbled something to the effect that Jesus had not abandoned her, and she walked out of his office—never to return. She could not explain clearly why she had broken off their relationship in this way, except to say that he had seemed unaware and unconcerned that she was falling apart before his eyes. The counselor made no attempt to contact Jane after their last meeting. A few weeks later she was hospitalized in a psychotic state. Her psychiatric records from that period indicate that she made statements concerning the Second Coming of Christ and the mystery of the Holy Trinity. Thus began the long series of psychotic episodes that were to disrupt her life over the next several years.

The delusions that appeared during this period never became fully systematized, but rather remained loosely organized and interconnected. Jane identified herself with the Holy Spirit, her former counselor with Jesus Christ, and the bishop for whom she had worked with God the Father. She also anticipated the Second Coming of Christ and looked forward to the end of the world. On the Day of Judgment, she was to be elevated into the Holy Trinity, along with her former counselor and the bishop. Sometimes she was overwhelmed by a feeling of great inner holiness and awaited a proclamation from Rome that she had been declared a saint. On one occasion she imagined she was flying through space to Rome, where she planned to sit on the lap of the Pope. On the other hand, she also frequently thought the bishop was about to be elected pope by the College of Cardinals.

Jane entertained the idea that she was pregnant, though still a virgin, and once told a psychiatrist she had experienced sexual intercourse with Jesus Christ. At other times she implied that she had been impregnated by the Holy Spirit. She often claimed to be experiencing an immense pain of some kind, sometimes linking this pain to the feeling that she had been abandoned by Jesus Christ. She also spent a great deal of time painting during this period when she was in and out of psychiatric hospitals. Her paintings were chiefly concerned with religious themes, e.g., the Crucifixion, the Resurrection, and the Holy Virgin, but there were other recurring images of the world being torn apart, roses dripping with blood, and vivid representations of fire with the words, "I AM PAIN," "I AM ANGER," or simply "I AM," scrawled across the canvases in large capital letters. As can be seen, these ideas and images are confused and even contra-

dictory at a number of points. There is nevertheless unity and coherence in the way in which they express the themes of Jane's life. Let
us now consider the subjective truths symbolically encoded in Jane's
delusions and describe how an understanding of these truths aided in
the conduct of her psychotherapy.

The Delusions and the Course of Psychotherapy

The psychotherapeutic approach taken in this case initially consisted
in building a relationship that the patient could experience as concretely real and reliably available. Jane at that time seemed to be more
involved with the products of her imagination than with any of the
actual people living around her, giving her new analyst the impression that for her the world of other human beings did not really exist.
In the beginning he did not respond directly to any of the voluminous
religious material that she expressed, but tried instead to shift the
focus of the sessions to more concrete aspects of their interactions. In
addition to spending many hours simply listening to all she said, the
analyst engaged her in conversations about her physical appearance,
discussed her daily activities in the hospital, and encouraged her to
participate with him in various art projects. Jane was never disturbed
by these interventions and, in fact, seemed to enjoy them more than
when her therapist tried to follow the streaming of her religious fantasies. Engaging in a direct dialogue concerning her delusions
seemed impossible, for such conversation led her invariably to experience disorganizing feelings of excitement and godlike power.

Although the concrete interventions of her therapist seemed to
serve as a means of establishing rapport with the patient, they by-
passed the central core of her religious preoccupations and thus were
not sufficient to bring her out of her psychotic state. One idea in
particular that seemed to gather strength over the first months of
treatment involved what Jane described as "my plan to reach my
gold." The word "gold," it was later understood, condensed the two
words "goal" and "God," expressing the idea that the goal of her
striving was precisely to become *one* with God. It is also worth men-
tioning that Jane experienced occasional visitations by Jesus Christ in
terms of dazzling flashes of *golden* light. What her plan entailed was a
program of meditation and prayer that she believed would exert a
peace-making force upon the world and ultimately bring about the
Second Coming of Christ. "Reaching my gold" meant being lifted up
into the Holy Trinity.

On the first occasion that her analyst expressed reservations about this plan, Jane forcefully denounced him for trying to interfere with her sacred mission on earth. She asserted in loud, commanding tones that if the analyst wanted to be a part of her life, he was obliged to participate in her plan and follow all her instructions regarding it. One such instruction was for him to immediately telephone her beloved former counselor and arrange for her to meet with him. She imagined this meeting as the first step toward bringing an age of eternal peace and tranquility to the human race. The meeting was also to be a prelude to her ascension into the Holy Trinity.

It was now dramatically clear that Jane had experienced the analyst's reservations about her plan as a threat to the organization of her world and that it was in response to this threat that she resurrected the tie to the counselor. In retrospect, though not recognized at the time, it seems likely that Jane had already perceived her new analyst's initial failure to respond to her religious preoccupations, along with his efforts to shift her attention to other matters, as a turning away from her reality and an imposition of his own. This repeated the trauma she had experienced when her adored former counselor turned abruptly away after she had opened her secret world to him. It is possible, looking back, that the disorganizing feelings that developed in response to her analyst's occasional direct comments on what he saw as delusions were the result of her sensing that his remarks were threatening to the constructions in which her last remaining hopes were then embedded. The expressions of Godlike power that ensued at such times, and the archaic longings for and delusions of merger with God, were, in all likelihood, urgent compensatory efforts to restore these structures in the face of the assault she was experiencing. It seems possible that had the analyst been able to comprehend this unfolding intersubjective situation, and to communicate this understanding to the patient, the delusional spiral might have been averted.

It was through the eventual understanding of Jane's efforts to involve her therapist in the enactment of her delusional plan that he finally recognized the implicit truths symbolized in her religious fantasies. His perception of these subjective truths in turn enabled him to adopt a stance with his patient that was responsive to her deepest needs. He grasped Jane's plan to achieve union with God through ascension into the Holy Trinity as a symbolization in religious images of her need to rematerialize a bond to a loving paternal figure—a need that had dominated her life since the time of her father's suicide. The tie to the father, it will be recalled, was the principal medium within which Jane's early self-definition crystallized. The circumstances and aftermath of his death presented her not only with the loss of a central selfobject, but also with the *invalidation* of her whole historical experience of their relationship. This invalidation arose first out of his implicit rejection of her in his willful act of suicide and, next, out of the family's relegation of the father after his death to the effective status of someone who had never been. The loss of the father, followed by the family's turning away from his life and death, together with the covert demand that she also renounce her tie to him, provided the specific context for Jane's first secret ruminations on the figure of Jesus Christ. Her embracing Jesus may therefore be viewed as an effort to preserve a remnant of the shattered and invalidated selfobject bond by encapsulating it within the symbols of the Catholic faith. The subjective truth inherent in Jane's delusional linking of herself to Jesus Christ was that the very substance of her being had been, and continued to be, bound up in the connection she had felt between herself and her beloved father. Later assertions that she had been abandoned by Jesus Christ equally reflected core truths of her existence, for such claims gave tangible form to the devastating experiences of desertion she had endured at the hands of her father, her family, her teachers, and her first counselor as well.

Jane's demand that contact be established with her counselor, the man whom she identified as the incarnation of Christ on earth, expressed once again her need to resurrect and concretize the lost prior selfobject bond, following her experience of her analyst as someone who was once again requiring repudiation of this vital tie. Her increasingly desperate efforts to involve her new therapist in the enactment of her delusional plan was understood as an urgent communication of her need for a different kind of response from *him*. He had never considered or observed the effect on her of his persistent efforts to redirect their conversations toward the concrete aspects of their interactions. Now, however, he recognized that she required a more powerful intervention, one that would establish the possibility of rematerializing the lost and deeply longed-for selfobject bond *within the transference*, rather than solely within her delusions. He also understood that his failure to comprehend the meaning of her urgent demands for help with her plan was being experienced by her as a new abandonment, repeating and magnifying the long history of abandonments that had so catastrophically affected her life. This could only further entrench the delusions that encapsulated both the history of desertion and her unmet archaic longing.

Bearing these general ideas in mind, Jane's analyst adopted a different strategy at their next meeting. Rather than allowing her to continue speaking of her religious plans and her goal of meeting with her old counselor, he stopped her from talking and insisted that for once she was to listen to what he had to say. He stated unequivocally that there was to be no meeting with her former counselor. He told her that he was bringing a new plan into operation, a plan in which she would become well again and return to live with the people who loved her. He added emphatically that he was himself the only person in this world she should be concerned about seeing, for it was in their work together that the goal of this new plan would be attained. In spite of Jane's initial resistance to these ideas, the analyst firmly insisted that she understand what he was communicating to her. She finally stopped objecting and began to cry. For perhaps twenty minutes she sat quietly in tears and then thanked him and ended her appointment.

The analyst's new understanding of Jane's need for him to assume a central place in her world marked the turning point of the therapeutic relationship and was followed by a dramatic diminution of her religious preoccupations in favor of a renewed interest in the actual persons of her social world. To Jane, the therapist's changed stance dramatized his understanding of her deepest longings and needs, and she responded by forming a profound idealizing relationship with him. Each day she brought paintings and other gifts, and when she was upset he became the only person who could console her. There were to be sure many times during the period after Jane's initial improvement when she would again begin to dwell on the figure of Jesus Christ and her own special place in the Holy Trinity. This occurred primarily when the new bond that had been established was threatened or temporarily disrupted, for example during separations. She constantly feared and anticipated desertion, and reacted in the early stages to even brief interruptions in their work as if the fragile bond connecting them had been completely ruptured, as it had been with her father. At such times it was necessary for her analyst to resume their frequent contacts and reaffirm his new and more active stance in the therapeutic relationship. As the bond was in each instance reestablished, the delusional concretizations receded and the progress of Jane's recovery continued.

After some months, during which the idealizing selfobject transference bond seemed to be stabilizing, Jane's mixed feelings of deep sadness and rage focused on her father began to emerge in the therapeutic sessions. Until this time Jane had been more concerned with Jesus Christ than with her father, and in discussing his suicide only spoke of how badly her mother had been injured. But now, with the increasing understanding of the devastating truths symbolized in her religious delusions and the concomitant restoration of the severed tie to her father within the therapeutic transference, she was able for the first time to become furious at her father for deserting her. Her hostility alternated with expressions of profound grief and loss. Having found a validating intersubjective context in the therapeutic relationship, Jane began a mourning process that had been blocked nearly twenty years before and, at the same time, revivified the archaic bond that would enable her to resume the arrested process of her own psychological development.

THE CASE OF ANNA

Anna, a nineteen-year-old woman who had been deeply psychotic for several years, entered treatment following her transfer from a residential school for emotionally disturbed adolescents to an inpatient psychiatric hospital. She introduced herself to her analyst with the words, "Doctor, I turn into anyone I meet. You won't let that happen, will you?" This danger actually seemed to materialize many times in the initial sessions when she began to call herself by her analyst's name and refer to him using her own.

The patient's experiences of self-object confusion pertained most fundamentally to her inability to maintain her own viewpoint and resist being overpowered by the perceptions and expectations of other people. She was perpetually vulnerable to being swept into others' perspectives on herself and her situation, and in the process was always losing a sense of who she was and of what she felt was true and real. The theme of vulnerability to self-object confusion and self-loss, introduced by Anna as her first communication to her therapist, came to be understood in the long course of her treatment as the central issue of her life.

What follows is an account of certain events that took place during the first year of Anna's treatment. This was the period during which the scope and significance of her many delusions were clarified and the foundations of a therapeutic bond were formed. The discussion is organized around a series of impasses that developed during the early stages of the analytic work. Each of these impasses involved specific communications from the patient that were repeated again and again, communications that initially seemed to her analyst to defy understanding and obstruct the development of a therapeutic dialogue. We will show how in each instance Anna's communications were finally understood as efforts to concretize symbolically and thereby articulate the most central subjective truths of her world. Our account focuses on the effect of the analyst's comprehension of Anna's statements on her struggle to crystallize and maintain a steady sense of her own selfhood. Information concerning the life-historical background of the patient's difficulties is also included in the discussion.

The First Impasse

Anna's first words to her analyst, as noted above, were to the effect that she "turned into" anyone she met. She presented this as something both inevitable and terrible, and made it clear that she desperately wanted her therapist to prevent it from occurring. Anna's extreme vulnerability to self-object confusion rendered ordinary conversation with her quite impossible during this early period. She could make an apparently reasonable beginning by answering a concrete question or two, but after only a few sentences began to call her analyst by her own name, refer to herself using his, and repeat various things he had said to her shortly before. Then, noticing that there had been an exchange of roles and names, she would say, "No, you're Anna, I'm George . . . No, I am George, I am Anna . . . Are you George? . . . Am I Anna? . . ." Such comments and queries would finally trail off into an inaudible talking to herself without any clarification having taken place. These incidents occurred frequently during the early sessions, reflecting the patient's inability to experience a consistently differentiated identity of her own. The exchanges of viewpoints also appeared to be symbolized in a series of nightmares she reported at the time. In these dreams she found herself inside a transparent globe, looking out across an expanse of space at another globe, and suddenly she was within the second globe looking back at the first one. Then she began to shift back and forth between the two in a terrifying sequence of increasingly rapid transpositions.

Anna's therapist first responded to her episodes of confusion by encouraging various activities in which they could participate without undergoing the mergers and identity-reversals that otherwise occurred. He joined with her in her favorite pastimes of drawing and painting, spent many hours reviewing poetry she brought to their meetings, and listened as she played her guitar and sang. The first impasse arose after several such sessions, when Anna began to repeat the words, "Hit me." Although she had initially been willing to participate in various activities with her analyst, now the meetings were increasingly dominated by her asking to be struck. She repeated these words to other hospital staff members as well. An odd-looking grin accompanied each of Anna's requests to be hit, and the incongruity between what she said and how she looked as she said it appeared bizarre and incomprehensible to everyone she approached. There was no humor or joy in that masklike expression, and if one asked why she smiled, her response invariably was, "Hit me."

The therapeutic sessions eventually came to consist almost exclusively of a going-around-in-circles about Anna's ever-renewed requests to be struck. The meetings would begin when she responded to her analyst's greeting by saying, "Hit me." She then often came over to his chair, sat down on the floor before him, and softly intoned the words, "Hit me, hit me, hit me." However he responded, these same words were repeated, and when the session was over and she was preparing to leave, she always turned for a last look into his eyes and said, "Hit me."

Anna's therapist was not immediately able to fathom the meaning of her requests. When he asked her why she wanted to be hit, she replied simply, "Hit me." If he voiced his own ideas about what might underly her constant requests, she answered only with those same two words. He tried, for example, to explore the many things that could conceivably make Anna feel she deserved to be struck. She always responded to these attempts by asking to be hit. He suggested that perhaps she believed it inevitable that he would strike her and, rather than wait passively for her fate, she was choosing to bring the anticipated blows on herself. She answered, "Hit me." Speculating on the meaning of her requests, he once suggested she might be feeling that her very existence was a crime of some sort, and that she should be punished just for being alive, occupying space, and taking up anyone's time. She replied, as always with that peculiar half-smile, "Hit me."

Finally, during one of their many meetings dominated by this issue, when all communication seemed to have ceased, the therapist interrupted Anna's repetitious request by telling her to write rather than speak. He added that he would answer in the same way. This intervention was based on the idea that perhaps there was something about speaking in a face-to-face encounter that made it impossible for Anna to express what she felt. It was hoped that the less direct medium of written communication might permit her to tell more of what she was experiencing. The first words Anna wrote on the paper her analyst provided were, "Hit me." He then wrote back, "Why do you want me to hit you?" She responded, again in writing, "Hit me." Then he wrote, "I don't want to hit you." Once more she scribbled on the page, "Hit me." At this point her analyst wrote, "I don't want to cause you pain." For the very first time she answered him differently, by printing in small letters in the upper corner of the paper, "Physical pain is better than spiritual death." Simultaneously, as she looked at him, the bizarre half-smile disappeared and was replaced by a facial expression in which he believed he saw immense despair.

Anna's requests to be struck were now comprehended as concrete symbolizations of her need to feel enlivened by the impact of her analyst's presence in her world. They were efforts to bridge the divide separating him from an alienated inner self that otherwise could be experienced only as emptiness and death. It was now clear that the activities encouraged by the therapist during the initial phase of therapy had failed to make contact with this deeply isolated inner self and that in asking to be hit she was communicating her longing for this absent contact. The urgency of her requests reflected her escalating terror that he would never be able to recognize his lack of connection with her.

The poetry Anna continued to bring to the sessions also made reference to her deathlike mode of being. A special feature of her subjective states was that they seemed to be occurring within a central part of her that she felt had never been perceived by other human beings, a part that she viewed as the true essence of her own self. She was subject within this inner region to a powerful sense of isolation, estrangement, and ultimately doubt as to her very existence. The following extract from her writing, composed years before her transfer to the hospital, give expression to some of these feelings:

> it all came down on me
> so i hid in my special closet
> but no one was around
> to report me missing . . .
> i am looking for my soul
> in an empty corridor of my mind . . .
> empty is my soul
> alone am i
> only can i exist
> like a dead piece of wood.

After Anna's "spiritual death" had been disclosed and understood, she never again asked to be hit. She remained vulnerable nevertheless to recurring episodes of numbing depersonalization, especially during periods of separation from her analyst. Even the interval of one or two days between their sessions became unendurable torture to her, threatening to plunge her back again into deathlike isolation and emptiness. During an early separation, lasting one week, she made numerous slashing cuts on her arms and chest with a stolen razor blade. The experience underlying this behavior, she later explained, had been an indescribably terrible "loss of all feelings." By inflicting pain on herself and causing her blood to flow from the cuts, she had been trying to "feel again" and return from death to life.

During subsequent meetings Anna began to verbalize directly the felt absence of her own self. She repeatedly said, "I'm not alive," "I don't exist," and "I have no self." She also often cried out the words,

"I'm not here, I'm not here!" Once she characterized herself as a "cavity in the world." These statements expressed her experience of herself in terms of a sense of insufficiency, absence, and nonbeing. Her analyst, recognizing that these negative descriptions embodied her efforts to articulate and convey what she authentically felt, sought to reinforce the bond that was developing between himself and his patient by communicating in all the ways at his disposal his understanding of what she expressed. Reactions of acknowledgment and understanding on his part always seemed to calm and reassure her.

The Second Impasse

After the resolution of the impasse brought about by Anna's asking to be struck, a new theme began to appear in her conversation. This was the idea that there were things she called "blocks" and "walls" located inside of her. The notion of "blocks" was associated with an elaborate delusional system that she revealed in discussions of secret meditations she had been practicing for the previous two years. She claimed these meditations helped her "dissolve and break down tremendous numbers of blocks and walls." A leap of extraordinary progress in this "dissolving" had taken place, according to her account, just prior to her transfer from the residential school to the hospital. She said she had ceased speaking for a full two months and devoted all of her energies to "dissolving the blocks and walls" that afflicted her. The final goal of her efforts, to be achieved with the elimination of the last "block" or "wall," was to undergo a transformation she described as "becoming born." The goal of being "born" contained for Anna all that seemed worthy of pursuit in life. She visualized it as reaching a pinnacle of human development, a nirvana-state beyond the capacity of ordinary people to attain or even imagine attaining.

The chief obstacle to "birth" resided in the "walls" and "blocks" that needed constantly to be broken down. Through many conversations with her analyst it gradually became clear that a "block," as she thought of it, was the result of an act of psychic violence against her by other persons. She specifically pictured this act as a ray or vibration of some sort emerging from a hostile individual's eyes, traversing space and impacting on her face, and then sinking through the layers of her skin and penetrating the surface of her brain. The final stage in this persecutory assault was the depositing of a tangible substance, referred to alternately as a "wall" or a "block," deep within her neural tissues. In a discussion of these matters Anna once drew a picture of a person's head showing such a "block" interposed between a darkened region at the center of the brain and the face. Near the darkened area at the brain's center she wrote the words, "soul-cave" and "heart-cave," while the face was given the label, "the dead surface." This diagram was actually a self-portrait, exhibiting the divided structure of Anna's self-experience.

The "dead surface," a term often appearing in Anna's conversations, referred sometimes to her face and sometimes to her whole physical body. In general the idea was that her visible embodiment in the world was a surface lacking depth, a nonliving mask or shield that had no connection to her "soul" or "heart-soul," which she located at the center of her brain. She also sometimes thought of this central soul-part as having a body of its own, one which could be "projected" into other places and times, and into "higher dimensions" as well.

Anna's image of "the dead surface" concretized her experience of herself in her social world. The person she felt she was seen as being had nothing to do with the person she believed she really was. Her deeper and more essential self, as she experienced it, was completely invisible to other people. The being of this deeper self was in fact defined through its negativity: it was absent, unseen, unborn; it was a bit of pure nothingness, an empty "cavity" in the midst of the positively existing universe.

Anna once claimed that she had been instructed how to create her "dead surface" by "members of a religious order," and often alluded to the presence of mysterious beings no one else perceived. These entities assisted her in "dissolving blocks" and advancing toward "birth." She further described them as "walking" her through life, conveying the impression that they were protective spirits watching over her and holding her as she moved through the course of her experiences. Anna referred to the guardian figures with the names of real persons she had known during previous eras of her life. Frequently, during the early months of therapy, one or another of the figures assumed control of Anna's body and spoke for her to her analyst and other people.

The second impasse in Anna's treatment developed when her delusions regarding the imaginary protectors and the "blocks" and "walls" became manifest within the therapeutic relationship. She first revealed the existence of the protectors who "walked" her through life by telling her therapist that he had been talking mainly to them from the outset, rather than to Anna herself. In a note from one of the figures, a young man known as "Tom," it was further explained that Anna was terribly frightened that her analyst did not realize that he had not always been speaking to her. For a long period most of the analytic sessions were conducted by this "Tom," who more and more clearly emerged as Anna's central protector. At one time she had known a real person having this name and had felt deeply loved by him. In her delusion of his continuing presence she thus retained a bond with someone she had experienced as connected to the most vital part of her.

The most difficult aspect of dealing with Anna's many delusions, from the standpoint of her therapist's experience of the treatment, was when she began to accuse him of projecting the "blocks" and "walls" into her. In the beginning, she had referred to this persecution in the past tense, as if it was something certain unnamed others had done to her long before. She originally explained these matters to her analyst in the belief that he could help her break down the many "blocks" that had formed and make progress toward "becoming born." She even once told him he was her "greatest birth guard." Now, however, she said he had started "blocking" her himself and was in fact undoing the results of years of her work of "dissolving." Often during the analytic sessions, in a seemingly innocuous conversation about the events of Anna's day, she suddenly stared intensely at him and said, "You're blocking me, you're blocking me! Stop it, please stop!" When these accusations first appeared, her analyst was not familiar with the various details of her delusions, nor did he have any understanding of their symbolic significance. When he reacted to Anna's claims by asking her to elaborate on what she had felt he was doing to her, she looked at him incredulously and repeated her demand that he immediately stop. She responded to his questions by saying, "Stop blocking me! Oh God, it's killing me! I was on the surface, but now I'm sinking. Going, going, going . . . gone!" The therapist found it extremely difficult to sit helplessly session after session, week after week, listening to Anna's ever-repeated pleas that he stop "blocking" her, especially when he could not identify the slightest aspect of his own behavior that corresponded to what she claimed. He knew she felt "rays" were flooding out of his eyes and piercing her head, but he could find no way to respond to what she said or alleviate her pain. It seemed to him that he was being accused of committing a psychic rape and murder of his patient's brain, and he finally reacted to the relentless onslaught of her claims by denying that any such thing was taking place. He said he was not "blocking" her, there were no "rays" coming from his eyes or his mind, and such things were physically impossible in any case and happened only in science fiction. Unable to comprehend her claims on any level other than that of their literal concreteness, he had begun to experience her communications as an assault on his self-definition and sense of what was real. His reaction of denying the validity of her delusions was thus brought about in part by his need to reaffirm the truth of *his* convictions. Anna's response to this denial was to lapse into muteness. For several of their meetings a pattern was followed in which, first, Anna would tell the analyst he was "blocking" her or "making walls"; he would deny the reality of her claims. Then she would become silent and turn away until their session was over.

The impasse was finally broken when the therapist recognized that a profound disjunction between their respective worlds of experience had developed. This recognition made it possible for him to decenter from the literal content of her delusional beliefs and to seek a new understanding of their meaning in the context of her life history. The most striking feature of Anna's history, as it was reconstructed in her therapy, was the way her caregivers had consistently invalidated her perceptions and undermined her strivings for self-demarcation and autonomy. Anna's family included herself, her parents, and a sister seven years younger. According to her mother, Anna as an infant "never nursed properly," "vomited back most of the food she was given for the first two years," and always "refused to cuddle." Anna was further described as engaging from a young age in "unprovoked acts to upset her parents," acts that over her first five years convinced her mother that she was emotionally ill. Anna reportedly reacted to her parents' first attempts to be affectionate with her as though they were intolerable intrusions, crying and turning away. She also rebelled persistently against their efforts to discipline her and teach her distinctions between acceptable and unacceptable behavior. The mother recalled an incident from when Anna was four that typifies the pattern of interaction dominating her early childhood years. One afternoon as Anna was being dressed and prepared to accompany her mother on a shopping trip, she suddenly stripped off her clothes, climbed into the bathtub, squatted down, and urinated. Her mother remembered her looking up with an expression of "pure spiteful-ness" and saying, "I will piss where *I* want to!" This behavior, affirming Anna's control over her own bodily functions, was regarded by her mother as an indisputable sign of mental illness, and precipitated the first in a long series of visits to child psychiatrists.

The relationship with the father was also fraught with difficulties. He was subject to severe depressions and came to rely on Anna to lighten his gloomy moods and support his tenuous self-esteem. Anna accommodated herself to her father's pressing needs and a quasi-romantic tie serving to fend off his depressions came into being. This bond was the most important of Anna's relationships between the ages of five and ten. Her father angrily excluded her mother from this special tie, often taking Anna aside and telling her it would be good if her mother died, since he and she had each other and that was all that mattered. At the same time he was unable to tolerate her expressing even the slightest negative feeling toward him. He experienced such disruptions of their tie as terrible emotional injuries. On one occasion when she refused to do something he wanted and angrily talked back to him, he tried to strangle her and had to be physically restrained by his wife. Reflecting back on these years during her therapy, Anna wrote a poem in which she described a choice between being a "live monster" or a "dead princess." Being her father's "princess" by fulfilling his expectations and archaic selfobject needs entailed a psychological death for her, produced by the cancellation of her own identity as a distinct person. Any effort to rebel against his expectations and establish a life according to her own design, on the other hand, led her to be perceived by him as something monstrous and destructive.

Anna's family moved from one city to another eight times during her first ten years. She never developed successful peer relationships during this period and, according to her mother, was always considered "odd" by other children. In addition to the interference in peer relationships caused by the family's constant moves, the parents often intervened directly when they did not approve of Anna's friends. Their interventions were motivated by fear for their daugher's welfare and a lack of faith in her ability to look after her own best interests. Anna told a poignant story of her parents' breaking off one of her friendships when she was nine years old. She had been seeing a great deal of a girl her own age who lived down the block and who was inseparable from a dog her family had owned for many years. One day Anna came home with a cut on her leg. When asked how she had been cut, she answered that she had been playing with her friend and the dog. The parents then jumped to the conclusion that the cut was a dog bite. Although she protested that she had not been bitten by her friend's dog, the parents nevertheless forced the other girl's family to arrange to have their pet quarantined and observed for rabies at a local animal hospital. After this incident the other family refused to allow their daughter to play with Anna and the two never spent time together again.

The first of Anna's psychotic experiences occurred when she was twelve and were triggered by the loss of a close romantic relationship with a boy she had met on the streets. This was during a year when, for the very first time in her life, she found a group of peers with whom she felt she truly belonged. She shared their interest in rock music, adopted their style of dress and speech, and resonated deeply to their irreverent attitudes toward the adult world. Unfortunately, these young people, including Anna's boyfriend, were heavily involved with drugs. Anna's parents again became alarmed at her choice of friends and especially at her experimentation with the drugs they supplied. Anticipating the terrible possibility of their daughter's life being ruined by addiction to psychoactive chemicals, they decided to bring an end to her romance and terminate all her contacts with her new friends. Although Anna struggled against their interference for a period, they were finally successful and her short-lived romance was broken off. She reacted to this disruption by falling into a paranoid state. She reported hearing voices talking about her in school, accused people of "watching" her, "jeering," and "making jokes," and thought various individuals were secretly "ganging up" on her in a conspiracy. These experiences so disturbed her family that they arranged for her first psychiatric hospitalization. Anna's long career in mental health institutions had thus begun.

With the aid of this historical information, Anna's therapist was finally able to grasp the significance of her delusions. He recognized that Anna's experience of herself and her world had been profoundly invalidated and undermined during her whole development. The devastating impact of what she had endured was vividly symbolized in a dream she brought to one of the therapeutic sessions. This dream followed immediately on a conflict-filled weekend spent at her parents' home. The conflicts were mainly with her mother, who had repeatedly reacted to Anna's oppositional behavior during the weekend by reminding her she was emotionally ill and pressuring her to take her prescribed medications. Anna had experienced her mother's reactions as annihilating rejections of what she was actually feeling during the time they were together. The home visit thus recreated long-standing cycles of action and reaction that had been centrally involved in the genesis of Anna's difficulties. The dream began with an image of a large standing mirror in her parents' bedroom. Anna felt she was somehow looking out at the doorway from within or behind this mirror. Through the doorway walked her mother, with her father in the background. Her mother was carrying a loaded revolver. She pointed the gun at the mirror (and thus at Anna) and fired. The glass shattered into thousands of fragments and Anna herself was no longer present. After a few moments a disembodied voice began to softly intone the words, "but a shadow on the wall, but a shadow on the wall." At the same time there was an impression of a faint silhouette passing quickly across the white wall next to where the mirror had stood. The effect on Anna of her parents' reactions was to shatter her selfhood and reduce her existence to virtually nothing, at most a fleeting shadow, a silhouette of something indistinct.

Anna's therapist now understood that she required immersion in a powerfully validating bond to an archaic selfobject in order to feel that she had any substantial existence. He recognized further that her vulnerability was such that even momentary lapses in attunement to her subjective states precipitated an experience of the annihilation of her very being. It now became clear that the guardian figures whom Anna characterized as "walking" her through her days embodied her efforts to construct a holding environment that would protect her from injury and destruction. The persecutory delusions regarding the "blocks" and "walls" were also intelligible in terms of Anna's efforts to defend her own psychological existence. A "block," it was now understood, was a concrete symbol of the impact on Anna of the invalidating failures of attunement of other people. It was just this devastating impact of the *analyst's* lapses that she was attempting to articulate by weaving him into the fabric of her delusional system. She experienced such failures as extreme violence against the being of her very self, and symbolized this violence by means of the image of rays penetrating her face and depositing inert matter at the center of her brain. The buildup of the "blocking" substances concretized the transformation of her sense of inner spontaneity into the inertness of dead matter. The work of "dissolving" and the preparing of the way for her "birth," by contrast, concretely dramatized her struggle to fight back against the violence and establish a sense of her own existence in the world as an enduring experience.

It was now possible to break through the impasse that had developed in the therapy. Anna's analyst saw that his rejection of her persecutory delusions was being experienced as a new persecution, utterly foreclosing the possibility of a healing dialogue between them. When he told her there were no "rays" coming from his eyes and penetrating her brain, he was depriving her of her only means of symbolizing and communicating the destructive impact of his and others' actions on her. The denials specifically invalidated her experience of the actual fluctuations in his attunement to her subjective states and the corresponding fluctuations in her sense of the existence of her own self. The denials thus recapitulated pathogenic patterns of interaction between Anna and her parents, who had consistently rejected her experience and pressured her all her life to conform to their image of who she should be.

What Anna required, at this stage of the treatment, was for her analyst to join her as she underwent the oscillations of being and nonbeing. When she felt the annihilating impacts of his empathic lapses and symbolized them with the image of "blocks" forming inside her, she needed him to acknowledge the connection between what he had done and what she was experiencing. She needed, in short, for him to understand that he and others had indeed been "blocking" her, i.e., persistently failing to understand her and support her capacity to experience the steady reality of her own being. The analyst therefore stopped denying the truth of her delusional claims and began to give a new reaction to her pleas and accusations. When she cried out that he was "blocking" her and that she was "sinking" and "dying," he told her that he was deeply sorry she was experiencing something so terrible because of what he had done. He added that he wanted her to know that he had never meant to hurt her and that he hoped they could find a way to undo the damage she had suffered. As her therapist gently spoke in this way, the penetrating rays from his eyes ceased to flow. The whole delusion in fact began to recede at this point, for now Anna was able to experience her contacts with her analyst as validating acknowledgment rather than persecution, and she reacted to his new communications by feeling restored to being. This restoration, repeated many times over the next few sessions, also had dramatic effects upon her other delusional ideas. The notions concerning her work of "dissolving" and "birth" disappeared as themes in her conversation. In addition, the guardian figures no longer took any role in the analytic dialogue, which now began to be conducted solely by Anna herself. The holding function of the figures therefore appeared to be passing over to the deepening bond between herself and her analyst.

Anna never again claimed her therapist or anyone else was transmitting "blocks" or "walls" into her. At a somewhat later stage of the treatment, she even said that "blocking" was an impossibility, since no one can actually project thoughts or anything else into the inside of another person. Anna's relinquishment of her delusions, reflecting a new consolidation of self boundaries, could occur only because the subjective truth encoded in those delusions had been fully acknowledged and understood within the therapeutic dialogue.

The Third Impasse

The third impasse in the flow of communication during the analytic sessions arose during the weeks after Anna's persecutory delusions receded. She was now able to participate in much more extended conversation with her therapist than before, for the most part staying within a framework of shared meanings and validities. There was, however, one group of new statements that she made that were opaque to her analyst, and when he was unable to respond adequately to these statements, they gradually became more frequent and eventually began to dominate the sessions. Anna asked her therapist: "Can you know my whole life?" At first he responded in the affirmative, saying he could know everything she told him and she could tell him the story of her whole life. This was not satisfactory, for she ignored his answer and repeated her question several more times. When her analyst asked her to further explain what she had in mind, she began to show alarm: "You *can* know my whole life, can't you? Do it now! I know you can do it. Please right now. Okay, go! Know my whole life!" As she said these things, she stared deeply into his eyes, waiting in eager anticipation for his response.

Over a period of weeks the therapist gathered a more detailed impression of what Anna was asking. She wanted him to somehow become aware of everything that had ever happened to her, from the inception of her life to the present moments of their ongoing contact. Nothing was to be excluded from this knowledge; no event, thought, or feeling, however trivial, could be left out. In addition, she expected him to develop this knowledge, not through any process of gradual discovery, but through a sort of blinding flash in which the totality of her experiences would be revealed to him. When he asked her if this all-encompassing, instantaneous knowing was indeed what she wanted and expected, she answered, "Yes, my whole life, at conscious, subconscious, and superconscious levels. Know it. Now!"

The therapist initially perceived these demands in terms of the supernatural powers they seemed to ascribe to him. He responded that it was not within his capabilities to engage in such limitless knowing. She rejected this answer, seizing his arm and shouting, "You *can* know my whole life. Do it! If you don't do it in the next ten seconds, I'll never speak to you again! Know my whole life. Okay, now! Ten, nine, eight, seven . . ."

Like the communications involved in the first two impasses, this one too was repeated meeting after meeting, week after week. Anna was unable to elaborate on the meaning of the need she was expressing, other than constantly to repeat her demand. The analytic sessions became filled with the tension of conflict and misunderstanding, but without any clarity emerging as to what this conflict between her and her therapist actually concerned. Finally, her analyst told her that he did not have any idea what she was talking about and implored her to give him some further indication as to how to help her. She answered, "Okay. Know my whole life. What are you waiting for? You must have some reason you are keeping me waiting. You can do it now. Go! Do it!" Each time the demands were made, Anna seemed to brace herself for something extraordinary, as if the response she was trying to elicit would produce indescribably far-reaching effects upon her. Each time, as the desired effects did not in fact materialize, this expectant attitude gradually gave way to one of bewilderment and then of bitter disappointment. Many of the sessions during this period ended with her telling her analyst to leave her alone.

One afternoon, following another of these difficult meetings, the therapist had the idea that perhaps the reason she needed him to know everything that had occurred in her life was because there was some particular thing that had happened which she could not bring herself to disclose. One way of guaranteeing that he would become aware of this specific incident would be for him to know absolutely everything there was to know. He speculated further that the hypothetical secret must have involved members of her family and somehow must represent a threat to them if brought into the open. It was characteristic of Anna never to act directly in her own self-interest if she thought her action might prejudice the rights or interests of anyone else. Dwelling on the possibility of there having been secret incestuous contacts with the father or others, or some other experiences she felt forbidden to reveal, he decided to discuss this matter with her directly. When she again began to press him to "know her whole life," he asked her if there was something important she had not been able to tell him. When she didn't answer his question, he asked her further if she wanted him to know her whole life so that he would understand something she was forbidden to discuss. Again she did not respond. Then he spoke specifically of the possibility of incestuous relations with her father and/or some other activities she felt she had to keep secret to protect someone. With a look of shock on her face, she answered at this point, "That's crazy! My father would never do anything like that. Can you know my whole life? I know you can. Go ahead, stop waiting. Now! Know my whole life!"

Anna's therapist now began to feel that he would never understand her and that all his efforts to build a psychotherapeutic relationship had been in vain. As he waited in mounting frustration and demoralization, a shift unexpectedly occurred in his way of listening to her demands. At the time they were sitting on the hospital grounds and she had once again begun to speak repetitously of her need for him to "know her whole life." His attention centered on her use of the word, "whole," and defocused the rest of what she said. It seemed to him she was saying, "whole . . . whole . . . whole . . . whole . . ." It then occurred to him that if he could know her *whole* life, her life would then become *whole* within his understanding. The self she would see reflected back to her by her analyst would thus be *whole*, rather than fragmented and incomplete. This idea, in turn, helped him to comprehend her endless demands as cries for help in overcoming a profound sense of inner fragmentation.

Anna's therapist had often seen the presence in her art of fragmentation and disunity themes. In addition to the earlier drawings, portraying the division between the "soul" or "soul-cave" and the "dead surface," she made many drawings and paintings of faces with the features scrambled about randomly. In these productions she often positioned one eye off to the side of the face and the other at the bottom, while the mouth would appear in the middle or at the top, and the nose was located off on the other side. Such artistic representations of her inner disarray were created concurrently with direct allusions in her conversation to a lack of wholeness and unity within herself. Once, for example, she claimed she was thirteen different people, rather than just one. When queried about this she explained that one person had lived from her birth until she was two, when her parents had moved for the first time. A different person had lived from the ages of two until four, when her grandfather died. Still another lived to the age of seven, when her sister was born. The story went on until precisely thirteen people had been described, each one living within an interval bounded on either side by a loss or discontinuity of some kind. Anna's past was not a continuous history, but rather a series of fragments having no subjective connection to one another.

It was through an understanding of this fragmentation along the axis of time that her analyst finally grasped the meaning of her demands that he "know her whole life." If he could somehow embrace the totality of her life experiences, past and present, then at the moment of that embrace the many unrelated pieces of herself would in his awareness come into connection with each other and form a whole. This was another facet of the holding function carried at an earlier stage by Anna's delusional guardians. The guardians, it will be recalled, were actual people she had known during various periods of her past. She had delusionally pictured these various individuals as ever-present companions and intimates, thereby mending the breaks in the historical continuity of her own self. The meaning of her demands at this stage of the treatment was that she had ceased to rely on the guardians and was seeking to find within the therapeutic bond a means for reassembling the broken fragments of herself into a single united whole.

With these ideas in mind, the therapist posed a question to Anna the next time she made her demand. He asked, "Is the reason you want me to do this because if I know the whole of your life you might then become whole within yourself?" She immediately answered with the words, "There might be something to that." During the next few sessions the therapist paid close attention to the problem of the experience of inner disunity and fragmentation. As he communicated his deepening understanding of what she had been trying to express, her expectations of him began to change. She ceased to ask him to "know her whole life," and eventually voiced an acceptance of the fact that neither he nor anyone else could actually provide what she had wanted. Relief from Anna's sense of being composed of disconnected fragments, as it turned out, did not depend on her analyst literally bringing the pieces of her life together within his psychological embrace; it was enough that he simply recognized and understood the state of self-fragmentation for which she had so desperately been seeking help.

The resolution of the third impasse marked the ending of the first of Anna's many years of therapy and also the disappearance of her floridly psychotic symptomatology. It was now clear to her analyst that she had been occupied throughout this first year with the task of developing and consolidating a consistently differentiated, internally cohesive, and historically continuous sense of her own selfhood. Many of Anna's communications during this early period, especially the ones involved in the impasses described above, were efforts to evoke validating and healing responses from her analyst and others; responses she could use to assist her in synthesizing the structure of her own subjectivity. These efforts appeared in a language of concrete symbols that provided her with a means of articulating experiences otherwise impossible to portray or communicate. Once the subjective truths contained in the concretizations had been understood within the analytic dialogue, Anna was able to dispense with her delusional preoccupations and turn her attention to continuing her growth and exploring the unrealized potentialities of her life.

SUMMARY

A specific structural weakness predisposing to psychotic states pertains to the inability to sustain a belief in the validity of one's own subjective reality. Delusion formation represents a desperate attempt, by means of concrete symbolization, to substantialize and preserve a reality that has begun to crumble. As the psychotic person becomes immersed in a psychoanalytic process, the therapeutic dialogue increasingly becomes shaped by the patient's urgent, primary, arrested need for the analyst's empathic attunement to restore, maintain, and consolidate his precarious belief in his own personal reality. To the extent that this archaic, validating intersubjective system is established, the delusions become less necessary and even disappear. Hence, it is essential to the psychoanalytic treatment of psychotic patients that the therapist strive to comprehend and interpret the core of subjective truth symbolically encoded in the delusional ideas. As our three cases demonstrate, the prominence and tenacity of delusional ideation will vary as a direct result of disruptions of the therapeutic bond and its subjective validating function, and it is crucial to the progress of treatment that this be recognized and brought into the analysis. Psychotic delusions, like other concretization products, cannot be understood psychoanalytically apart from the intersubjective contexts in which they arise and recede.

REFERENCES

Atwood, G., & Stolorow, R. (1984). *Structures of Subjectivity: Explorations in Psycho-analytic Phenomenology.* Hillsdale, NJ: The Analytic Press.

Brandchaft, B. (1983). The negativism of the negative therapeutic reaction and the psychology of the self. In A. Goldberg, ed., *The Future of Psychoanalysis.* New York: International Universities Press.

_____ & Stolorow, R. (1984). The borderline concept: Pathological character or iatrogenic myth? In J. Lichtenberg et al., ed., *Empathy II.* Hillsdale, NJ: The Analytic Press.

Breuer, J., & Freud, S. (1893–95). Studies on hysteria. *Standard Edition,* 2. London: Hogarth Press, 1951.

Freud, S. (1911). Psycho-Analytic notes on an autobiographical account of a case of paranoia (dementia paranoides). *Standard Edition,* 12:9–82. London: Hogarth Press, 1958.

_____ (1924). Neurosis and psychosis. *Standard Edition,* 19:148–156. London: Hogarth Press, 1961.

Gill, M. (1982). *Analysis of Transference,* Vol. 1. New York: International Universities Press.

Hall, J. (1984/85), Behind the mask of the persecutor: The idealized selfobject. *Annual of Psychoanalysis,* 12/13:239–263.

Josephs, L., & Josephs, L. (1986). Pursuing the kernel of truth in the psychotherapy of schizophrenia. *Psychoanalytic Psychology,* 3:105–119.

Kohut, H. (1959). Introspection, empathy, and psychoanalysis. *Journal of the American Psychoanalytic Association,* 7:459–483.

_____ (1971). *The Analysis of the Self.* New York: International Universities Press.

_____ (1977). *The Restoration of the Self.* New York: International Universities Press.

_____ (1984). *How Does Analysis Cure?* Chicago: University of Chicago Press.

_____ (1985). *Self Psychology and the Humanities,* C. Strozier, ed., New York: W. W. Norton.

Magid, B. (1984). Some contributions of self psychology to the treatment of borderline and schizophrenic patients. *Dynamic Psychotherapy,* 2:101–111.

Meares, R. (1977). The persecutory therapist. In *The Pursuit of Intimacy.* Melbourne: Thomas Nelson.

Niederland, W. (1974). *The Schreber Case*. New York: Quadrangle.

Rosenfeld, H. (1966). *Psychotic States*. New York: International Universities Press.

Schatzman, M. (1973). *Soul Murder: Persecution in the Family*. New York: Random House.

Schwaber, E. (1983). Psychoanalytic listening and psychic reality. *International Review of PsychoAnalysis*, 10:379–392.

Searles, H. (1959). The effort to drive the other person crazy—An element in the aetiology and psychotherapy of schizophrenia. In *Collected Papers on Schizophrenia and Related Subjects*. New York: International Universities Press, 1965.

_____ (1963). Transference psychosis in the psychotherapy of chronic schizophrenia. In *Collected Papers on Schizophrenia and Related Subjects*. New York: International Universities Press, 1965.

Socarides, D., & Stolorow, R. (1984–85). Affects and selfobjects. *Annual of Psychoanalysis*, 12/13:105–119.

Stein, M. (1966). Self-observation, reality, and the superego. In R. Loewenstein et al., ed., *Psychoanalysis—A General Psychology*. New York: International Universities Press.

Stolorow, R., Brandchaft, B., & Atwood, G. (1983). Intersubjectivity in psychoanalytic treatment: With special reference to archaic states. *Bulletin of the Menninger Clinic*, 47:117–128.

_____ & Lachmann, F. (1984–85). Transference: The future of an illusion. *Annual of Psychoanalysis*, 12/13:19–37.

Trop, J. (1984). Self psychology and the psychotherapy of psychotic patients: A case study. *Clinical Social Work Journal*, 12:292–302.

Chapter 7

Reflections on Self Psychology and the Psychoses

PSYCHOSIS AND FAILURE OF COGNITIVE DEVELOPMENT
Michael Franz Basch

The power of the selfobject theory of motivation has exceeded the hopes of even its originator. Kohut was confident that his contribution had widened the scope of psychoanalysis to include narcissistic personality disorders, but he believed that neither borderline nor psychotic disorders could be analytically treated (Kohut, 1971). Those disorders reflected a basic lack of cohesion of the self and were therefore considered to be beyond the pale of psychoanalysis.

The work of Adler, Atwood, Brandchaft, Lachmann, and Stolorow apparently persuaded Kohut that borderline problems were, after all, potentially available to psychoanalysis, for he mentions this possibility, albeit quite cautiously, in *How Does Analysis Cure?* (1984). But here are two contributions giving the clinical evidence that the pathology of psychotic patients can now be understood in the framework of the selfobject transference and successfully analyzed. How can this be? How can patients who do not have a cohesive self respond to the demands of the analytic situation? According to our theory, these patients are not anxious about the danger of fragmentation of the self; they are fragmented, or in a state bordering on fragmentation, and attempts at analysis would only add more stress and simply make a bad situation worse. The answer that always seems to lie at hand when analysts are puzzled by clinical results that they cannot account for with their theory is to say, "It's nice work and very necessary, but it's not analysis." That is the opinion many members of the establishment have concerning Kohut's and our work with narcissistic personality disorders. It never seems to occur to them that maybe the theory is wrong and needs to be amended.

Freud was not comfortable and generally had no success with patients who had what we today call narcissistic personality disorders, because he did not understand the nature of their defenses as well as he did secondary repression, the paramount defense of psychoneurotics. As a result, what psychoanalysis was, and who could be psychoanalyzed, came to be defined in terms of the defense of repression. However, Kohut's work with narcissistic personality disorders dealt primarily with the defense of disavowal, though he was not aware of that when he first made his clinical discoveries. Kohut insisted, quite correctly, that since he had obtained his treatment results with narcissistic personality disorders through the method of empathy and introspection, these were analytic results even though they differed from what was traditionally achieved in the successful analysis of psychoneurotic patients.

Not surprisingly, Kohut's theory of the self was based on his work in removing the roadblocks to maturity of patients with narcissistic personality disorders, and the concept of a cohesive self came to be defined in those terms. This meant that persons who could be said to have a cohesive self were those who, if it became necessary, could defend their integrity through either repression or disavowal. It follows, given that definition, that borderline patients and psychotics who cannot utilize these defenses (a limitation that, I suggest, is responsible for the course their pathology takes) do not possess cohesive selves and theoretically are unanalyzable.

I think Kohut, like Freud, was unnecessarily pessimistic about the potential efficacy of his discoveries because of the limitation placed on all theories of development based on retrospective evidence obtained in clinical work with adult patients. As clinicians we get a picture of the developmental process that is of necessity distorted and restricted. Fortunately, we now have the advantage of being able to step outside our own field and its particular methodology and check our findings against those of related but methodologically distinct disciplines, especially relatively recent investigations into infant and child development. From these observations we can learn that Kohut's contribution to our understanding of the transference situation, the selfobject theory of motivation, is as powerful as it is in its clinical application because it complements what research has revealed about the development of thought.

In systems theory, information is defined as anything that makes a difference to a system confronted by alternatives. Extensive research has shown that some stimuli make more of a difference to infants than do other sensory signals. Bright colors are preferred to gray, structure to formlessness, and the new to the familiar. Above all, signals given by other human beings capture the baby's full attention and interest in preference to all others. All this predisposes the infant to explore the world and make contact with the adults on whom his well-being depends. This is not learned behavior, but instinctual in the true sense; that is, the infant's preferential reaction to certain stimuli is determined by the genetically transmitted blueprint that sets our young on the road to becoming functioning human beings, very much as lambs are programmed at birth to become sheep, and tadpoles frogs (Basch, 1977).

Papousek (1969) has reported an experiment corroborating that the supraordinate striving that leads to actualization and coordination of the infant's potential is what White (1959) has called effectance pleasure—pleasure in being a cause. Papousek, using milk as a reward, first conditioned preverbal, four-month-old infants to turn to the left when a bell sounded and to the right for a buzzer. Both bell and buzzer rang in the midline, so the infants did not simply turn to the source of the stimulus but, rather, had to learn the response called for by different sounds. Interestingly, the infants, when satiated and no longer interested in drinking the milk they had earned by their performance, still responded appropriately to the signals, demonstrating obvious pleasure at their performance. Papousek concludes: "So it looked as if some motivation other than hunger was involved—some demand to respond correctly or to solve a problem. And the congruence between the infant's plan or expectation and the real events seemed to please him" (p. 255). Papousek suggests that what adults interpret as the infant's striving for competency is on the neurological level "the response to incongruity" (p. 264).

Over the years, further experimentation by Papousek and others corroborated that, just as in later life, the infant's basic goal is to function competently. Or, as Bower put it, what is basically rewarding for the infant is the establishment of contingent control over events in the external world (cited in Broucek, 1979, p. 312).

White (1959) makes it clear that the striving for effectance as a motivation for behavior is not a new idea: Among others, Groos (1901) wrote of the child's joy in being a cause; Bühler (1924) called this phenomenon *Functionslust* (the pleasure of functioning); Hendricks (1942) postulated an instinct to master.

The primary function of the brain is to create order, and it is this function that is represented by competence on the experiential level. Neurologically, the ordering function is carried out through negative or deviation-correcting feedback cycles. The establishment of order based on the patterns of expectation of that particular brain leads to effectance pleasure. The infant can achieve order and experience effectance pleasure in two ways. He can fulfill his needs through his own efforts, or, as is more frequently the case in the early years, he can use the inherent, automatic, and, at first, involuntary affective reactions to signal his need for help (Basch, 1976). If he then recruits an appropriate selfobject response, relieving the tensions he experiences, then the baby will also have achieved competence. Though unable to help himself directly, he has communicated effectively and restored order in that manner. All these activities lay down patterns of expectation in the brain, rules for problem solving that form the preverbal, affectively toned, sensorimotor foundation for character development. New patterns of expectation and modification of old ones occur as the infant copes both with inevitable frustration and also independently explores himself and the world during periods of optimal equilibrium with the surround.

Significant failure, for whatever reason, in the process of building up a network of adaptive patterns, may well lead to either maladaptive feedback cycles and/or a restricted set of coping mechanisms as the infant has to concentrate more on dealing with distressing affect to the exclusion of exploration and experimentation in the environment.

Early in life, cognitive development lags far behind the capacity for affective communication, and the only mechanism for coping with hyperstimulation is withdrawal—turning the head away, closing the eyes, falling into a stupor, or going off to sleep. Used appropriately, withdrawal spares the organism unnecessary hyperstimulation from the external world. When, however, the infant's own activity becomes a source of frustration and pain, withdrawal limits, in part or massively, the baby's attempts at affective communication and interferes with further development in that area. That is, once an affect pattern is associated primarily with pain and frustration, a pattern of avoidance is laid down that is activated whenever the affects concerned are mobilized.

I suspect that it is at this earliest level of affective maturation that Galatzer-Levy's patient suffered the massive empathic failure that determined the course of his self-development. Judging from the infant research done by Daniel Stern (1984), I suspect that, given what came out in the course of therapy of this manic patient, his parents were too anxious to be attuned to their baby—that is, to follow in voice, with gestures, or in other ways his affective states and, using such cross-modal communications, to make affect a part of shared experience for him. As the parents subsequently acted out with the patient, they could communicate with him effectively only on the sensorimotor, the nonreflective, level of physical pain, responding in soothing fashion to distress caused by somatic disorders. As a result, the normal progression from affect, to feeling, to emotion, and finally to the capacity for empathy with others, never took place (Basch, 1983a). The tensions this highly creative man experienced could not be channeled into appropriate affective communication; he had, as the analyst tells us, no words with which to describe the autonomic responses to stimulus gradients and intensity that, as Tomkins (1962–63, 1970, 1980, 1981) has taught us, constitute basic affect. Predictably, when reflection and symbolic representation became a possibility in what Piaget (1969) calls the preoperational period—around the second year of life, a time when imaginative play, dreams, and fantasy become a possibility and serve as a means for controlling affective tension—this patient could not develop these filters for grandiosity. He either had to retreat into a chronic depression, which, when it threatened to become overwhelming, led (probably because of a hereditary predisposition to that disorder) to manic states.

The analyst's empathic grasp of this patient's developmental arrest and its consequences as it was played out first in the defense transference and later, when that had been surmounted, in the transference proper (an archaic merger and then a mirror transference), resulted in the undoing of that developmental arrest and a visible progression of affective development. Although it is not spelled out in Galatzer-Levy's paper, I suspect that what evolved and now sustains the patient is an alter ego transference. Through the analyst, the patient has for the first time received confirmation that he belongs to the human race, even though his creative gifts may set him apart in certain respects from his fellows.

With time the brain's maturation permits the development of increasingly sophisticated cognitive mechanisms. In the so-called preoperational phase (from age two to five or six), the beginning of the symbolic function lets an initial *concept* of self as distinguished from others come into existence. But that self is conceived as the center of all experience; the other is never an entity in his own right. At this stage, cause and effect are never decentered. The child is the cause of everything, and everything that happens is experienced as affecting the child personally. There is, for example, no such thing as chance.

With the development of concrete operations and the beginning of logical constraints on thought in the sixth year or so, the separation of self from the other becomes a possibility.

As I have already mentioned in the case of withdrawal, what we experience as resistance or defense in the clinical situation are the normal cognitive mechanisms with which the brain fulfills its function of creating order out of the sea of stimuli that constantly impinge upon it. It is only when psychological development has been impeded that the activity of these mechanisms appears destructive rather than constructive. So it is with disavowal, a major defense discovered by Freud (in 1927), a mechanism that probably becomes operative with the onset of what Piaget calls the concrete operational phase. Whereas in infancy no concept of self as self existed, and in the preoperational phase of childhood the self and the world were indistinguishable, now disavowal, by making it possible to evaluate experience in terms of its degree of significance or lack of significance for the self, makes possible a separate self and two stores of memory— the semantic that deals with facts as facts, and the episodic, which, by permitting an affective connection, relates experiences significant for the self to the self (Basch, 1983b).

In narcissistic personality disorders we encounter a warding off of memories that rightfully involved the self though the creation of an affective blockade in response to a selfobject failure of traumatic intensity; that makes mobilization of affect appear potentially disorganizing or even fragmenting. Kohut called this the vertical split, the patient presenting a false self to consciousness and to the world, always vulnerable and in danger of having the earlier self and its affective needs intruding and disturbing the pathological balance that had been achieved. In other words, narcissistic personality disorders suffer from excessive disavowal.

When the opposite situation exists, when disavowal fails, the result, as Freud (1937, 1940) intimated, is psychosis. Unable to separate the self from the affective overstimulation directed toward it, the brain attempts to preserve its ordering function by reverting to the kind of thinking that is present in the preoperational phase, where everything is related to the self and explained in idiosyncratic ways. Freud called this primary process thinking. When it governs an adult's life we, the observers, experience it as delusional thinking. This was of course the situation in the case described here by Stolorow and his coauthors. The patient was never permitted to develop a protective barrier for the self, an empathic wall as Nathanson (1986) has called it; he could not use disavowal to separate his concept of self from his mother's intrusive demands. It may well be that there is an organic component predisposing one to react the way this patient did to his mother's inability to tolerate a child separate from her; other children exposed to such stresses may react differently because of a different chemical makeup. Be that as it may, what is of importance for us is that, relying on the psychoanalytic method of introspection and empathy, the analyst was able to grasp the symbolic significance of the patient's delusions, the latter representing a reaction to a failure in empathic mirroring, and by giving the patient's delusions understanding and credibility, supply that which made attempts at delusional adaptation no longer necessary. We do not know enough about how the case proceeded to know what the outcome was. Hypothetically speaking, what should have happened is that the patient developed the cognitive capacity for protecting his self-concept from untoward intrusion. Traumatic overstimulation would then, one might speculate, have resulted in disavowal of the meaning of the traumatic experience for the self, rather than in a fragmentation of the self necessitating delusional attempts at self-restoration. Paradoxically, the result of the analysis of this psychotic patient would be not the resolution but, rather, the institution of a defensive structure, giving the patient, as it were, both the permission and the wherewithal to develop an enclave of privacy, safe from intrusion of what had been overwhelming stimulation.

To return now to a question raised earlier: Are the therapeutic efforts described in this volume psychoanalysis, or are the results, elegant as they are, accounted for "only by reparenting" and a so-called emotionally corrective experience? No more, I would say, than the analysis of a psychoneurotic patient is only a matter of reparenting or the provision of a corrective emotional experience. The analyst who understands his neurotic patients' need to be accepted in spite of their incestuous wishes and their conviction that they cannot possibly be so accepted, reworks, through interpretation guided by empathy and introspection, *that* particular empathic failure. The analysts reporting this work here were able to do the same for patients in whom crucial empathic failures had occurred at different, earlier points in development.

The clinical significance of Kohut's contribution in freeing us from the constraints of the instinct theory is that, at least in principle, we are now free to work analytically with all patients and may hope to achieve results similar though, given the differences in development and choice of pathology, not identical with those Freud first made possible for the neurotic patient.

Our clinical horizons are changing; with that so will our theoretical formulations and our definitions as to what constitutes psychoanalysis.

REFERENCES

Basch, M. F. (1976). The concept of affect: A re-examination. *Journal of the American Psychoanalytic Association*, 24:759–777.

———— (1977). Developmental psychology and explanatory theory in psychoanalysis. *The Annual of Psychoanalysis*, 5:229–263.

———— (1983a). Empathic understanding: A review of the concept and some theoretical considerations. *Journal of the American Psychoanalytic Association*, 31:101–126.

———— (1983b). The perception of reality and the disavowal of meaning. *The Annual of Psychoanalysis*, 11:125–154.

Bower, T. G. R. (1977). *A Primer of Infant Development*. San Francisco: W. H. Freeman.

Broucek, F. (1979). Efficacy in infancy: A review of some experimental studies and their possible implications for clinical theory. *International Journal of Psychoanalysis*. 60:311–316.

Freud, S. (1927). Fetishism. *Standard Edition*, 21:152–157. London: Hogarth Press, 1961.

———— (1937). Constructions in analysis. *Standard Edition*, 23:255–269. London: Hogarth Press, 1964.

———— (1940). An outline of psycho-analysis. *Standard Edition*, 23:141–207. London: Hogarth Press, 1964.

Kohut, H. (1971). *The Analysis of the Self*. New York: International Universities Press.

———— (1984). *How Does Analysis Cure?* Chicago: University of Chicago Press.

Nathanson, D. L. (1986). Denial, projection and the empathic wall. In E. Edelstein, ed., *Denial: A Theoretical Clarification*. New York: Plenum.

Papousek, H. (1969). Individual variability in learned responses in human infants. In R. J. Robinson, ed., *Brain and Early Behaviour*. R. J. Robinson, ed., New York: Academic Press.

Piaget, J. & Inhelder, B. (1969). *The Psychology of the Child*. New York: Basic Books.

Stern, D. N. (1984). Affect attunement. In *Frontiers in Infant Psychiatry*, Vol. II, J. D. Call, E. Galenson, & R. L. Tyson, eds. New York: Basic Books.

Tomkins, S. S. (1962/63). *Affect, Imagery, Consciousness*, Vols. I & II. New York: Springer.

———— (1970). Affects as the primary motivational system. In M. B. Arnold, ed., *Feelings and Emotions*. New York: Academic Press.

———— (1980). Affect as amplification: Some modification in theory. In R. Plutchik & H. Kellerman, eds., *Emotions: Theory, Research and Experience*. New York: Academic Press.

———— (1981). The quest for primary motives: Biography and autobiography of an idea. *Journal of Personality & Social Psychology*, 41:306–329.

White, R. W. (1959). Motivation reconsidered: The concept of competence. *Psychological Review*, 66:297–333.

THE SEVERE REACHES OF PSYCHOLOGICAL DISORDER
Paul H. Tolpin

There has always been considerable skepticism about the possibility of successful *psychoanalytic* treatment of borderline conditions or the major psychoses. Kohut conceptualized the therapeutic difficulty in these illnesses by positing a failure in the formation of a cohesive nuclear self in both—more pervasive and undefended in the psychoses than in the borderline states. This failure seemed practically to be basically unrectifiable—though *psychotherapeutic* efforts were seen to be effective in strenghthening defensive structures of the personality. This strengthening might allow some patients to manage their profound vulnerabilities with greater success.

We do not know whether Kohut would have held as strictly to his early position on this issue today and there is some indirect evidence that he might have been less conservative about the possibility of greater success in the treatment of some of these patients.

Whatever the opinions or positions of others—Stolorow, Atwood, and Brandchaft as well as Galatzer-Levy—have boldly crossed the frontier into the new territories and have discovered exciting new formations to be considered and form judgments about. Let me begin by summarizing the closely argued, six-point section of Stolorow's and his colleagues' paper entitled "Schematic Conceptualization of Psychotic States and Their Treatment." They say, and I am paraphrasing here: The essential structuralization of a sense of self, which depends on a firm belief in one's own subjective experience, fails if early childhood caretakers are not validatingly attuned to the child's *perceptions and emotional reactions.* Lacking that validation the child is left in doubt about his own subjective reality and it will be vulnerable to dissolution in later years. When attunement is "consistently absent or grossly unreliable" there may result a predisposition to delusional psychotic states. The treatment of such psychotic states in the adult requires the therapist's recognition of the core of subjective truth of the psychotic delusions which concretize a triggering moment of crumbling reality in order to preserve that reality. The understanding and implicit affirmation of the truth of the patient's subjective or personal reality, leads to an increasingly positive therapeutic bond, the consolidation of a reliable sense of self and an improvement in his psychotic state.

In an overall way I have relearned from the authors' arguments what validation in infancy and childhood effects. And I am also in agreement with the authors' related therapeutic advice about the adequate conveyance of the understanding of the core of truth in delusion to the patient. Still, at the same time I am uneasy about some aspects of both ideas.

One of my questions is about the idea of a one-to-one relationship between pathologically harmful caretaking and doubts about one's own subjective reality. Validating attunement by caretakers leads to a sense of general or basic well-being. Yet how does it lead to a child's belief in his own subjective reality? It seems to me that most aspects of subjective reality, a quite specific concept of a different order than

well-being, depend on validation by others, though how one is responded to by others certainly contributes to the form of one's subjective reality. Perhaps I am missing the point here but since it is clearly
a critical point in the schema on which other points are constructed I
would like to hear more about it from the authors. Perhaps examples
of the process would clarify what they have in mind.

My next question relates to the first and ties in to the authors'
theory of treatment. Treatment, they say, requires "the therapist to
strive to comprehend the core of subjective truth symbolically encoded in the patient's delusional ideas and to communicate this understanding . . ." [to the patient]. They continue, "Empathic decoding of the patient's subjective truth . . . establishes the therapeutic
bond as an archaic intersubjective context in which his belief in his
own personal reality can become more firmly consolidated." Once
again I am in general agreement with the authors' suggestions while
feeling uncomfortable with their elaborations of them which tie them
into their concept of the patient's personal reality. I think there is little
question that one of the essentials of treatment is that the therapist
understand the origin and meaning of his patient's psychological
realities—whether or not they are presented in the form of psychotic
delusions. I think the author's rich clinical material, particularly the
case of Anna, beautifully illustrates the effect and effectiveness of
grasping the meaning of a patient's psychotic delusion. Kohut's telling reminder of just that point throughout his work should remain an
object lesson for all of us, including those the authors mentioned in
their section subtitled "Obstructions to the Search for Subjective
Truth." Two of Kohut's best-known examples of this are: (1) Miss F.'s
cry of No, No, No when Kohut went beyond her description of some
recent events in her life and added a thought of his own which inad-
vertantly recapitulated the injuries of her mother's self-absorption
(Kohut, 1971); (2) Kohut's reunderstanding of Mr. Z.'s dream of the
return of his father overladen with gifts—not terrified because of
castration anxiety as such but terrified and locking the door because
the father's return was emotionally overwhelming to him (Kohut,
1979). Clearly, understanding is essential; that is empathic, nuanced
understanding of how the patient really lives in and experiences the
world around him in his own idiosyncratic way. Understanding of
the core of truth in psychotic delusions is a particular and particularly
important aspect of working with psychotic patients just as dreams or
other forms of thinking are in neurotic patients—and in psychotic
patients as well. It is important because, as the authors indicate, in
some psychotic patients delusions are a royal road to the origins of
their pathology. While the clarification of the symbolic meaning of

delusions in the treatment of patients with psychotic delusions is an important step in treatment, it is limited to a "moment," as it were, in the treatment situation—just as the understanding of dreams is in the treatment of nonpsychotic (as well as psychotic) patients. The repetition of such moments related to delusion formation as well as those arising from other pathological experiences with others are necessary for the establishment of a therapeutic bond.

However, whether the delusion is the critical nucleus of the psychotic state, as the authors contend, or is an expression of a particular aspect and moment of self-disintegration is an important point. The underlying core of the psychotic state is rather the essential lack or relative failure of the self to have achieved reliable cohesion and some kind of basic or primal self-confidence. The lack of both is a consequence of a variety of caretaking failures that shape the bedrock stability of the personality. Failures of self-integration may lead to psychotic delusions. Some of these express the precipitating moment of collapse in relation to selfobject failures. But some delusions are like self-state dreams. They are in effect self-state delusions which express the *experience* of a crumbling or disintegrating self. And there are delusions which, like dreams, express a frightening vision of an absent selfobject-world or the consequences of that. All of these would have to be recognized at appropriate times—and in appropriate ways conveyed to the patient. But it is the general as well as the specific caretaking lacks that will have to be recognized, responded to in treatment, and they will be addressed by the therapist in a number of ways not only or even mainly via the discernment of the truth in the patients' delusions. If treatment is to have a chance to be successful, the understanding of the meaning of delusions, along with a variety of other therapeutic activities, will lead to revival of the possibility of renewed engagement in depth with the therapist. When that is achieved the further development and strengthening of the patient's cohesive self and essential self-confidence is possible. The enhancement of both of these psychological qualities will help to improve the patient's sense of the validity of his own subjective experiences. While the authors perhaps overemphasize the therapeutic effectiveness of the comprehension and empathic decoding of the patients' delusions, they have highlighted an important aspect of treatment of psychotic disturbances that have not previously been adequately understood.

Galatzer-Levy's account breaks new ground in the application of self-psychological insights to one of the major psychoses: manic-depressive illness. He does this by way of empathic immersion in and the careful analysis of the character of several manic-depressive patients he has had in treatment for a number of years. He extracts from his work with them a cluster of personality traits, sensitivities, deficits, and defenses—as well as related traits and attitudes he has sensed characterize the parents of these patients. He is also mindful of the psychobiological givens in his patients which clearly play an important if not decisive role in the development of the manic-depressive disorder.

In brief, Galatzer-Levy argues that had it not been for a unique and unfortunate combination of biological and psychological tendencies in both the parents and their children, manic-depressive illness would presumably not have developed. With the use of medication to control the underlying biological tendencies to extreme states of mania, or depression and grandiosity, psychoanalytic treatment of the illness was possible—using the insights of self-psychology that are particularly attuned to selfobject experiences—particularly in terms of separation anxiety and its consciously unperceived effects; and in the patients' inability to link affective reactions to experienced but consciously unrecognized psychological injuries. Galatzer-Levy found that his patients were not only periodically or only relatively depressed but that they lived in a baseline state of chronic depression-depletion marked by more episodes of increasing depression that was often aborted by a grandiose manic reaction to the threatened depressive collapse.

The kind of treatment Galatzer-Levy instituted followed the general theory and clinical insights of self-psychology as it applied to this group of patients. It was reasonably successful over a fairly long period of time. The one patient Galatzer-Levy reported in most detail remains in periodic contact with him because he requires the experience of Galatzer-Levy's continued availability. That should not surprise anyone who has treated highly vulnerable patients whatever their diagnostic category.

Galatzer-Levy develops a unifying hypothesis that is meant to explain his patients' psychopathological development. He says the patients had a biological endowment with unusual intensity of affects in the area of grandeur and depression. Their parents could not relate to or empathize with these though possibly they could have dealt with ordinary degrees of such psychological states. Instead they encouraged defenses against the experiencing of psychological intensities. The patients became strangers to their own affective world.

Galatzer-Levy has demonstrated not only the value of the use of self-psychological insights in manic-depressive illness but also of the use of untrammeled thought—and how it can enlarge the possibilities of understanding human psychology. His recognition, for example, of his patient's inability to experience play-reality is not particularly self-psychological but it is an example of sensitive psychological investigation like the crucial negative insight in the detective story in which the dog did not bark. Still, what do I think about the validity of his findings and their relevance to manic-depressive illness?

Certainly his constructions are plausible. Given the biological tendency to depression and mania, it does seem to fit that the constricting limitations instituted by early caretakers in relation to the development of psychobiological elaborations of particular, intense emotional states, could lead to a brittle personality organization, which operates in a psychologically binary fashion, e.g., the patient's premature ejaculation, lack of language for affects (that is, not just not knowing the designating words but not knowing affect degrees or shadings), lack of understanding of play-reality, which is a relatively sophisticated composite psychological experience, and so on. And the parents personalities, which allow them to respond affectionately to physical but not emotional distress—all these would seem to fit in with a kind of manic-depressive illness—a psychological illness that has wide swings of untempered affect and a basic difficulty in tension regulation. And certainly the successful therapeutic work described by Galatzer-Levy, which particularly addressed these issues and emphasized the recognition, understanding, and experiencing of affective states in general and of manic or depressive or magical grandiose thinking in particular, is equally impressive. Regarding the latter, Galatzer-Levy's interpretation of Mr. L.'s delusional, magical thinking in reaction to an impending vacation interruption—I am paraphrasing here: You want to control my mind because my continued attention and understanding are vital to you and you are afraid you'll lose that during the vacation—is a particularly cogent and impressive example.

Still with all this there are some questions and doubts. The first is the most obvious: Are the psychological peculiarities of Galatzer-Levy's patients specific for manic-depressive illness or for a type of manic-depressive illness? Is it not likely that the same or a similar constellation of findings in both patients and their parents could lead not only to manic-depressive illness but to some other kind of psychopathology? If that is true, what makes for the difference in the manifest disorder? Is it only the overwhelming biological tendency or is it other unrecognized, specific and/or nonspecific factors in the parent-child interaction that lead the patient in one direction or another? Or is there a necessary coalition of a biological tendency and specific psychopathological events that lead to manic-depressive disease?

The next point is not a question so much as a doubt. Despite the distinct value of Galatzer-Levy's findings in both his patients and their parents, which are invaluable clues to the givens and form of the patient's pathology, are they sufficient without the addition of what is implied but not clearly stated in his report? I would suggest that the noted specific pathology of the parents is only part of the picture of the failure of optimal responsiveness. That is, in addition to the specifics regarding affect suppression, conventionality, and so on, these parents were presumably lacking in more general responsiveness to their children. Just what form this might have taken is difficult to guess. I would speculate, however, that it lay in the area of effective object or selfobject relatedness of some diffuse but profound kind so that their offspring were not only unacquainted with the psychological elaboration of affects but were also unacquainted with the elaboration of some kinds of self-selfobject experiences which, in a healthy sense, would have addicted them to the need for relations with other people in their adult life—however problematic that might be. A corollary point is how much the parents anxiety-prone personalities from early on affected the anxiety-proneness of their children. This tendency might have amplified the children's responses to their parents more specific pathological attitudes in other areas mentioned.

My next to last point relates to the previous one regarding the quality of self-selfobject relations and the effectiveness of treatment. I believe that Galatzer-Levy's specific understanding and interpretation of the deficiencies in the patient's childhood experiences with selfobjects were critical for the treatment process. But I want to emphasize that the effect of these therapeutic interventions—for example, the linking of intense affects to language, which encouraged the capability for enlargement and further structuralization of the patient's deficient or distorted self-organization—particularly for patients like those Galatzer-Levy treated, whose involvement with selfobjects was so fragile and so dangerous, would not be confined to or even dominated by the content of the interpretation alone. Rather the overriding experience of a relationship with a reliable, responsive selfobject whose *engagement* with the patient was experienced as a replacement for the weaker or absent mirroring, idealizing, alter ego, and a variety of other strengthening, maturing experiences of childhood would be the sine qua non of effective treatment. The details of that engaged therapeutic relationship are conveyed by the understanding and interpretation, and by other less concrete and unconceptualized attitudes, which a competent therapist conveys to his patient. These unnamed qualities experienced by transference-hungry, even though highly defended, patients make it difficult to assign the role of the primary effective agent in effective therapies. Is it the words or the music of the therapeutic effort? Or is it a false question that cannot be answered in any simplistic way? The latter would seem to be the eminently sensible conclusion, but the recognition of varying importance of the components of therapeutic activities has to be kept in mind. And I think that is particularly pertinent with seriously ill patients Galatzer-Levy has been studying.

One last point regarding the specificity of the psychological factors Galatzer-Levy has suggested are linked to manic-depressive illness. I think it should also be kept in mind that the illness is one of the two most frequently diagnosed major psychoses in the U.S. and Great Britain and even with the uncertainty of fashion in diagnosis it seems likely that biological factors clearly play a fundamental role in the disease. But further, does it seem possible that the specific kinds of parental pathology and the consequent pathodynamics of the patient would be as relatively narrow as Galatzer-Levy suggests? It seems unlikely to me that all families of or all patients with manic-depressive illness have the kind of interacting psychological formations Galatzer-Levy has outlined. Rather it would seem that Galatzer-Levy has tapped into a particular kind of manic-depressive patient, and/or that his findings are secondary products of a more general kind of pathogenesis that organizationally makes use of the character pathology he has described.

I believe that the authors of both chapters have presented us with conceptual tools that can add significantly to our therapeutic skills. They have, as Stolorow et al. have so felicitously stated, brought the insights of self psychology to bear on "the most severe reaches of psychological disorder."

References

Kohut, H. (1971). *The Analysis of the Self*. New York: International Universities Press.
——— (1979). The two analyses of Mr. Z. *International Journal of Psycho-Analysis*, 60:3–29.

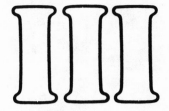

Clinical
Contributions

Chapter 8

Dream Interpretation Revisited

James L. Fosshage

Despite proposed theoretical and clinical modifications emanating from ego psychology, object relations theory and self psychology (for a review, see Fosshage, 1983), Freud's biologically dominated conception of dreams as primarily energy discharging and wish fulfilling in function has remained central to the classical psychoanalytic models of dream formation and dream interpretation. Although the shift from the topographical to the structural models of the mind (Freud, 1923; Arlow and Brenner, 1964), has emphasized in dreams the omnipresence of conflict between the three psychic agencies (id, ego, and superego) the primary impetus for the dream, from a classical vantage point, remains the wish that represents an instinctual drive, infantile in origin and seeking gratification throughout one's life (Altman, 1969). And clinically, although dream interpretation has increasingly focused on the latent conflict, in contrast to simply the

Portions of this paper were presented at the conference entitled "Dreams: New Frontiers," sponsored by the American Academy of Psychoanalysis, in Philadelphia on March 9, 1985, and at the Eighth Annual Conference on the Psychology of the Self entitled "Frontiers in Self Psychology," in New York on October 5, 1985. Theoretical sections of this paper appear in Fosshage and Loew, 1987. Adapted by permission.

latent wish, no dream is considered fully analyzed until the infantile sexual or aggressive wishes have been uncovered.

Consistent with the entirety of his personality theory, Freud anchored his clinical finding of latent wishes in dreams in a metapsychological model, i.e., the drive-discharge model, dominated by the biological and physicalistic models of his day. With the recognition that the in-depth scientific investigation of mental states requires that we remain in the realm of psychological discourse, a number of authors with the classical psychoanalytic tradition have contributed to the establishment of a psychoanalytic psychology free from and unfettered by the biological and physicalistic-energy models (Gill, 1967; Holt, 1967; Klein, 1967; Gedo and Goldberg, 1973; Kohut, 1977, 1984; Loewald, 1978; Stolorow and Lachmann, 1980; Atwood and Stolorow, 1984). In a similar vein, I have proposed a revised psychoanalytic model of the psychological function of dreams (Fosshage, 1983, 1987). My purpose here is to set forth briefly this model and to compare the clinical applications of the classical and revised models through a reformulation of a detailed clinical illustration initially presented from the classical perspective.

THE REVISED PSYCHOANALYTIC MODEL

Within the classical model, dreaming is viewed as predominantly the product of a regression to a primitive mode of mentation called primary process. Primary process is economically (energically) defined as mobile cathexes that press for immediate discharge. Because this mode of mentation theoretically never changes or develops and, thus, remains forever primitive (i.e., unbound energy always presses for discharge and lacks organization), dreams, dominated by primary process mentation, are also viewed as regressed and comparatively primitive products. Although the structural model opened the door theoretically to the participation of complex secondary process ideation through the participation of ego functioning in dream formation, the view of dreams as regressed, primitive primary process products predominates—and the higher-developed and more complex forms of cognition are by and large excluded from dreaming mentation.

Out of the empirical observation of dreams, creative productions, and psychotic mentation on the one hand, and through the theoretical extrication of primary process from its energy-based definition on the other, primary process has gradually become reconceptualized by some as a form of cognition which serves an overall organizational function of integration and synthesis (Holt, 1967; Noy, 1969, 1979). In keeping with these theoretical contributions, I have proposed that primary process be redefined as follows:

> primary process [is] that mode of mental functioning which uses visual and other sensory images with intense affective colorations in serving an overall integrative and synthetic function. Secondary process, on the other hand, is a conceptual and logical mode that makes use of linguistic symbols in serving an integrative and synthetic function. These processes may be described as different but complementary modes of apprehending, responding to, and organizing [the experiential world]. . . . (Fosshage, 1983, p. 649).[1]

It is posited that both forms of mentation develop in organizational complexity more or less throughout one's lifetime. In dreaming, both modes are clearly operative, although primary process or representational thinking (using Piaget's term) is usually predominant.

In keeping with this reconceptualization of primary process I have proposed that *"the supraordinate function of dreams is the development, maintenance (regulation), and, when necessary, restoration of psychic processes, structure, and organization* (Fosshage, 1983, p. 657).[2] Dreaming, as with waking mentation, is an affective-cognitive activity that, in serving an overall organizational function, ranges from the elemental to the most highly complex forms of mentation. The complexity ranges between what might be seen as the elemental repetition of a day's event, similar to a momentary daydream, and the most intricately, imagistically dominated scenario and complex logical problem-solving efforts. Occurring at night, when external input is limited, places dreaming mentation advantageously for dealing with insufficiently attended-to subjective concerns. In providing this organizational function dreaming mentation, as waking, both utilizes and

---

[1]Similarly, McKinnon (1979) describes two cognitive-affective modes of organization, the Visual-Spatial semantic form and the Auditory-Sequential semantic form, which correspond respectively with primary and secondary processes. On the basis of infant research, Lichtenberg (1983) also differentiates between these two modes of mentation.

[2]Stolorow and Atwood (1982), independently arriving at a similar formulation, refer to the maintenance and consolidation of psychological organization through the dream's concrete representations. Jung (1916) was the first to view dreams as regulatory and developmental, i.e., "compensatory" and "prospective," in function. Ullman (1959), Palombo (1978), Breger (1977), and Jones (1980) speak of the adaptive function; French and Fromm (1964) of the conflict-resolving function; De Monchaux (1978) of the trauma-integrating function; and Greenberg (1985) of the production of schemas (for a more complete review, refer to Fosshage, 1983).

maintains our primary organizational principles, i.e., the thematic ways in which we organize our experience (Atwood and Stolorow, 1984).

Dreaming mentation frequently continues the management of sexual, aggressive, and narcissistically related processes which have been stimulated, but insufficiently modulated, during the day. Kohut (1977) noted this regulatory function in some dreams, called "self-state dreams," in which the dream would manifestly attempt to deal with an "uncontrollable tension-increase or . . . [a] dread of the dissolution of the self. . . . by covering frightening nameless processes with nameable visual imagery" (p. 109). Within the revised model wish-fulfillment, central to the classical model, is no longer viewed either as a defensive process or as a fantasied gratification of libidinal or aggressive impulses with the primary function of discharge, but rather as an avenue of regulation and management of affective-cognitive experiences.

Dreaming mentation not only serves to maintain organization, but contributes to the development of new organizations, a crucially important dream function that has remained unrecognized within the classical model. Dreams frequently further the consolidation of emergent affect-laden images of self and other. The fundamental motivational principle posited by Kohut (1984), namely, "the self" striving to realize its "nuclear program of action," can be viewed as operative in dreaming mentation, as in waking, to bring about incremental developmental movements. Because these developmental movements may first appear in dreams, their recognition is crucially important in order to further the consolidation of ongoing changes.

Dreams also continue "the unconscious and conscious waking efforts to resolve intrapsychic conflicts through the utilization of defensive processes, through an internal balancing or through a creative, newly emergent reorganization. . . ." (Fosshage, 1983, p. 658). In contrast to the classical intersystemic conflict model, wherein conflicts are viewed as ubiquitous in dreams with little movement toward resolution, with the revised model conflicts are not seen as always present or the most salient issue in dreams, but, when they are, the higher-order function of conflict resolution is always operative, even if not successful, just as in waking mentation.[3]

With regard to the manifest-latent content distinction that is central

---

[3]I am not suggesting that dreaming mentation is always successful in its functioning, just as is the case with waking mentation. An obvious example is the nightmare, wherein dreaming mentational efforts are unsuccessful in regulating intense anxiety-producing processes. Clinically, of course, we must remain focused on the dreamer's experience to elucidate the salient issues and the dream's function.

to the classical model, because the revised model posits that dreams serve developmental and maintenance functions, *"there is no theoretical necessity to posit the ubiquitous operation of disguise and transformation of latent into manifest content"* (p. 652). For example, Kohut (1977) clinically noted that associations did not lead away from the manifest content to a presumed latent content in self-state dreams. Defensive operations are utilized in dreaming, as in waking mentation, only in response to anxiety-producing conflict. When intrapsychic conflict is present, however, the use of defenses—resulting in a manifest-latent content discrepancy—varies, as with waking mentation. with the intensity of the conflict and the dreamer's recognition, clarity, and acceptance of the conflict. Rather than assuming from the vantage point of the classical model the omnipresence of defensive functioning and the corresponding differentiation between manifest and latent content, it is proposed within this model that, instead of utilizing the terms "manifest" and "latent content," we refer more precisely to *the dream content* that may or may not involve defensive functioning. When defensive operations are present, they will be empirically discovered (not assumed a priori) through the dreamer's associations.

Dream images are poignantly meaningful representations that serve as thematic or organizational nodal points. The primary clinical task, in contrast to the translation of dream images, is to amplify and elucidate the meanings of the chosen images. For example, in contrast to the common assumption that the analyst is always, at least latently, in the dream, with the revised model the analyst is never *assumed* to be present in the dream unless he or she actually appears. However, because the primary organizational patterns are operative in both dreams as well as in the transferential relationship,[4] the analytic discussion, without requiring translation, can focus on the particular organizational pattern as it emerges in the dream as well as in the transference. When the dream image is not translated, its significance will be better understood and the appearance of the identical organizational principle in the transference will be thoroughly understood when it is operative. To assume incorrectly that a particular organizational theme is operative in the transference, and has precipitated the dream, is restrictive and potentially undermines the richness of object relations and organizational complexity, and/or of reorganizational developments. Thus, associational activity is more focused, aimed at elucidating the images within the context of the dream and the experience of the dreamer within the dream. To re-

---

[4]Stolorow and Lachmann (1984) redefine transference as the operation of primary organizational principles within the analytic relationship.

main at the phenomenological level elucidates the poignant meanings of dream images, increases the dreamer's participation and conviction in the understanding of the dream, and minimizes the potential imposition of the analyst's idiosyncratic organizations of the dream data.

Within this model, dreaming, rather than providing a royal road to latent wishes and intersystemic (id, ego, and superego) conflicts, is accorded a far more profound role in its developmental, regulatory, conflict-resolving, and restorative functions. Dreaming mentation—as waking mentation—utilizes, maintains, and transforms a person's primary organizational principles. The view that defenses are operative in dreaming mentation only in particular instances of intense intrapsychic conflict enables us in the clinical arena to observe more directly—i.e., usually without translation—the meanings of particular dream images and themes. The recognition that dreaming, at times, can initiate and further emergent psychological organizations in keeping with developmental strivings and, in so doing, can express representationally incremental developmental achievements, facilitates the use of dreams in analysis to enhance this consolidation process.

A CLINICAL ILLUSTRATION

For comparison of the clinical applications of the classical and revised psychoanalytic models, I have chosen a dream of a patient presented by Ralph Greenson (1970)[5] a highly respected classical analyst who was especially well known for his work with dreams. My reformulation of the understanding and interpretation of the dream is not to be considered exhaustive, for I have intentionally limited myself to address the most salient features of the dream, a process which, of course, is usually paralleled in the clinical situation.

The patient, Mr. M., was a thirty-year-old writer "who came for analytic treatment because of a constant sense of underlying depressiveness, frequent anxiety in social and sexual situations, and a feeling of being a failure despite considerable success in his profession and what appeared to be a good relationship to his wife and children" (Greenson, p. 534). The second dream of Mr. M., which is

[5]I wish to express my gratitude to Mrs. Hildi Greenson, Executrix of the Estate of Ralph Greenson, and to the *Psychoanalytic Quarterly* for permission to reprint the clinical material from Dr. Greenson's (1970) article, "The Exceptional Position of the Dream."

the one I focus on, occurred about two and a half years after his first dream. Greenson writes:

> The patient had to interrupt his analysis for six months because of a professional assignment abroad and returned some three months before [having] the dream. During this three-month interval of analytic work Mr. M. was in a chronic state of quiet, passive depression. I had interpreted this as a reaction to his wife's fourth pregnancy, which must have stirred up memories and feelings in regard to his mother's three pregnancies after his birth. It seemed clear to me that he was reexperiencing the loss of the feeling and fantasies of being his mother's favorite, the only child and the favorite child. The patient accepted my interpretations submissively and conceded they had merit, but he could recall nothing about the birth of his three siblings nor his reactions, although he was over six when the youngest was born. My interpretations had no appreciable influence on his mood.
>
> Mr. M. came to the hour I shall now present, sadly and quietly, and in a somewhat mournful tone recounted the following dream:
>
> "I am in a huge store, a department store. There are lots of shiny orange and green plastic raincoats on display. A middle-aged Jewish woman is arranging other articles of clothing. Nearby is a female manikin dressed in a gray flannel dress. I go outside and see a woman who looks very familiar but I can't say specifically who she is. She is waiting expectantly and eagerly for me near a small surrey, putting clothes in it. I feel sorry for the poor horse and then realize the surrey is detached from the horse. I lift up the surrey to connect it and I am surprised how light the surrey is, but I don't know how to hitch it up to the horse. I also realize then that I was silly to feel sorry for the horse."
>
> Mr. M.'s associations were as follows: "The three women in the dream were so different from one another. The older Jewish woman was a motherly type, working, doing, arranging, like my own mother used to before she became bedridden. The manikin reminds me of how I used to think of gentile girls when I was a kid; beautiful, pure, and cold, like my wife. But they taught me different. The best sex I have ever experienced was only with gentile girls. Jewish women just don't turn me on. They never did. Since my wife's pregnancy our sex life is practically nil. She isn't feeling well and I must say I'm in no mood for sex. I would like to be close to her in bed, but I don't want her to think it is a sexual demand so there is no talking even. I'd like to just be close and cuddle. My wife is so quiet of late. I feel she is getting revenge on me for all my past wrongs. I never realized before I had had such a bad temper and that she had been and still is so afraid of me. [Pause] I feel so alone in that big house of ours. I work like a horse to pay for it. Maybe I am the horse in the dream that I felt sorry for."
>
> I [Greenson] intervened. "It might be so. You think he had such a big load to carry, but then you lift up the buggy and you are surprised

to discover how light it is." [Greenson immediately addresses what from his and my perspective is the most striking feature in the dream.] The patient interrupted me. "That buggy is so light, it's a baby buggy, it's a baby carriage. No wonder it was so light, it was so tiny, and the woman was putting clothes in it, like diapers." [Pause] I interrupted. "A baby buggy is very heavy for a little boy, he has to work like a horse to push it." [Greenson here shifts the focus to the historical context.] Mr. M. burst in with, "I can remember trying to push my baby sister in her buggy but it was too heavy for me. Now I see my father carrying the baby carriage downstairs as if it were a toy. I can even remember my brother and me together trying to push it." [Mr. M. easily relates to his past and confirms Greenson's portrayal of the boy's experience of the baby buggy as heavy. The crucially important intonation and affect are absent, but I wonder if Mr. M. is not recalling his father's ease in handling the baby carriage with some admiration, a point that I will discuss later.] [In contrast,] I [Greenson] interpreted and reconstructed: "I believe you have been depressed ever since your wife got pregnant because it stirred up memories of how you reacted when you were a small boy and your mother got pregnant and delivered your brother and sisters. You didn't want to face the fact that your father was hitched up to the coming of the babies. You wished you could have been the father of the babies. But you weren't—you didn't know how to do it as a little boy and you felt left out in the cold, detached. You have been depressed about this ever since." [Through this theoretically dominated reconstruction of the oedipal rivalry and defeat, Greenson shifts the focus away from the dream element with its much lighter affective tone, expressed in such statements of the dreamer as "I am surprised how light the surrey is," and supplies instead an explanation of feelings of depression and defeat, a focus which corresponds with the patient's waking, in contrast to dreaming, affective state. Following the interpretation, Mr. M. seems to comply and to feel like a defeated man.] After a pause, Mr. M. said, "I've always felt I'm not a real man. I act like one, but inside I still feel a real man should be like my father; strong physically, tough, and unafraid. I can fly airplanes but my hands sweat whenever I want to screw my own wife [pp. 540–542].

Using the classical dream model Greenson presents his rationale for the reconstruction of the oedipal defeat: "I could see how the dream work had condensed, reversed, and disguised the agony of feeling abandoned, unloved, inept, and depressed by pictorializing an attractive woman waiting eagerly for him to join her" (Greenson, p. 543). Greenson clearly views the attractive woman waiting eagerly for the dreamer to join her as a wish-fulfillment which, serving a defensive function, conceals the underlying feelings of abandonment and depression. To posit the ubiquity of the manifest and latent content distinction paves the way for "free," i.e., free from content, and theoretically dominated translations of dream images, changing in this instance the central affective tone of the image itself. The consequent negation of the positive, affectively toned dream element corresponds with Garma's (1978) formulation that any solution in a dream is but a "fictitious solution," a wish fulfillment that is a disguise and not to be trusted. Similarly, despite the fact that the patient associatively related the middle-aged Jewish woman to his mother, Greenson states that the "familiar but unrecognizable woman is the mother of his childhood years, whom he has tried to ward off in his memories, in his sexual life, and in the analysis." (If this were true, namely, the eagerly awaiting woman were an accurate portrayal of his mother, the patient very likely would not be in his present predicament.) And, despite the fact that the dreamer's last statement was, "I also realized then that I was silly to feel sorry for the horse," Greenson concludes that the patient is "full of jealousy, envy, and depression, and [feeling] sorry for himself" (Greenson, p. 543). Contradicting the dreamer's associations and the dreamer's experience in the dream, Greenson, through the use of the classical dream and psychosexual developmental models, has translated the dream figures, altered a primary affect in the dream, and construed the dream function to be primarily defensive in that the dream conceals the patient's underlying "jealousy, envy, and depression."

Greenson continues:

> In the next hour the meaning of the green and orange raincoats became clear. The patient spontaneously recalled some dirty jokes from early puberty in which the terms "raincoat" and "rubbers" were used to refer to condoms. He then remembered finding condoms in his father's chest of drawers and later stealing some for his own use, just in case an opportunity presented itself, which, he wistfully said, "didn't occur for several years." By that time the rubbers, the raincoats, had disintegrated in his wallet. It is worth noting how the hidden old shreds of "rubbers" in the patient's associations were changed into the shiny new raincoats on display in the dream. Here you can see the attempt at wish-fulfillment in the manifest content of the dream: "I can buy conspicuous sexual potency in a store or in analysis." Later it also became clear that I too was the poor horse who had him as a big load to carry and also I was the 'horse's ass' who could not help him make proper sexual connections with his wife or any other woman [p. 542].

Mr. M. associates raincoats, in what might be viewed as the theoretically "expected" direction, to condoms; but, despite the possible analytic influence on associational activity, the theme of inadequacy and defeat reemerges. Greenson, once again, understands the shiny new raincoats as a defensive disguise of the shreds of old "rubbers". Translating the department store to refer to the analysis, Greenson interprets Mr. M.'s attempt to buy sexual potency through the analysis as a wish-fulfillment which, in this instance, represents an infantile desire to be ultimately renounced. This formulation, from my vantage point, would have, at least momentarily, crushed Mr. M.'s hope to gain sexual potency and, more generally, self-potency through the analysis, a wish which, rather than a representative of an infantile drive, is more accurately viewed as an expression of a *developmental striving*. Indeed, Mr. M.'s view of the analyst as "the 'horse's ass' who could not help him make proper sexual connections with his wife or any other woman" followed and might have been his reaction to the disheartening interpretation and ensuing empathic rupture.

Using the revised psychoanalytic model of dreams minimizes (but, of course, does not eliminate) the possibility of arbitrary and theoretically dominated translations of dream personages and events and enables us *to remain close to the experience of the dreamer*. From this vantage point let us first examine the patient's associations and then readdress the dream. In his initial associations, prior to the analyst's interventions, Mr. M. mentions his mother and gentile girls, but focuses primarily on his current life situation. A repetitive sequence emerges in which Mr. M. expresses feelings of having, of being responded to, and of satisfaction, followed by experiences of abandonment and disappointment: "The older Jewish woman was a motherly type, working, doing, arranging, like my own mother used to *before* she became bedridden." [italics added] He then anticipates a lack of responsiveness: "The manikin reminds me of how I used to think of gentile girls when I was a kid; beautiful, pure, and cold, like my wife"; but was pleasantly surprised, "they taught me different." With satisfaction Mr. M. recounts, "The best sex I have ever experienced was only with gentile girls"; but he immediately follows with a sense of disappointment, "Since my wife's pregnancy our sex life is practically nil." He begins to defensively maneuver, "And I must say I'm in no mood for sex"; but his needs and desires immediately reemerge, "I'd like to just be close and cuddle." However, disappointment ensues once again, "My wife is so quiet of late," and he begins to blame himself, "I never realized before I had had such a bad temper and that she had been and still is so afraid of me." He ends up feeling "alone in that big house of ours" and burdened, "I work like a horse to pay for it"; and makes the poignant connection between his waking and dreaming experiences, "Maybe I am the horse in the dream that I felt sorry for." This thematic experience of the ruptures of the needed responsiveness from others (as ruptures in the self-

selfobject matrix) leaves him feeling depleted and depressed. In order to protect himself from further disappointment, he avoids asserting his needs, "but I don't want her to think it is a sexual demand so there is no talking even" (p. 541).

With Mr. M.'s waking thoughts in mind let us turn to his dream. In light of the fact that Mr. M. had been a child of impoverished parents and was embarrassed by his shabby, dirty clothing, the dream interestingly opens in a huge department store where there were "lots of shiny orange and green plastic raincoats on display." Although we need the dreamer's elaboration of his mood at this point and thoughts as to his reaction to and the meaning of the raincoats, the dream appears to open in a "bright" mood with a sense of plentitude in the world, i.e., a huge department store, and with a busily caring, middle-aged, motherly Jewish woman. In contrast, and paralleling the sequential unfolding of his associations, a female manikin dressed in a gray flannel dress stands nearby—epitomizing a cold, lifeless, and unresponsive female. However, the dreamer proceeds to go outside and encounters a woman "who looks very familiar" and who "is waiting expectantly and eagerly for me near a small surrey, putting clothes in it." The dreamer envisions a responsive and caring woman, a woman who eagerly awaits him. His associating the surrey to a baby buggy suggests that the familiar woman and he are securing baby clothes for their expected child and, in contrast to his own childhood deprivation, they are preparing to provide more adequately for the expected baby—a hopeful and psychologically reparative enactment. The act of providing is experienced momentarily as a heavy burden, "I feel sorry for the poor horse," an old configuration that must have developed out of his childhood experience in which, feeling abandoned by his mother, he had to attend to his younger siblings. However *something new occurs*. The dreamer "realizes the surrey is detached from the horse. I lift up the surrey to connect it and I am surprised how light the surrey is. . . ." The horse is no longer connected to the burdensome surrey of the past so that the dreamer realizes "that I was silly to feel sorry for the horse." The dreamer is experiencing something new, namely, the lightness of the surrey, and, although he does not know yet quite how to make this connection, he is in the process of an important discovery. In contrast to organizing his current experience according to the pattern of abandonment, deprivation, and burdensomeness—a pattern previously established in childhood—the dreamer, instead, is envisioning and experiencing imagistically an eagerly caring woman, preparations of baby clothing, and a potential lightness in the previously burdensome task of being a father and a husband—a developmental step of no small magnitude. Through this internal reorganization Mr. M. is in the process of emerging from his depressed, anxious, and weakened state and consolidating a more positive, potent sense of himself. Using the classical model, the dream was viewed essentially as a disguise of his underlying depression; using the revised model, it is viewed as a mentational attempt to reorganize in keeping with developmental strivings in order to emerge from a depleted, burdened, and depressed state.[6]

What are the transferential implications of the dream? From my vantage point the dreamer is primarily engaged in an intrapsychic reorganizational effort to emerge from a depleted and depressed state. Primary developmental strivings are potentially partially rekindled and supported within the self-selfobject matrix of the analytic relationship. Despite the reported ineffectiveness of Greenson's interpretations prior to the dream, a sufficient self-selfobject connection arising from Mr. M.'s developmental motivation, and Greenson's availability, must have been established to enable the dreamer to report his dream and, perhaps, even to dream it. The organizational sequence of hoped-for responsiveness followed by anticipated and ensuing disappointments, evident in Mr. M.'s dream and associations involving his current and past life, undoubtedly must also have operated frequently within the transferential relationship (e.g., his more energetic responses to Greenson's initial interventions and his apparent depletion following the oedipal interpretation). This scenario can be addressed as it occurs within the analytic relationship, as well as in the relationship to his wife, without requiring translations, and what from my vantage point would be distortions, of the dream images. At the moment the dreamer is internally capable of envisioning an eagerly awaiting woman that results in a new lightness of the buggy. To shift the focus to the self-selfobject matrix in the analytic arena could potentially undermine the dreamer's emergent capacity to envision this more hopeful situation by subtly locating the impetus

[6]Discussion following the presentation of this paper pointed on several occasions to a misunderstanding that I would focus exclusively on the developmental strivings and progressive movements in dreams. I believe that this misunderstanding was based, at least in part, on the presentation of only one clinical illustration, Mr. M.'s dream, that exquisitely demonstrates the achievement of novel reorganizations brought about through dreaming mentation. In other dreams, however, the maintenance or regulatory functions may predominate and developmental strivings would not otherwise be apparent. And, in still other dreams, intense affect-ridden conflicts may overwhelm effective psychological functioning so that no function is clearly identifiable. Dreams, in these instances, poignantly portray the experiential position and predicament of the dreamer, whether it be a state dominated by acute anxiety or intense despair.

of the developmental movement within the experience of the analyst's responsiveness. The crucial importance of the analyst's responsiveness notwithstanding, it is the patient's motivational thrust and capacity that enables him to make use of the analyst's responsiveness and availability. In this instance, to emphasize the patient's experience of the analyst as affirming, or even his use of the analyst to provide a mirroring selfobject function, shifts the focus away from the patient's current internal self-cohesive capacity and potentially could undermine the further consolidation of that capacity. Thus, in this instance, the recognition and implicit affirmation of the internal incremental developmental achievement both provides a sufficient responsiveness to continue the maintenance of a viable self-selfobject connection within the analytic relationship and furthers the self-consolidation process.

With regard to interventions, following Mr. M.'s initial associations where he ended up with the old scenario feeling burdened and lonely (additional confirmation that this old scenario was more available to him in his waking mentation), I would have inquired, "But how did you feel when you discovered that the surrey was light?" And at another point I would have asked, "How did you feel about the woman waiting expectantly and eagerly for you?" With these questions I am attempting to reconnect the dreamer experientially to these important new, affectively potent developments in the dream and to further their elucidation and consolidation. We would probably arrive together at a formulation something like, "In the dream you are realizing something new—the surrey is not heavy, but light, and although you didn't quite know how to hitch this new surrey or realization up to the horse, you realized that there is no need to feel sorry for the horse—that the horse is not burdened after all." I would use as much as possible the intense affect-laden images of the dream, or, in other words, primary process mentation as our mode of communication, so that the patient can experience these new developments as fully as possible in his waking life. In order to utilize and integrate both waking and dreaming mentation, I would inquire if he had been aware in his waking life of experiencing or envisioning feeling lighter and less burdened in relation to his expectant wife. And toward further integration of these changes, if Mr. M. had said as he did to the analyst, "Now I see my father carrying the baby carriage downstairs as if it were a toy," after requesting elaboration of his feeling about this scene, I would have embraced (i.e., if I sense the affect correctly) the admiration and identification with his father in saying, "You seemed to have admired your father and to have wanted to be like him at that moment, and in the dream you have envisioned that you too can be like your father and can easily carry that light surrey."

I have posited that the supraordinate function of dreaming is to develop, maintain, and regulate psychological processes and organization. Of course when regulatory and developmental strivings have been seriously undermined, the dream, as with waking mentation, may poignantly express states of depletion, fragmentation, and exitless despair. Mr. M.'s dream, however, exemplifies how we are able to reorganize and further incremental developmental movements through dreaming mentation. The crucially important recognition of these reorganizational and developmental efforts with the aid of the revised psychoanalytic model enables us to embrace these efforts as they appear in dreaming mentation and, thus, through the utilization of dreams to further the developmental process. With regard to the previously analyzed dream, the fact that the woman is unknown and that the dreamer does not know how to hitch the light surrey up to the horse, suggests that he has yet to integrate these new possibilities, requiring all the more our therapeutic use of this dream to consolidate further this new, and in this instance, uplifting reorganization.

REFERENCES

Altman, L. (1969). *The Dream in Psychoanalysis*. New York: International Universities Press.

Arlow, J., & Brenner, C. (1964). *Psychoanalytic Concepts & the Structural Theory*. New York: International Universities Press.

Atwood, G., & Stolorow, R. (1984). *Structures of Subjectivity*. Hillsdale, NJ: The Analytic Press.

Breger, L. (1977). Function of Dreams. *Journal of Abnormal Psychology*, 72:1–28.

De Monchaux, C. (1978). Dreaming and the organizing function of the ego. *International Journal of Psycho-Analysis*, 59:443–453.

Fosshage, J. (1983). The psychological function of dreams: A revised psychoanalytic perspecfive. *Psychoanalysis and Contemporary Thought*, 6:641–669.

_____ & Loew, E., ed. (1978). *Dream Interpretation: A Comparative Study*. New York: Spectrum.

_____ _____, ed. (1987). *Dream Interpretation: A Comparative Study*, rev. ed., Great Neck, NY: PMA Publications.

French, T., & Fromm, E. (1964). *Dream Interpretation: A New Approach*. New York: Basic Books.

Freud, S. (1900). The interpretation of dreams. *Standard Edition*, 4 & 5. London: Hogarth Press, 1953.

_____ (1923). Remarks on the theory and practice of dream interpretation. *Standard Edition*, 19:109–121. London: Hogarth Press, 1961.

Garma, A. (1978). Freudian approach. In J. Fosshage & C. Loew. ed., *Dream Interpretation: A Comparative Study*. New York: Pergamon Press.

Gedo, J., & Goldberg, A. (1973). *Models of the Mind: A Psychoanalytic Theory.* Chicago: University of Chicago Press.

Gill, M. (1967). The primary process. In *Motives and Thought: Psychoanalytic Essays in Honor of David Rapaport*, R. R. Holt, ed. New York: International Universities Press.

Greenberg, R. (1987). The dream problem and problems in dreams. In M. Glucksman, ed., *Dreams in New Perspective.* New York: Human Sciences Press.

Greenberg, R. (1987). The dream problem and problems in dreams. In M. Glucksman & S. Warner, ed., *Dreams in New Perspective.* New York: Human Sciences Press.

Holt, R. R. (1967). The development of the primary process: A structural view. In R. R. Holt, ed., *Motives & Thought: Psychoanalytic Essays in Honor of David Rapaport.* New York: International Universities Press, pp. 345–383.

Jones, R. M. (1980). *The Dream Poet.* Cambridge, MA: Schenkman.

Jung, C. G. (1916). General aspects of dream psychology. In *The Structure and Dynamics of the Psyche. Collected Works*, Vol. 8. New York: Pantheon, 1960.

Klein, G. (1976). *Psychoanalytic Theory: An Exploration of Essentials.* New York: International Universities Press.

Kohut, H. (1977). *The Restoration of the Self.* New York: International Universities Press.

———— (1984). *How Does Analysis Cure?* Chicago: University of Chicago Press.

Lichtenberg, J. (1983). *Psychoanalysis and Infant Research.* Hillsdale, NJ: The Analytic Press.

Loewald, H. (1978). Primary process, secondary process and language. In *Papers on Psychoanalysis.* New Haven, CT: Yale University Press, 1980.

McKinnon, J. (1979). Two semantic forms: Neuropsychological and psychoanalytic descriptions. *Psychoanalysis and Contemporary Thought*, 2:25–76.

Noy, P. (1969). A revision of the psychoanalytic theory of the primary process. *International Journal of Psycho-Analysis*, 50:155–178.

———— (1979). The psychoanalytic theory of cognitive development. *The Psychoanalytic Study of the Child*, 34:169–216. New Haven: Yale University Press.

Palombo, S. (1978). The adaptive function of dreams. *Psychoanalysis and Contemporary Thought*, 6(4). New York: International Universities Press.

Stolorow, R., & Atwood, G. (1982). The psychoanalytic phenomenology of the dream. *Annual of Psychoanalysis*, 10:205–220.

———— & Lachmann, F. (1980). *Psychoanalysis and Developmental Arrests.* New York: International Universities Press.

Ullman, M. (1959). The Adaptive Significance of the Dreams. *Journal of Nervous and Mental Diseases*, 129:144–149.

Chapter 9

Pathognomic Mirroring and the Organization of Experience: A Developmental Factor in Self Pathology

Doren L. Slade
Lisa J. Moskowitz

The "different baby" of self psychology is born with a harmonious and vigorous self (Tolpin, 1984), dependent on continuing, optimally sustaining selfobject experiences from birth to death. The centrality of the concept of self and the individual's requirement for attuned responsiveness provides the basis for a uniform, encompassing theory of psychological development in both health and pathology. More severe psychopathology results from repeated, traumatically unattuned disturbances in selfobject experiences during earliest development leaving structural deficits in the self. Defensive structures emerge in response to these structural deficits as perservative attempts at balancing a precariously cohesive or distorted sense of self. The selfobject matrix for the developing child forms a mutually influencing affective field, culminating in the self's organization of experience which cannot be empathically comprehended beyond the field's subjective boundaries. The central focus remains the experiencing self as distinct from interaction with objects that do not function at that moment as selfobjects; that is, they do not function to sustain the self.

As development proceeds, selfobject experiences provide the specific affective and cognitive coloration characteristic of the organization of experience of the individual. Structuralizations of self-experience within the selfobject bond begins at birth, quickly becoming part of the baby's already complex psychological structure. The final firming of critical functional capacities like self-soothing and self-demarcation begin to conclude in late adolescence. The experience of reliably attuned engagements during healthy development allows the baby to gain, lose, and regain a sense of self-cohesion (Tolpin, 1984). These attuned engagements are self-confirmatory and the baby will develop a reliable sense of self and a reliable sense of competence vis-à-vis the world. Thus, these interactions create and serve to maintain the effectively stable structural properties of the person's self-experience revealing, as Stolorow states so clearly, ". . . the multidimensionality of the self deriving from a multiplicity of selfobject experiences at various levels of psychological organization" (Stolorow, 1986, p. 394). Repetitive selfobject experiences of attunement and unattunement affectively organize memories and expectations regarding maintenance or loss of cohesion in the self-organization. As Tolpin states, the baby will expect to self-right unless interfered with through failures in providing essential selfobject functions.

By implication, selfobject disorders create corresponding self-disorders. Repeated traumatic empathic breaches during early development that include failures in healing disjunctures in this basic experiential dyad, are pathogenic by failing to provide optimal developmental opportunities necessary for consolidation of the self. On the other hand, the three-step process of empathic engagement, disengagement and reengagement, which comprises optimal developmental opportunities, is central to restarted development in treatment in the healing of empathic disjunctures promoting transmutting internalization of the analyst's selfobject functions.

When our "different," now developmentally thwarted baby grows up and enters treatment, the implications for the selfobject transferences are multiple. The patient spontaneously presents specific self-deficits once the empathic responsiveness of the analyst fosters the emergence of unmet needs in this new selfobject bond. Empathic disruptions can only be optimal if the patient feels attuned to and understood in his subjective experience and can achieve a sense of cohesion again. For the patient, the analyst must function as a reliably needed selfobject capable of sustaining empathic immersion in the patient's earlier, pathogenic selfobject experience. The patient can only experience thwarted needs injuriously and defensive configurations became intricately interwoven with thwarted need experiences in the self-organization. This process of empathic resonation allows for the experience of reliability within the selfobject bond and eventually within the self. Thus, the opportunity for restarted development is offered, producing further structuralizations of self-experience.

The baby's affects serve from the first days of life, a most critical function. Affects are the basis for the baby's instrumental behavior toward its earliest caregivers and thereby organize experience. The baby will attempt to elicit developmentally necessary and empathically informed selfobject responses that match and help regulate the baby's affective states (Beebe, 1985). When empathically responded to, these affects form the baby's sense of efficacy in the world and allow the baby to self-regulate, to find solutions to problems it experiences within and also in its environment. This needed protomirroring process provides primary self-confirmation in reflecting back to the baby its existence, its innate sense of vitality, and its sense of competency. The baby also has the need for admirable qualities to look up to, and through fantasy merger experiences with caregivers, feels uplifted and soothed, promoting an inner sense of infallibility and well-being that fosters a competent curiosity aimed toward the larger universe. These early uplifting selfobject experiences later resonate in meaningful cultural ideals and symbols which are available to support and sustain the older child and adult. Unlike the infant's withdrawal without disengagement, which Beebe (1985) refers to as "protodefensive activity," the adult with deficits in self-confirmatory functions is capable of a more complete or total disengagement following empathic breaches. In the adult this more total disengagement, clinically the "breaking of the connection with the analyst," is usually pathological and erodes the patient's self-esteem because it calls into operation the structures of defense characteristic of that individual. This form of disengagement represents a disavowal of subjective experience, rather than an assertion of selfobject needs. The continued engagement of the infant, that is, its innate tendency to reach again, enables the building of self-structure, albeit with a specific affective tone and pattern of experiencing the self in interaction with others which becomes part of the individual's personality. Thus, the original thrust toward self-confirmatory mutual engagement between infant and caregiver serves for the adult a self-affirmatory function precisely because it now contains a historical inner experiential content regardless of its negative or positive coloration. Consequently, even painful repetitions form and are maintained as part of the enduring organization of experience and sense of inner continuity. In treatment, a new self-confirmatory opportunity is offered if the needs of the patient are not being coopted by the analyst's superimposition of her own subjective reality on the patient. If this does not occur, then reaching experiences remain syntonic and eventually become sustaining in and of themselves. In effect, the self-confirmatory experience of reaching and being responded to in a more attuned way, eventually obviates the need for the more perfectly attuned response so critical in the fantasy mergers of infancy.

Lastly, there are alter ego needs which we see experientially as the need for attuned accompaniment. These involve the confirming, soothing experience of belonging with other human beings with whom there is mutual understanding and sharing of beliefs and feelings. As Kohut (1984) elucidated looking, talking, and feeling in familiar ways prevents the fragmenting experience of total, inhuman isolation and the loss of one's sense of human participation in a reliably known universe. Each of these needs has its own line of development in which the baby vigorously reaches for phase-appropriate selfobject responses confirming, both cognitively and affectively, the baby's effectual nature and importance. These later become discrete feelings and meanings in the individual's organization of subjective experience.

The experience of vitality or enfeeblement, the capacity for a sense of reliable cohesiveness and balance, represents the presence or absence of deficits in the self-structure. Self psychology's "different baby" expects to remain cohesive, to have the innate capacity to self-right, to maintain its balance through the mirroring, soothing, and accompanying engagements with its selfobjects and is surprised when it does not (Tolpin, 1984). This baby expects to get, upon its initial signaling and later active demanding, all that it needs. Certain pathogenic patterns in protomirroring and mirroring experiences create a discrete configuration that we call pathognomic mirroring. This results in a recognizable and potent obstacle to the fulfillment of the self's intrinsic program by producing a propensity for the dissolution of self-experience stemming from an absent or profoundly insufficient self-confirmatory capacity.

The individuals focused on in this paper live in constant threat of, at times, severe and potentially protracted experiences of nothingness created by eroding self-doubt in an extreme form. They constantly ask the analyst to define their inner experience for them and are more than willing to defer to what the analyst says—rather than believing in the subjective validity of their own affective states. This represents a refusal to be subjectively alone in their own feelings and thoughts developmentally colored by past misattunements and deficits in affect regulation. Their primary organization of experience is negatively colored and founded on a distorted sense of self-worth. These patients are surprised to find the unexpected, sustaining attunement in the soothing, confirming words of the analyst. They are

further surprised by the empathic response thev receive to the unbearable vulnerability they feel as a result of the analyst's confirming
mirroring. Thus, these patients are in desperate need of validation
with which they are unable to affectively connect within the selfobject
context of the empathic bond with the analyst. They have supreme
difficulty in revealing what one patient called the "forbidden territo-
ry," the subjective experiences which resonate with early selfobject
disturbances. And while demanding interpretive responses to their
productions, these patients often feel humiliated or overstimulated
by verbalized attunement. On the other hand, when validating interpretations are not offered, the response is anger and disappointment since, as a group, they tend to be therapeutically ambitious and
in desperate need of reducing panic states associated with feeling. It
was in further selfobject transference manifestations that we found
that these individuals did not expect a response centering on them,
but rather felt impelled to be the responsive caretakers to the selfobject analyst. Enactments of this inversion in selfobject functions includes bringing coffee to early morning sessions for the analyst, offering to make tea or chicken soup if the analyst has a cold, and being
the model patient by complying with presumed expectations based in
fantasized needs of the analyst. We questioned ourselves as to
whether these responses could have been an expression of concern
out of anxiety over possible loss of the selfobject—in actuality the
destruction of the selfobject bond; or were they a sign of enhanced
empathic capacities, or the emergence of the grandiosity in flight
from the need for a mirroring, attuned engagement centering upon
the self? It was also thought that this behavior might indicate the
beginnings of a loss of balance in the patient's sense of self.

What we came to understand is that the original selfobject experiences did not provide basic affect-regulating and self-confirming
functions essential to forming a reliably cohesive sense of self characterized by self-confidence and an ability to recognize, float in and
affirm subjective experience. These selfobject failures created developmental disruptions that often outweighed the patient's innate
reaching capacity, although the patient remained tentatively capable
of moving toward an empathic selfobject bond as did become available with the analyst. The baby's healthy thrust to develop a sense of
competency in its selfobject ties, became, in these patients, a grandiose delusional belief in the total power to control everything they
need by contorting the sense of self to conform to a projected version
of the fantasized selfobject. We believe this to be an endopsychic
response to profound helplessness generated by the patient's ineffec-
tual appeals for self-confirming responses in earliest development

and in the primary organization of experience. The patient assumes in their selfobject experience, that the caregiver is in the same need state. The patient scans the analyst until focusing on a need, more or less readily apparent or projected, which the patient will respond to through mirroring or actual enactment. This is experienced by the patient as essential to the sustenance of the selfobject bond. The patient never experiences consciously, either his own invalidating compliance, or the archaic cooptation of his needs in his original selfobject experience. The joy in the mirroring selfobject connection is transformed into a delusional excitement, at first mistaken for joy, in experiencing mythical control over and merger with the confirming selfobject function. Pathogenic protomirroring and mirroring experiences leave only the baby's capacity for fantasy, enabling it to recreate an experience of affirmation and self-regulation of previously unconfirmed affective states and now defensive self-regulation.

Fantasizing comes to play a more and more significant role in the continuing engagements between the infant and its caregivers. In the absence of confirming support of the baby's need to create order and regulate its affective states, the baby, once representational thought is possible, is able to utilize fantasy to encapsulate and give meaning to its frustrating and painfully distressful subjective experiences. Eventually, a fictional version of competency and order is created in which the baby can now affirm its own existence and the impact it has on the provision of its selfobject functions. This ficticious version emerges in a series of primary, developmentally specific and phase-appropriate grandiose convictions about the nature of the self and the ability to influence the caregivers affective participation in the person's existence. The hallmark of these grandiose convictions, as seen in the transference, is the deletion of the actual mutuality involved in the original dyadic engagements between the infant and its caregivers. This deletes the experience of needs in the self with the corresponding sensations of helplessness and disappointment regarding the original selfobject experience, which is maintained in regard to all subsequent selfobject connections. Thus reliable attunement, essential to the development of a reliably cohesive sense of self, is ultimately replaced by a reliable complex of convictions and reinforcing defensive procedures, reaching at times delusional proportions. These address this now-symbolically encoded deficit and the faulty selfobject experiences creating it.

A very clear example of the endopsychic processes we are describing is seen in the case of a twenty-six-year-old woman who is the second of seven children from a family who moved to a new state in order to make a fresh start with a different business. The failure of the father's previous business put grave strains on the marriage; and, for the mother, having multiple children was her only means of confirming her self-worth. All seven children were born within nine years. After the birth of the fifth child, the mother found a part-time job that eventually led to her own full-time career. The patient often spoke of the feeling of being used by her mother to carry out the many tasks needed to maintain both the household and the younger siblings—tasks, the patient felt, her mother should have performed. While her older brother was allowed to pursue his own interests independently of family obligations, the patient felt herself becoming interchangeable with her mother—without receiving any admiration for the sacrifice. Desperately seeking moments uncrowded with noise and competing needs, the patient never felt centered upon and often fled to the soothing quiet of a large oak tree behind the house, hiding in the branches for as long as she could. She often was angry and quarrelsome with her siblings and her mother. This eventuated in a form of punishment that provided the patient with the opportunity to reinforce her internal defense against the painful helplessness of overstimulation. As she put it, she was given time to herself in the bathroom, where she was sent for often over an hour, so that she could develop a better attitude. Significantly, she had mixed feelings about this experience. She reported that a gradual sense of excitement would develop and replace her panic as she arranged and rearranged all the towels in the bathroom. At times she imagined the towels to be the towels of a secret family she hid inside herself. This towel family valued her above all the other children as an especially needed family member and not the especially unworthy child she worried that she was; they participated in her experience of her own greatness, which became her secret. Gradually, as her excitement grew, she imagined what it would mean to her mother to be without her. She felt she was depriving her family of her needed presence, thereby inverting the punishment to one that she administered to them, although this thought was accompanied by guilt and fear that they could indeed not really manage without her. In the patient's fantasy construction, the punishment became her choice, rather than the choice of her unattuned parents. A delusional sense of competency came to replace her experience of helplessness in relation to her attunement needs and her chaotic capacity to regulate her affective states. With the acquisition of ficticious choice through this fantasy operation, a reordering of the selfobject universe occurred. She felt affirmed in her power without actually being confirmed or centered upon—a delusional experience devoid of the actual dyadic engagement generating it. Reporting this punishment without affect until later in the treatment, it reminded her of Cinderella, though she did not understand why, since that story had the happy outcome of Cinderella's being able, after much suffering, to go and live with the prince in his palace!

These grandiose beliefs and convictional assumptions about the nature of the self and the world are crystallizations of absent or insufficient self-confirmatory and affect regulatory functions. Delusional convictions become sustaining: they affirm subjective experience by providing an experience of fictional self-confidence that affectively diminishes the subjective experience of self-doubt. In other words, delusions provide meaning and help contain confusional panic states accompanying self-doubt. These characteristically include various forms of self-reproach. The meanings offered, however, almost invariably include an intense, near-paranoid focus on the object—once the patient is confronted with the elusiveness of his or her own inner experience. In synoptic form, in the inversion of selfobject functions, the set of meanings and feelings in the experiencing self are almost immediately replaced by the presumed cognitive and affective attributes of the object. As one patient was able to articulate; "It feels like you become me so I don't have to feel the terrible panic I feel when I don't know what I feel." This patient's desperate plea for interpretations is experientially an intense reaching for the selfobject analyst to save him from the archaic experience of invalidating engagement which makes the sensation of floating in his own experience intolerably dangerous to his sense of cohesion; that is, it leaves him to feel infirm in a need state. Thus, asserting one's needs becomes intensely frightening, and will typically result in self-invalidation as a means of self-preservation. This invalidation is often attributed to the analyst, and fosters the reaffirmation of the original conviction that survival depends upon attunement aimed at meeting the needs of the analyst-as-selfobject.

Delusional configurations elaborated from fantasy operations like those described above, can be further elaborated given a more profound or enduring absence of affective confirmation until they reach full delusional proportions. We are referring to configurations not completely unlike Deborah's private world of Yr as depicted in Green's novel *I Never Promised You a Rose Garden*. Yr and its inhabitants provided for Deborah all the self-affirming mirroring, idealizing, and alter ego functions not provided for her in her earliest selfobject experiences. Participation in such pseudo-selfobject functions totally occupies the patient cognitively and affectively, and nearly eliminates the original need for attuned responsiveness providing vital selfobject functions. Clearly, the isolation these individuals maintain in their lifestyles serves to reduce the possibilities for dissolution of self-experience through contact with others whom they expect will demand that their needs take precedence. The patient expects rejection, humiliation, or punishment of the self in its need states, a by-product of pathognomic mirroring.

Examination reveals that the maternal selfobject of these patients does not have the capacity to empathically mirror most of her baby's affective states. The mother can only identify and therefore mirror those affective states that she does not disavow in herself. Affective states in the baby arise spontaneously and send the mother into a panic out of her own inability to accept these feelings as part of her own subjective experience. In order to sustain her own precarious sense of cohesion, the mother defends against the baby's affects. The baby's affect states may be ignored, denied, pulled back from, responded to harshly or heightened as part of the mother's unconscious defensive operation. Thus, affect states in the baby are either implicitly or explicitly deregulated and invalidated. She attempts to make her own subjective reality the only one. Her unattuned responses to the baby and her incapacity to maintain her own sense of balance in the self, are reflected back to the baby who, in its attempt to elicit self-confirmation, experiences the mother's engagement as an attack on its very existence.

We believe that the mother in these cases is neither overtly nor latently psychotic. Kohut's (1977) descriptions of narcissistic vulnerabilities and the defensive structures typically accompanying these vulnerabilities conform to our patients' descriptions of their mothers and the selfobject experiences that would follow, which are reflected in the content of the patients' selfobject transferences in treatment. Disavowed failures in responsive mirroring in the mother's organization of experience remain unconscious and are reactivated by the birth of her baby when she, like the baby, becomes the center of attention and empathic concern in her family and amongst friends. Once left alone with the baby, the mother is presented with the baby's innate vigor and capacity to reach for her. The baby's attempts at self-regulation places the mother unconsciously in touch with her enfeeblement and self-doubt in regard to being all that she thinks her baby needs her to be. The baby's repeated reaching and withdrawals panics the mother, flooding the baby with her uncontained feelings. The baby, in its need for a self-confirmatory response, loses inner balance and attempts, through reengagement, to regain its own balance. In effect, the baby attempts to self-right but is not supported. The mother's incapacity to self-right and her concomitant disapproval and disengagement from the baby increases the baby's imbalance. This mismatching thwarts the baby's self-regulation and precludes an experience of confirming attuned responsiveness. It also diminishes the mother's sense of joy in the baby's responsiveness to her presence. Neither the mother nor the baby can completely pull back or disengage from what is now a pathogenic process. The mother's need for self-confirming mirroring becomes the paramount feature in the baby's selfobject experience. In the baby's developmental strivings, which normally promote matching behavior, this baby learns to respond in such a way as to promote in the mother affective states most calming to itself. Mirroring does indeed take place but includes an inversion in selfobject mirroring functions: for this baby, there can be neither safety nor joy in needing. What emerges in the baby is an extremely tentatively cohesive self-organization. Subjectively unconfirmed throughout development, the individual loses larger and larger portions of subjective experience to defensive operations, which are designed to preserve the precarious organization of the self but become pathogenic in themselves. A reliably positive sense of self does not occur.

We have noted in the gathering of clinical data from these patients that as they grew, they became more and more externally compliant, and as adults, are in constant fear of disapproval. They do not present needs for attuned selfobject responses for fear that this will harm or destroy them. As with patients we spoke of earlier in their responses to the analyst's having signs of the flu, the process of inversion in selfobject functions becomes a critical repetition. The child-now patient, attempts to function again as the confirming, validating and soothing selfobject to the mother-now analyst and cannot disengage from the original pathogenic matrix.

A patient entered treatment after a previously unsuccessful analysis that ended because she felt criticized and humiliated by the analyst's interpretations and was unable to rectify the situation short of ending the treatment. She appeared from the beginning to be confused, not in touch with her affective experiences and emotionally brittle with a high level of narcissistic vulnerability. Yet she was able to perform the duties on her job although she did not derive any satisfaction from them and could not be proud of her work. She lived alone, with only minimally supportive relationships in her life, and felt unable to be close to anyone. She felt painfully aware of a need to be important and loved. She came to sessions three times a week and was always worried about being late or missing sessions altogether because she found public transportation to be unreliable. Upon exploration, she felt that her relationship with the new analyst was in jeopardy every time she was several minutes late; and she developed severe anxiety and panic while obsessing about the analyst's being gone from her life. In sessions she was always polite and usually overly attentive to the analyst. She talked freely about her work as a copy editor for a large firm—though she remained saddened by the loss of her dream of becoming a concert pianist. A persistent complaint centered on feelings of profound anxiety, which would be replaced by depression that seemed to overcome her without apparent reason. She talked tentatively about feeling secretly apart, that she was "faking it," and that her existence did not seem real or substantive to her. Although she had no actual contact with her retired parents, she seemed emotionally involved in their existence to the point that it was at times difficult to distinguish her references to the past from current fantasies or feelings in experiences with them.

She was only a year old when her parents opened their own household goods store, enduring for another decade all the stresses involved in a new business—including working late and on weekends. The patient spent most of her time with her immigrant grandparents, who offered her minimally sustaining support for her developing self. When her parents picked her up on their return from work, they would destroy her excitement by arguing over the day's business transactions. A very bright and curious child, she learned to read early and would hide away for hours reading books. This provided her with a means of self-soothing in an otherwise unreliably involved and emotionally charged environment. The patient remembers feelings of guilt and terror whenever she spontaneously felt excited about expressing herself. To this day she finds it very difficult to feel good about anything she does creatively—except her private fantasies which occur when she is playing the piano. The patient's mother wished her daughter to play from the time she was very young and there was always enough money for the best lessons available. Playing the piano represented a lost talent of her mother's, which existed now only in the mother's grandiose, exhibitionistic fantasies—an archaic remnant of her own father's dreams for himself and for her that were destroyed by the war in Europe. When the family was able to flee to safety in America without severe loss—while the patient was growing up—the grandfather had already abandoned his piano playing. The patient's mother insisted on deep commitment to playing. Showing real talent, the patient enjoyed sharing this dream and excitement with her mother. In fact, playing classical music provided a source of mutually inflated grandiose fantasies of renown, a collusion between the patient and her mother in fantasies of greatness and the power to influence the international music world. It was essentially only in this context that the patient and her mother were attuned to each other's emotional lives. However, the gleam in her mother's eye seemed to vanish whenever the patient wanted to play a piece of music she had just learned, or by herself independently of her mother's participation. She found it difficult not to feel guilty enjoying music for herself by herself. She attempted to attend a nearby college so that she could continue with her current music teacher, and when the teacher obtained a faculty position at a college far away, she followed. She described herself at college as being in a constant state of panic and fragmentation without knowing why, but managed to finish and receive her degree. An unsuccessful love affair with a fellow pianist made her withdraw into herself and she became suspicious of men—fearing that they were only interested in her musical talent and not in her for herself. She returned from college to find that her mother had converted her bedroom into a music room. Gradually she felt herself sinking into unspeakable anxiety states in which she would close herself off in the music room for days without being able to play. She ultimately fled her home, taking her piano with her to an apartment she rented after obtaining a job in the firm where she still works.

The only visible show of affect in this patient occurred when she talked about the music she played—now alone in her own living room. She admitted that, in treatment, she would block out interpretations by reciting certain pieces of music in her head. It was later revealed that playing music either on her piano or in her head would allow her to become the very composer whose piece she was playing. This experience was soothing to her and confirmed her sense of self-worth by being able to turn on the music affectively representing the "turning on" of the self, an experiential selfobject deficit. These disturbed early mirroring experiences clearly contributed to the patient's anxiety states, her external compliance, and her need to act appropriately at all times. As early experiences, they took on their actual significance after several incidences occurred in treatment involving the patient's compelling need to be helpful in any way to the analyst. Her helpfulness appeared in the form of empathically responding with concern to what she experienced as needs in the analyst, or by being solicitously understanding about vacations, emergency phone calls, or changes in schedule. This culminated in one particular event when the patient noticed that an arm on the analyst's chair was loosening and asked for a screwdriver to fix it. Good at mechanical things, she became suddenly enraged when the analyst did not provide the screwdriver. The analyst remarked that the patient must have felt distressed about things not being in perfect order in her office and that things in their relationship might also need fixing. The patient only became calmer when the analyst stated that it

was understandable to want to be helpful, but it was also understandable to want to be taken care of. The patient felt strangely relieved
and was finally able to say that she felt terrified when unable to be
helpful to the people she needed but did not know why. It became
apparent that this patient had minimal affective connection with her
experience of needing as needs became reactivated in this new selfobject bond. What she was able to articulate was her initial experience of
feeling chaotic, confused, and helpless. She reported that she felt
"out of control," a sensation that invariably made her feel victimized
by her partner in the interaction. The analyst realized that the patient
felt thwarted in reenacting her need for self-confirmation through this
archaic mode of pathognomic mirroring; and this resulted in the
puncturing of her ficticious capacity to control the analyst and thereby affirm her own existence. This resonated with the fragmenting
terror originally associated with her deficit in the selfobject experiences with her mother who was unable to validate the patient's self-
experience. Thus, this form of delusional encodation occurring in this
patient prevented the establishment of an inner sense of affective
continuity in time and space, making it particularly difficult for the
analyst to be accepted as a mirroring selfobject.

Delusional encodation of experience utilizes ideosyncratic sets of
symbols, personally given meaning which can be in the form of
thoughts and assumptions, places, concepts, events and emotional
responses, and so on, in order to obscure the contextual meaning of
traumatic subjective experiences. In some patients, delusional convictions do not obliterate consensual reality; they rather obfuscate inter-
nal-subjective reality as it pertains to injuries sustained in pathogenic
selfobject experiences. The formalized internal subjective reality for a
particular individual like this patient is derived from the organization
of experience for the purpose of defense against traumatic self states.
However, if the individual's mother is so narcissistically disturbed
that she can neither recognize nor join her baby in any of the infant's
affective states, then the necessity for an all-encompassing delusional
barrier against this level of toxic invasion will be generated as preser-
vative to the infant's most basic psychological structure. We also believe that other resources potentially confirming to the child's early
affective states, such as a sufficiently reliably attuned and available
father, must be absent for the more profound levels of self-distur-
bance to occur. In such individuals, delusions will generally be uncontained and psychotic states will occur as the normative mode of
experience and response as seen in the following case.

A patient in treatment for five years was anorectic and almost
constantly in a state of fragmentation, with full-blown paranoid delu-

sions and occasional hallucinations. The hallucinatory experience often included seeing faces staring at him through windows in his apartment or being invaded by a neighboring family whose structure duplicated that of his own natal family. In his 29th month of treatment, he began coming four times a week for sessions paid for by his father because he himself was unable to keep on working. When he arrived for the first of these sessions, he noticed on the analyst's desk a small pile of stamped letters and offered immediately to mail them. The analyst said, "Thank you very much. It is very kind of you but I am planning to mail them later." On hearing this, the patient jumped up and began to cough violently, jerked his handkerchief from his pants pocket, and loudly and repeatedly began to blow his nose. Without a word, he left the office, leaving the analyst alarmed at the intensity of his reaction but certain that the patient was responding to her refusal to let him mail the letters; in the past, she had also gently refused to let him enact meeting other needs he believed her to have. The patient did not appear for any further session that week, but did return at his appointed time the next week. He seemed agitated and terrified and began the session by telling the analyst that he had just put lyrics to a song he had written, and had mailed them at the post office by special delivery in a self-addressed envelope. His purpose, he continued, was to obtain a copyright. The patient spoke angrily and at great length about his lyrics being stolen. Actually, the lyrics were to songs published around the time of the patient's birth. He complained bitterly about the inefficiency of the post office and the expense involved in accomplishing anything for himself. The analyst felt that the patient had encoded the crippling selfobject experience of feeling that no one had concern for him or his productions, which he felt deserved special handling. The analyst became aware that the patient had expressed a need by offering to mail her letters, which provided a sense of sustaining, affirming engagement within the caring, resonating presence of the analyst. Further analysis revealed that the lost lyrics were a delusional encodation of both his lost sense of self and the loss of hope for an empathic, reliable person who would provide missing selfobject functions to confirm and sustain him. The patient felt that the analyst's denial of his request to mail the letters was the same as his mother's refusal to resonate with, soothe or mirror him. He also connected the analyst's refusal to his mother's punishment for any spontaneous expressions of the self which did not participate in her affective states. It is clear that this patient pulled the analyst's letters into his own delusional thoughts because the analyst's action around them thwarted both a developmental need and the structures of defense built up around them. The patient needed the analyst to confirm the self-experience and not the experience of delusional power expressed through this inversion in selfobject functions, which had originally created his delusional defensive structure. In this selfobject transference, the patient showed his profound terror of losing his fragile sense of self-cohesion both by not coming to session and then, verbally, through encodation of his subjective experience upon his return. Through the analyst's empathic attunement to the patient's terror—and her admiration of his capacity to disengage and reengage with her—the patient began to slowly feel safe enough to explore the archaic affective components central to this event and others affectively similar to it. He came to feel that it might be possible to survive continuing engagements with the analyst involving his affective states which did not directly address or focus on presumed needs of the analyst before even considering his own. His archaic inability to disengage from his mother had previously left the patient feeling invalidated inducing panic and chaotic affect states that further threatened his fragile sense of balance. He could not comprehend his needs and helplessness but affirmed his fancied power to protect himself and the selfobject bond upon which he remained dependent. He was then able, after some time, to address his delusional convictions in treatment although he remained, for a much longer period, within his protective stance vis-à-vis the world.

This patient's delusional defense which became central to his organization of experience is also seen in his desperate attempts to halt his enmeshment with his mother by sending his vitality away in an envelope in the hope that it would be returned with a copyright; that is, as belonging irrevocably to him. His expectations revealed, in the selfobject transference, his terror of having his vital inner resources stolen once again in a selfobject context against which he could not protect himself. The needs he offered to his mother for her response would be returned, as he feared with the analyst, but no longer reflecting him. Rather, they would reflect her own disavowed emptiness, chaotic anxiety and grandiosity which required constant mirroring. The patient's resonation with his terror and helplessness would provide the patient with a sense of meaningful continuity, and enable him to begin again a long and painful journey toward establishing a cohesive sense of self.

In this group of patients as a whole, we have noted that the deep emotional connection with the maternal selfobject is enduring, in spite of their growing awareness of invalidating early selfobject experiences that had left them in doubt about what they were actually feeling. Concomitantly, these individuals have the most difficulty in accepting the analyst as a confirming selfobject. These two processes are directly associated with pathognomic mirroring. They produce the fragmenting helplessness defended against by believing that the patient's actions can sustain the affective existence of the selfobject bond. These patients are convinced that continuing affective participation in their lives is directly dependent upon their ability to provide nonself-centered selfobject functions. The organization of experience around a fantasy of reliable albeit delusional competency is essential to defending against affective continuity, resulting in an enduring propensity for traumatic self states. The critical experience in these traumatic self states, we believe, is initial self-doubt evolving very rapidly into total self-invalidation which these individuals attribute to uninvolved third parties as seen above in the rejecting lover for the pianist or the post office for the paranoid patient. These patients also frequently blame themselves for being "out of control" which is typically the self experience following the unconscious process of self-invalidation.

A patient in treatment for six years initially presented a complaint of severe anxiety attacks and an inability to sleep. She also had "weird" thoughts that she was unable to share with anyone for fear of humiliating rejection, leaving her unable to either let the thoughts go or to understand their existence in her. She described confusional states that left her helpless to be able to buy food at the supermarket because she could not decide what to eat and felt overwhelmed by the choices she had to make. A student at a major university, she often felt suffocated in her apartment. This feeling forced her into the street, where she could not avoid the intense experience of being penetrated by people staring at her, or seeing corpses lying in the street which she was unable to judge as actually there or a product of her mind. When she left her apartment, she would return to it several times to be sure she had turned off the lights, left the oven off, and double-locked the door. This patient often felt she lost her own sense of self-experience, fearing she could not come to sessions. She feared that her "bad self" would contaminate the analyst upon whom she depended to help her sort out her confused thoughts. The analyst noted that an exacerbation of these decohesive experiences occurred most often when the patient had succeeded in accomplishing something for herself that did not center upon either her mother, with whom she had frequent contacts, or the analyst. She needed reassuring soothing from the analyst that she would not die if she acted on her own needs independently as she gradually became aware of them. Focus on her subjective experiences revealed the coloration of engagements with her mother as captured in the following description:

Mother was in bed for several weeks having hurt her back and Dad was away. Our school was having a party and I wanted to go. So did my sister. But somehow the idea of leaving her there alone was something I couldn't stomach and I knew my sister would never consider staying home. So as if it were the most natural thing in the world to do, I didn't go to the party and was on call for mother instead. I guess I probably felt like she would die if I didn't stay. I knew that the thought of choosing someone or something over her filled me with dread. I suppose I was afraid she'd kill me or something even though she never hurt me. I knew other kids could just get up and leave and I envied them. It was like I was her anchor or something, keeping her from flying off to Oz.

In conclusion, patients enmeshed in pathognomic mirroring from their earliest selfobject experiences are left without definite or enduring outlines for self structure. They cannot make sense of their subjective experience, nor can they easily reach for self-confirming, developmentally enhancing selfobject ties because they cannot attribute any value to their own feelings—to themselves, and how they experience themselves interpersonally. They cannot rely on a sense of self to provide guiding meaning in their powerful and frightening self-doubt. Self-invalidation precludes experiencing their own needs while they must focus on the intrusive and crushing needs of others, especially those on whom they are dependent for attuned responsiveness. This results in a psychological environment that is random yet ordered through fantasy with fictitious elaborations on the meaning of personal and interpersonal events. Pathognomic mirroring also leads to a quality of inconsolability in these patients at the moment of deepest need for the soothing experience of empathic confirmation. In working through the subjective experiences associated with these self-deficits, the talents and skills that appear lost forever in delusional convictions of competency emerge in these patients along with an increased sense of vitality, enabling them to experience pleasure in their own productions. A greater capacity to use the analyst as a confirming selfobject, specifically providing mirroring functions, creates for the first time a belief that their own creative talents, heretofore affectively disavowed, are an important and uplifting part of the self.

We have also noted that these individuals are especially bright and sensitive with heightened attunement to their environment. This matching capacity, we believe, helped promote receptivity to their caregivers' often unspoken needs and attunement demands to which a less affectively available child would not, perhaps, have responded so totally.

REFERENCES

Beebe, B. (1985). *Mutual Influence in Mother-Infant Interactions and the Precursors of Psychic Structure.* Presented at Eighth Annual Self Psychology Conference, New York City.

Green, H. (1964). *I Never Promised You a Rose Garden.* New York: Signet.

Kohut, H. (1977). *The Restoration of the Self.* New York: International Universities Press.

——— (1984). *How Does Analysis Cure?* ed. A. Goldberg. Chicago: University of Chicago Press.

Stolorow, R. (1986). Critical reflections on the theory of self psychology: An inside view. *Psychoanalytic Inquiry,* 6:387–402.

Tolpin, M. (1984). *The Self and Its Selfobject—A Different Baby.* Presented at Seventh Annual Self Psychology Conference, Toronto.

Chapter 10

On Ambition and Hubris: A Case Study

Frank M. Lachmann

A patient, a 39-year old woman, reported to me the following dream: "I came to your office, and you told me that you had cured Anne Bancroft." The patient then offered various associations to this dream. She thought of two movies in which Anne Bancroft had appeared. "The Miracle Worker" and "The Graduate." In the previous session, she had described a flirtation with a considerably younger man with whom she was working and had referred to herself as "Mrs. Robinson," the character portrayed by Anne Bancroft in "The Graduate." She then discussed some difficulties with respect to her work and in this context described Mrs. Robinson as a ruthlessly ambitious woman, who pursued her desires without concern for the effect on others. She admired her determination in her pursuit of the young college graduate and wished that she could pursue her work with similar determination. Yet there was something frightening about the unconflicted boldness and cold-blooded determination of Mrs. Robinson's designs. Anne Sullivan, Helen Keller's caretaker, portrayed by Anne Bancroft in "The Miracle Worker" was another matter. She epitomized total commitment and devotion, which the patient valued and easily recognized as part of herself. That character embodied both the patient's early relationship to her husband and, especially, her relationship with him after he developed a life-threatening illness only three years after they were married.

"I can only love like Anne Sullivan," the patient said, "I don't feel I can be Mrs. Robinson. I can be totally devoted. Even before my husband's illness, I knew he needed a lot of love and affection, and I was all over him. When we were first going together, he said, 'Being loved by you is like being a hamburger—smothered with onions.' When I was the 'miracle worker' I felt all good. That's how I get my self-esteem."

In referring to the smothering quality of her attachment to her husband, the patient elaborated her conflicts between her attachments and her emerging ambitions. The intensity of her attachment created difficulties as such and also conflicted with her ambitious strivings. Her light touch, however, reflected the insightful perspective she had gained at this point in the analysis.

To the patient, Mrs. Robinson and Anne Sullivan were the personifications of incompatible and contradictory ways of relating to the world. To compromise her Anne Sullivan ideals would mean to lose a valued and familiar sense of herself. To renounce her attempts to acquire aspects of Mrs. Robinson would stifle her emerging ambitions. Furthermore, relinquishing her commitment to her Anne Sullivan ideals carried the meaning of turning into a Mrs. Robinson. Ultimately, this would constitute a humiliatingly experienced capitulation to her father and a deeply felt betrayal of herself and her mother. The patient's Mrs. Robinsonlike pursuit of goals meant a compliance with her father's devalued view of her "artistic" talents, which to her father were impractical but which were idealized by her mother.

In offering these associations, the patient defined ambition from her subjective vantage point. Ambitions were bold pursuits without concern for consequences or one's effect on others. Ambitious people were callous and unconflicted in their determination to obtain what they wanted. For the patient these strivings were specifically associated with work and the pursuit of a career. What to the eye of an observer might have been seen as mature goal-directed efforts were felt by the patient to be "hubris," her dread of aiming too high, of striving ambitiously at the expense of her attachments, so that the wrath of the gods would be incurred.

Essentially, the Anne Bancroft dream pointed to a dilemma: How to live with incompatible ideals and goals? Was the dream-wish an attempt to reconcile and resolve these conflicted goals or to tolerate these divergent themes?

If this conflict were unique to the patient, a discussion might follow in which only her specific dynamics, the origins of her conflicts, and her treatment would be detailed. However, I believe that this brief vignette points to broader issues. Whereas this patient's struggle certainly is a reflection of her individual psychopathology, her conflict in the juxtaposition of ambition and attachments is also a gender-related issue shared by many women and therefore poses special challenges to clinical practice and theory.

The patient was in a five-year analysis with me at the age of 19 and in a second analysis at age 34; that is, the second analysis began ten years after the termination of the first. The contributions of Edith Jacobson had served to guide me through the patient's first analysis. But, just as Mr. Z (Kohut, 1979) did not find the same analyst upon his return to analysis, neither did my patient. During the twenty-year period from the start of the first analysis to the conclusion of the second analysis, my clinical and theoretical perspectives were influenced and, I believe, enriched by contributions from both within psychoanalysis and from related fields. (For a discussion of the "new directions" for psychoanalysis see Basch, 1985; Lachmann, 1985).

During the past decade, the findings and formulations of developmental and social psychologists have challenged two biases which had become embedded in psychoanalytic thinking. First, there was the view that ambitions as related to career and work activities were normal for men, but when sought by women signified a specific kind of psychopathology: masculine strivings. The equation ambition equals masculinity not only achieved theoretical respectability but also found a place in the fantasy life of many people. A second view proposed that women ought to be able to be ambitious like men. The former view held that when women experience themselves as conflicted with respect to ambitious strivings; such conflict should be resolved in the direction of renunciation of such strivings. The latter view held that when women experience themselves as conflicted with respect to ambitious strivings, such conflict reflected their psychopathology and could, through further analysis, be resolved in the direction of enabling such women to proceed ambitiously and unconflictedly. Both views were based on extrapolations from a model of male development, and neither did justice to the specific priorities by which women organize their experience. To do justice to their specific priorities, the conflict between attachments and ambitions must be acknowledged as, at some point, irreducible, and depending on life circumstances, requiring a self-organization capable of tolerating and negotiating these ever-conflicting ideals and goals.

By and large, Jacobson (1964) discussed ambitions in nongender-related terms. When she suggested that ambitious fantasies are a prerequisite underpinning for the motivation to engage in work, however, the question of how these fantasies differ for men and women was left open. From her standpoint, ambitious strivings find expression in competitive struggles and rivalries, which, in turn, lead to identifications with competitors and rivals. Problematic, however, in Jacobson's model was her emphasis that development should proceed in the direction of increasing individuation through separation between oneself and the world of objects. Her emphasis was such that dependency, attachments, and symbioticlike and merger wishes were relegated to a position of lesser priority in the psychological organization of the healthy adult and were not recognized as occupying different priorities for men and women. Jacobson posited the roots of a woman's feminine identity to be in her early relationship with her mother and the firming and consolidating of that identity required continual gradual steps of separation from her. A function of a girl's relationship with her father was his availability as a rival for her mother. In her identification with him, she widened her separation from her mother and thereby gained her autonomy, independence, and self-reliance. These formulations of Jacobson provided the clinical theory for my understanding and interpreting the productions of the patient as they emerged during the first of her two analyses.

The patient initially sought treatment at age 19, after she dropped out of college. She had become increasingly uninterested in academic work and felt that there was nothing she wanted to do. She was cutting herself off from her friends and had become involved with her boss, a married man, while working as a secretary.

When the patient was six years old, her parents divorced and her father remarried. The patient remained with her mother and took it upon herself to maintain contact with her father. A close relationship between mother and daughter held until, when the patient was ten years old, her mother began a love affair with a married, well-known, and considerably younger artist. The patient felt disappointed and rejected by her mother but defended herself against these feelings by assuming an "accepting" and "protective" stance in relation to her. Her sense of herself as her mother's caretaker was furthered, and her closeness to her mother was thereby secured.

By the time the patient had reached adolescence, she had, on the one hand, lost both her parents and, on the other hand, acquired too large a cast for her oedipal drama. Nevertheless, to some extent she was able to maintain her mother as a source of comfort. Yet her mother became increasingly unavailable—especially with respect to actual caretaking, the preparation of meals, and the purchasing of clothing. To replace the lost closeness with her mother, the patient turned toward occult interests. In tarot cards, mysticism, the Cabala, and, later, through studying the psychology of Carl Jung, she sought to replace her missing attachment with a sense of "oneness on a cosmic level."

The patient described two traumatic incidents in the course of her first analysis, the deeper significance of which—with respect to her attachments and ambitions—was not understood until the second analysis. The first incident was as follows: The patient's mother and the mother's lover spent most of their time on the double bed in the mother's bedroom. They ate their dinner, watched television, and spent their evenings on the bed. When the patient wanted to be with her mother, she had to join them on the bed. Frequently, all three would be lying on the bed, the patient's mother in the middle. On one of these occasions, the lover embraced the mother but brought his hands past her and grabbed the patient's breasts. The patient was a fully developed young teenager at the time. She felt humiliated and thought she had done something wrong. Of course, she said nothing to her mother so as not to threaten the mother's tenuous attachment to her lover, nor her own tenuous attachment to her mother. Understandably then, she emphasized in her recollections that she felt ashamed for having worn a flimsy nightgown at the time and felt guilty because she believed that she behaved provocatively.

The second incident occurred some time later and involved her father. The patient had been ill and was in bed in her father's house. He wanted to entertain her by playing a game. He had been a medical student for a brief time and had kept a medical text with illustrations, cross-sections of various parts of the body. The patient was to show her father various diagrams and cover the captions. He would then have to identify the body part from its cross-sectional view. She recalled how impressed she was with her father's knowledge until she showed him a particular diagram and he confessed he did not know what it was. He asked her to name it for him, and once again she felt humiliated. She had to tell her father it was a penis. She felt she was being provocative and aggressive in that she had exposed her knowledge of sexuality to her father. Among numerous issues, this incident synopsized for the patient an important dimension of her relationship with her father. She must not pose challenges to him which might make him feel humiliated and diminish him in his own eyes and in hers.

These two incidents brought together the major dimensions of the patient's relationship with each of her parents. It later became evident that the incidents not only encapsulated the themes of the patient's prior experiences with her parents but affected her subsequent relationships, the quality of her attachments, her problems with ambition, and the vicissitudes of the transference. During the first analysis, they shed light on the preoedipal and oedipally derived conflicts. During the second analysis, they highlighted the interrelated nature of the patient's self-pathology and her oedipally derived conflicts.

A summary of the first five-year analysis must of necessity be schematic. Initially, the transference was understood as shaped predominantly by the patient's relationship with her father. She feared that she would be rejected or abandoned because she would be found unacceptable—morally, intellectually, and mainly sexually. As these concerns were described and connected to her various experiences, her enactment of triangular relationships in her life diminished. The exploration of this transference then enabled her to turn to and expose her more shame-filled experiences in relation to her mother. This phase of the treatment was ushered in with a dream: "I went to Bloomingdale's and I was naked in the elevator from the waist up. I felt uncomfortable and wondered if that was indecent exposure." Other dream images referring to "Bear Mountains," a double bed in my [her analyst's] office, and various threesome relationships suggested that the experiences with her mother and her mother's lover—particularly the incident in which her breasts were grabbed—were being worked through (Freud, 1914). At this time in the analysis the focus was on uncovering the consequences and derivatives of the traumatic experiences that occurred in her mother's bedroom which the patient was unconsciously repeating in her life. The predominant configuration of the transference thus shifted and she described the following dream: "I called you to ask if I could bring my quilt to the session. You said, 'sure.' Then I had my legs over the arm of a chair, and you said, 'You'd better put the quilt over your legs. I can see.'" While bringing her quilt to my office could be understood as a move toward turning my office into a bedroom, the emphasis here was on the quilt as a "comforter" and in finding a safe setting in which she could gradually modulate her humiliating shame and her guilt-ridden "indecent exposure." In the dream she depicted me as saying, "I can see," unlike her mother who specifically did not see, did not acknowledge her developing sexuality, and did not see what her lover was doing. The suggestion that she place the quilt over her legs, she felt, was depicting me as "tactful." She felt "protected" rather than "exposed." In the analysis we understood that she now differentiated herself from the mother who "exposed" herself and differentiated me from the mother who "did not see" and the father who "exposed" her.

Of the various implications of this line of exploration relevant for the issues under discussion were the following: the patient's shame with respect to her sexual development had served to ward off competitive feelings toward her mother and to maintain a sense of closeness with her. Diminution of her sense of shame enabled her to enjoy her sexuality and to begin to integrate a previously split-off grandiose, exhibitionistic self-concept, her "bare mountains." Her attachment to her mother was thereupon less suffused by her sense of guilt over her triumphant "indecent exposure." Recollections of repetitive childhood nightmares emerged. They were later understood as expressive of her confusion as part of the threesome on her mother's bed and her rage upon her nightly expulsion. Diminishing her stance as her mother's caretaker, she was able to venture toward a bolder appreciation of her own sexuality.

Though the patient's dream images had been replete with sexual references, her sexual experience had been very modest. We understood her flirtations with married men—a superficial identification with her mother—as prompted by her terror of her own sexual feelings, prompted by images of being "grabbed" in her mother's presence. However, to have sexual relations, to have her own sex life, would have meant that she had forgiven her mother for not "seeing" and for flaunting her "affair." To the patient, not to participate in sex constituted a constant silent reproach to her mother and hence a residual subservience to her.

Early in the analysis, the patient's interests in the occult were understood as the (re)establishment of a tie that had been ruptured by her mother's affair. She reported a dream: "I came to your office, and all your patients were witches." The reference to the witches related to an aura of the supernatural, which she equated to feeling at home, that is feeling accepted by me in my office. But the witches also referred to my other patients, who had now become frightening rivals whose power she feared. However, in referring to my other patients as witches, she also conveyed that she thought she was better looking than they. While retaining my selfobject function as a source of comfort, the patient also experienced me as an oedipal object whose women were both potentially dangerous but with whose women she could now compete.

Gradually the patient achieved a less anxious, better integrated sense of herself. Oedipal phase issues now dominated the dream imagery. She dreamed that she wanted to go to bed with me, and that I wanted to go to bed with her. After four years her references to feeling inadequate, rejected, and frightened had receded. She now depicted herself as sexually comfortable and capable of more adult relationships. No longer did she dream of sitting on the lap of her mother's lover and kissing him as though she was a little girl. She told me about a dream that took place in her mother's bed, "You and your wife were there. I had overstayed my welcome, your wife was annoyed and wanted to get rid of me." She could now depict herself as an adult contender but could not yet own the initiative to separate nor entertain the wish to get rid of a rival. Defensively, she still had to depict herself as being the rejected one.

Subsequently the patient described an experience with her boyfriend. She felt a particular sense of pleasure during intercourse from the gentle pressure of his body upon hers. She then spoke of feelings that she had recently experienced in her analytic sessions, which she could now articulate more fully. She wished that I would put more pressure on her by introducing new ideas and even contradicting her rather than appearing to be in unison with her. This wish signalled a major developmental shift, and this was acknowledged to her. However, I also noted her reluctance to take the initiative, wanting me to take the initiative, just as she had previously depicted my wife as taking the initiative. Her fear of contradicting me, preferring that I contradict her, could now be explored. In these explorations the two traumatic incidents were implicated, though the accent fell on her dread to repeat the sexually humiliating situation with her father, in which she felt obliged to take the initiative. Gradually, her avoidance of circumstances in which she would have to take the initiative was transformed. Through acknowledgment of her exhibitionistic strivings, her sense of herself as being capable of engaging in and competing in the world was enhanced. She then reported a dream in which she depicted her mother as crying because "I had disrupted everything when I left her. I became annoyed at my mother and said, 'Why don't you grow up?' My mother understood. It was the right thing to be telling her." The continuing development in the direction of separation and individuation, assertion, and initiative indicated that the seeds of ambition had been planted prior to the termination of her first analysis.

In the first analysis, these oedipal and preoedipal themes were examined and integrated by the patient into an enlarged perspective of herself. Major improvements were noted in her relationship with men. Her sense of herself changed from having initially felt fortunate if a man paid her any attention to recognizing herself as a vivacious and attractive woman. Her relationships with women had been characterized by openness and affection all along, and these qualities remained. Her enactments of oedipal-like triangular relationships ceased. Psychosomatic symptoms (spastic colon, headaches) became both rare and mild when they did occur. With respect to her work life, she felt satisfied with her status as a committed painter, able to support herself modestly. She exhibited her paintings and occasionally sold one. The first analysis ended when her sense of herself as a sexually and personally alive and well-functioning woman was attained.

The patient's problems had been understood along lines outlined by Jacobson. Having retained her father as a highly eroticized love-object, she could not identify with him as a rival so as to further her separation from her mother. Through the analysis of her erotic tie to her father and her defensive idealization of him, as this material emerged in the transference, her capacity to separate from her mother increased. Both her father and her mother's lover had remained overly stimulating erotic figures in her psychic life; and to that extent she had not been able to selectively identify with their ability to deal with the world in practical terms. Through such identifications she would have both furthered her independence from her mother and would have acquired a sense of herself as goal-directed and capable of mastering the world of work. The mother's subservience to her lover and, in effect, sacrifice of her daughter, offered a model to the patient. This underscored the self-effacing qualities of attachments to men and was a model for relegating herself to the background. In the analysis of the transference the preoedipal and oedipal themes were reworked. Fears of abandonment and rejection alternated with fantasies of the analyst/father as seductive. Later, the defensive attachment to, subservience to, and protection of the analyst/mother became evident with rageful, competitive, and rivalrous feelings being warded off.

The second analysis at age 34 was prompted by a life crisis. Her husband's illness forced her to (re)consider issues having to do with work and its financial consequences and, more generally, with ambitious strivings and a career. Prior to that time, these concerns could remain at the periphery of her life. Since her husband's illness also exacerbated the caretaking-being-taken-care-of dimension of their relationship, his remission, about one year after the second analysis began, necessitated a reconsideration of this aspect of their relationship as well.

In the first session upon her return, the patient reported a dream: she was wheeling me about in a wheel chair. I looked pale and weak, a reference to her husband's illness. Though he was not incapacitated at the moment, she dreaded that this might occur. More importantly, this dream reminded her of a dream she had had just after her last session ten years ago. It was a nightmare: she was taken off a dialysis machine. She linked the two dreams in that she felt, immediately after termination, that she had been taken off a life-support system and worried that she might not survive without it. We speculated that some issues might indeed not have been understood and addressed sufficiently in her first analysis. Specifically, it appeared, self-support or "life support" were depicted as external to her. There were, of course, other themes that emerged from the "wheel chair" image: being my caretaker, controlling my movements so that I could not abandon her, or so that we would not be precipitously separated as was depicted in the "dialysis" dream. The "wheel chair" image also previewed the Anne Sullivan theme that crystallized years later. Initially this image highlighted the quality of her attachments and her role as a caretaker in relation to her husband.

Among the issues that the patient discussed upon her return to analysis were her husband's illness and its effects on their relationship. Soon, the roots of her problems with respect to settling on a career direction came to the fore. She revealed an interest in working in the theater, which she had rejected in the past, in part, because of its association to her mother's family. As this studiously neglected interest emerged, she further revealed that she feared, if left unchecked, she would become a ruthless, pushy competitor, who would "cheerfully step on people's fingers as (she) climbed up the ladder of success." Inadvertently, she hummed a few bars from a song during one session. It turned out to be "Twinkle, twinkle, little star." By that time it was clear that she did not aspire to be a "little" star but a dazzling one. Her reference to "ruthless, pushy competitors," who lacked concern for others, previewed the Mrs. Robinson theme that crystallized later.

The analysis addressed her frequent description of any achievement or aspiration as "little." She, personally, did not really think that her successes in acting school were all that "little," but she feared revealing her estimation of her accomplishments and her future plans lest she be accused of "hubris." To avoid that charge, she maintained the fiction that she was still "little." In this context, to be lively and exuberant, about which she felt socially comfortable, was felt to be dangerous and could bring forth swift condemnation from gods and "grown-ups."

In exploring her dread of hubris, the patient described, for the first time, a playground visit with her mother in childhood. She recalled her mother's panic when she engaged in physical activities and her mother's intense anxiety when she climbed the monkey bars. Torn between calming her mother and enjoying her own ascent, discouraged by her mother's panic, she refrained from climbing "too high."

She speculated that if her mother had only felt more confidence in her ability to handle herself, and had only shown some trust in her ability to gauge dangers as she climbed the monkey bars, she might now be feeling less intimidated as she faced her "ladder of success"—and less in dread of being condemned for hubris.

The material that emerged during the second analysis illustrated that indeed separation had been successfully achieved; the patient and her mother lived satisfactory, independent lives and enjoyed a relationship balanced between affection and occasional squabbles. The extent to which the mother was needed as an archaic, mirroring selfobject, a protective presence, however, required further work. This specific self-selfobject bond had remained vulnerable, and the patient protected her mother from anxiety in order to maintain her as a source of comfort and support.

In retrospect, in the first analysis, object-related dimensions of the transference were clarified, and an idealizing transference was, quite likely, subsumed within the analysis of the oedipal transference. However, a silent mirroring transference may have been precipitously ruptured (as depicted in the "dialysis" dream) by or during the termination of the analysis. The recall of the playground visit provided new details in that it linked her upward striving with a continual self-requirement that she look back to see if her mother's face showed fear and disapproval.

As her theatrical career began to "twinkle," Anne Bancroft appeared in the patient's dream. The dream was understood as addressing an aspect of the transference. The patient felt that I had an agenda for her as did her father, namely, for her to become just like Mrs. Robinson, settle down, and get to work. She felt distrustful toward me. The transference dilemma was that when she was about to ascend the "ladder of success," I was either experienced as her anxious, disapproving mother, or her humiliating, approving father. She agreed that, with a touch of Mrs. Robinson, she might feel less intimidated when pursuing her own ends but would simultaneously be complying with her father's explicit, but, to her, demeaning expectations of her. The dream also reflected the persistence of two irreconcilable priorities in the organization of her experience. Her concern, care, and compassion regarding the needs and feelings of others were acknowledged as indeed likely to be experienced as clashing with her ambitious strivings. These strivings were now becoming more apparent and less suppressed in her life and were crucial in her evolving work life. The dilemma was acknowledged as an irreconcilable conflict, which enabled her to explore how it became exacerbated, how personal issues heightened it. She was thus enabled to gauge how and when to proceed with her career in the context of her attachment to her husband and his occasionally erupting health problems.

By the third year of the second analysis, the patient had embarked on a career. She had completed a respectable course of study in acting and directing, had earned much praise, and had succeeded in landing jobs commensurate with her talents and training. She handled her responsibilities well and thereby earned increasingly more responsible assignments. She contrasted the backing she received from relative strangers to the sense that she had never felt backed by her father. She acknowledged, however, his inconsistency: that in concrete situations he could be supportive. He did show enthusiasm for her art work—when actually confronted with one of her paintings—and did applaud her directorial work when he saw a play she had directed. But, she noticed, he did not express confidence in her and in her ability to provide for herself in the future.

The patient's mother related to her daughter's talents as though they were the mother's own private domain—as though they existed only between mother and daughter and had no reality in the world at large. Her father doubted whether her talents had any commercial value and encouraged her to take a secretarial job and be done with it. Thus, when it came to integrating ambitions with her talents, skills, and interests, she had two obstacles to overcome: work was experienced by her as neither real nor valuable.

Exploration of the theme that her mother was exclusively interested in her feelings and her father could not address them at all, helped the patient recall, for the first time, an aspect of her father's visits to her mother's house after their divorce. He would stay exactly two hours and then leave, no matter how much she, his daughter, protested—not even an extra five minutes. Her father's coldness and his attempt to treat the divorce in a matter-of-fact way were interpreted by the patient as his guilt over the divorce. Prior to the divorce, he had taken some interest in her beginning school and in her mathematic-like activities; after the divorce, she felt that he showed neither an interest in nor encouragement for her academic work. Her father's rigidity prompted her to feel that it was hopeless to try to be better organized. Equating reality and the world of work with a rigid, uncompromising, insensitive stance gave work, reality, and organization a bad name. The patient had always sensed that her father was disappointed in her, and she now explored her disappointment in her father. Remnants of her archaic idealizations of him were transformed into a less intimidating appreciation of him.

When the opening night of a play she had directed was in the offing, the patient wondered if she should invite me. If she did, she would certainly only send me one ticket. She did not want me to bring my wife. In depicting how this preplay drama would unfold, she imagined introducing me to her mother, who would be in the audience. Her mother would be extremely friendly and complimentary toward me, expressing gratitude and admiration. Her mother would be her usual charming, gracious self; the patient imagined I would be as much taken by her mother's charm as were all people who met her mother on such social occasions. I said to the patient that while this would start out as "her" night, it would quickly become "my" night and, then, just as quickly become and remain "her mother's" night. As she imagined it, she would become a member of the audience while her mother would assume center stage.

The patient was struck by the extent to which she accepted a place "in her mother's shadow" without question. She believed that her mother would not deliberately elbow her out of the way, but it was surprising to her that her mother, who was so concerned about her feelings, would never have been aware that she was being "pushy" in upstaging her daughter. The patient sensed that her mother needed this admired position, and that she had needed her to retain it. The patient's fear of hubris, of "climbing up," thus also contained the dread that her mother would have to be pushed out of the way. These insights also suggested that her mother's readily given acknowledgments of her daughter's achievements were understandibly experienced by the patient as somewhat shallow and thus never diminished her feeling that she was "incapable." The patient better understood why she experienced her own accomplishments as "little" and, as so, fleeting; and had needed to retain her mother as a modulator of self-esteem especially with respect to self-support.

Gradually divested of its pejorative, hubristic connotations, ambition had acquired a new meaning in the expanded context of the patient's subjective world. The conflict between ambitions and attachments on the broader level provided an ever-present background accompaniment to her career successes. When it became necessary to do so, she was able to fire some actors who were not contributing their best effort to a play she was directing. But, she added half-humorously, she still had great difficulty killing a cockroach. Half-humorously I asked her if she were afraid that such an act would make her appear too aggressive, as a killer, in her eyes? "No," she said, "I identify with the cockroach and the actors I fire. It's hard for me to see them as expendable. Should I enjoy firing someone? I can fire someone, now, but I feel a kinship toward them. It's the way I know myself. Do you want me to give up my identity?"

In her fantasy that I attend her play-opening alone, the patient acknowledged her competitiveness. However, in her fantasy I am also seduced by her mother. While this seduction was understood as a restoration of her mother to a position of preeminence, this was not the major point. The transference issue was addressed: that my presence did not enable her to feel that it was *her* big night, and that I became the recipient of admiration. Just as she had forfeited her upward climb in the playground in deference to her mother, she forfeited her night. Pursuing this issue shifted the spotlight back to her, and, in feeling so acknowledged, questioned her self-sacrificing support of her mother's need to be admired and its transferrential counterpart. The maintenance of an archaic mirroring selfobject transference had necessitated her relinquishing her own right to be admired and had restricted her ambitions.

The patient's conflicts with respect to attachments and ambitions receded to the level of difficulties of everyday life. Actually, and in metaphor, she was able to fire bad actors though with some discomfort. She continued to negotiate her attachment to her husband and the requirements of her career. In the diminution of the smothering quality of her attachments, both her relationship with her husband profited and her ambitious strivings became less encumbered with pejorative imagery. A residual tension between her attachments and her ambitious strivings remained and, I believe, inevitably will remain.

CONCLUSION

Two psychoanalyses of a woman have been described from the perspective of her dilemma and conflicts between attachments and ambitious strivings. Initially these problems were addressed from the standpoint of unresolved oedipal and preoedipal issues. Through the addition of a self psychological perspective in her second analysis, the remaining personal conflicts with respect to ambitions were addressed. She developed a well-functioning set of skills and talents which provided her with personal satisfaction in her work life. Her problems with respect to attachments and ambitions were understood from the vantage point of her subjective experience and from a perspective that acknowledged gender-specific issues in the priorities by which she organized her subjective experience. The discomfort she felt with respect to her incompatible ideals and goals, attachments and ambitions, required an integrated self-organization capable of tolerating such diversity and conflict.

Two gender-related biases within psychoanalytic theory were described. An early view held that career-oriented ambitious strivings in women were evidence of pathology and need to be renounced. A second view held that any conflict with respect to the pursuit of realistic ambitions was based on unresolved personal problems. The interaction between personal dynamics and gender-related priorities must be studied and explored in each case. An empathic immersion in a patient's subjective experience requires the inclusion of a gender-specific perspective. Psychoanalytic treatment can then address the personal themes that restrict or encumber the patient.

REFERENCES

Basch, M. (1985). New directions in psychoanalysis. *Psychoanalytic Psychology*, 2:1–14.

Freud, S. (1914). Remembering, repeating, and working through. *Standard Edition*, 12:145–156. London: Hogarth Press, 1958.

Jacobson, E. (1964). *The Self and the Object World*. New York: International Universities Press.

Kohut, H. (1979). The two analyses of Mr. Z. *International Journal of Psychoanalysis*, 60:3–27.

Lachmann, F. (1985). Discussion of "New directions in psychoanalysis" by Michael Franz Basch. *Psychoanalytic Psychology*, 2:15–20.

Theoretical
Contributions

Chapter 11

Selfobject Failure and Gender Identity

Leslie M. Lothstein

While the literature on childhood gender-identity disorders and childhood transsexualism is quite extensive, it is also fragmented and lacks a sound underpinning (Sperling, 1964; Greenson, 1966; Zuger, 1966; Harrison, Cain, and Benedek, 1968; Kohut, 1969; Green, Newman, and Stoller, 1972; Bloch, 1974, 1978; Volkan and Kavanaugh, 1977; McDonald, 1981; Loeb and Shane, 1982; Pruett and Dahl, 1982; Green, 1985; Meyer and Dupkin, 1985). Indeed, some of the key concepts, such as *core gender identity* (Stoller, 1966, 1968, 1970; Gershman, 1970; Kleeman, 1971), are even put forth without reference to such events as the simultaneous development of the *nuclear self system*.

Given the temporal relationship between core gender-identity development and the organization of the nuclear self system it would appear that Self Psychology theory (Kohut, 1977, 1984) could provide us with the necessary and sufficient theoretical underpinnings for a theory of gender-identity development (especially via the concept of a selfobject cf. Coen, 1981; Tolpin, 1971, 1978; Basch, 1981, 1984a,b; Stepansky and Goldberg, 1984; Stolorow, 1984; Stolorow and Lachmann, 1980).

THE PROBLEM FOR SELF PSYCHOLOGY

Lang (1984) noted that while an "awareness of one's gender (ought to) occupy a central place in one's sense of self" there has been no concerted effort by self psychology to elaborate "on the significance of gender identity in the nuclear self, nor of the specific processes by which [that] aspect of the self is consolidated within the matrix of selfobject relationships" (p. 51). On several occasions, however, Kohut (cf. Clower, 1977) alluded to the significance of gender identity as related to the development of the nuclear self. He did not, however, expand those ideas into a coherent theory. On one occasion, in response to Stoller's notion that gender identity was fully formed by age two, Kohut stated, "one should instead speak, for example, of activity or passivity as precursors of masculinity or femininity" and not of "full gender identity" by age two. Essentially, Kohut believed that "the nuclear self and its needs . . . (could only) be understood in the abstract as androgynous; that is, the supraordinate urges and motivational forces are in principle the same for both men and women, as are the processes of self-structure formation" (Lang, 1984). Kohut (1977) elaborated on this argument and stated that the nuclear self, which, having already been laid down "now receive[d] an important imprint determining its shape—it will . . . be more definitely a male or female self" (p. 240).

Lang (1984), extrapolating from Kohut's statements on gender-identity and the nuclear self, stated that the contents of the self (that is, the nuclear self as male or female) was never fully developed by Kohut or self psychologists because it was viewed as "secondary and not especially interesting (to the) theoretical concerns of a psychology of the self." However, a few psychoanalysts conversant with self psychology have felt that these issues merited discussion (cf. Mahler, Pine, and Bergmann, 1975; Lachmann, 1982).

Through the presentation of clinical case material from three young children with severe gender-identity disorders I will argue that the male aspects of the self are "consolidated within the matrix of selfobject relationships" and that selfobject failures around gender-identity issues may lead to severe disorders in gender- self or gender-identity functioning (especially for those boys who are raised in families which bluntly interfere with their son's male development). I will also argue that an analysis of the "contents of the self" as male or female may provide us with new insights into the structuralization of the nuclear self, and the later development of the self as male or female, and ought to become an integral part of self psychology theory.

CASE MATERIAL

The three male children who are the focus of this study exhibited a spectrum of psychological symptoms; and had either threatened or attempted to mutilate or amputate their genitals. In each case, the experience of tumescence was greeted with intense rage, anxiety, shame, guilt, and despair; feelings which led to self-destructive acting out directed primarily toward their genitals (with the aim of ridding the self of the penis and its dreaded erection). Each of the boys (two whites, 4 years 7 months, 5 years; and one black, 4 years 8 months) also expressed an intense wish to be a girl and engaged in a number of cross-gender behaviors (some of which were supported by one or both parents).

THE CASE OF ELLIOT

Elliot (age five) is a husky and affectionate child whose gender problems were manifested in several ways. He wore girl's clothing, make-up, and toenail polish; stated emphatically that he was a girl, and attempted to amputate his penis.

Elliot said, "When my penis goes up I get mad and angry. I hate it when it goes up. I want to shoot it off with a gun. I want to get rid of it. I want to shoot myself and die." He also beats on his penis when he becomes erect. Once he tried to cut off his penis but he was thwarted. When asked why he was so angry at his penis Elliot squealed, "I want to be a girl, I want to be a girl, I want to wear skirts and spin around." His mother had a program for Elliot's gender development, which she saw as a bulwark against his becoming too "macho" or masculine like his father. She hoped that if she allowed him to be "feminine" he would become a gentle and nurturant person, traits that she felt men lacked.

Elliot's home life was in chaos. His father, Mr. E., a retired Marine drill sergeant, was a pathologically jealous man with a violent temper. At times he became so enraged with Elliot that he lunged at him and shook him violently.

Mr. E. had previously been married and had four older children. One son, who lived with his mother, liked to dress up as a woman. He had a high-pitched voice and feminine features. Another son, Evan, while running away from home, was killed when his car was struck by a train. Just prior to that tragedy, Mr. and Mrs. E. had filed for separation. It was during their trial separation that Evan was killed and Mrs. E. became pregnant with Elliot. It seemed as if Elliot were a replacement for Evan.

This was Mrs. E.'s first marriage, and she was only three months into their marriage when Mr. E. (then age 42) had his first myocardial infarct. Eight years later, Elliot was born. Mrs. E., an ex-nun, is an intelligent, obese, but seductive woman. She is the oldest of five siblings. Mrs. E. described her mother as always being "diabolically" opposed to her. "I was frightened of her and never close to her at all. She never kissed me." Her mother favored the boys and showed them more affection. Her father, however, was described in glowing terms as "my whole family . . . a philosopher, who taught me how to be tough and saw that I did things in spite of what I wanted to do."

Mrs. E. recalls mystery, intrigue, and secrets surrounding both her father and many family members. Most of the males in her family had tragic lives, and two brothers died violently. Mrs. E. views herself as caring but tough. She said of herself, "You needed a set of balls to do what I was doing and I had them." At 18 years of age she entered the convent; ten years later she abandoned her vows because she wanted to marry.

Mrs. E.'s pregnancy with Elliot was the result of a contraceptive accident. She nursed Elliot for six months and describes him as "eating every hour and a half." She breast-fed reluctantly and was resentful of the demands the baby placed on her. "The total dependence stage bothered me," she said. "I don't like anyone, baby or adult, to be that dependent on me."

Apparently Elliot was poorly circumcized and has difficulty pulling his foreskin back because "my penis hurts." His mother continues to clean his penis and puts ointments on it. Elliot's home life is permissive and overstimulating; he shares his mother's bed and bathroom, and she even showed him how she inserted tampons.

According to Mr. E., Elliot's feminine behavior emerged around age two and were supported by his mother. He passively stood by as his wife dressed Elliot in skirts and blouses, bought him dolls and dolls' dresses, helped him put on makeup and toenail polish. Although his father tried to discourage Elliot's effeminacy, he was fearful that he might do something "to hurt the child" (perhaps in reference to his son Evan's violent death) and let his wife raise the child.

Elliot was in once-weekly therapy. During the first phase of treatment, he would not separate from his mother and dragged her into the room. He showed little interest in the toys and either performed or danced for us or climbed on to his mother and attacked her. He was very exhibitionistic and practiced cheerleading steps and songs. He sang in a high-pitched voice and was self-absorbed in his fantasies of being a cheerleader. Occasionally he did cartwheels and then took off his shoes and socks to show off his toenail polish.

The second phase of treatment began when he was "weaned" from his mother and was able to be alone with me in the treatment room. Elliot came to therapy with a backpack filled with food. Although he ate gobs of candy (bought by his mother), he never seemed to get filled up. In his play he was preoccupied with the doll house. He obsessively arranged the dolls' beds and crammed them in the rooms. Indeed, he filled all the beds with dolls. Everybody was sleeping with everyone else.

When he became anxious he would virtually fly around my office—climbing on furniture, leaping off the chairs, bumping into things, and eventually trying to hit me or soil me with craft materials. His play suggested that he was re-creating some conflictual themes related to his overstimulating home environment and especially primal scene material. His "femininity," however, had a strikingly phallic cast.

When I finally produced some new girl dolls for Elliot to play with, he looked at me with a tenderness that I had never seen before. He felt understood and appreciated. It was as if a storm had lifted. His chaotic, uncontrolled behavior, his lack of frustration tolerance, his inability to bear anxiety, his poor concentration ceased, and his attention span dramatically increased. The dolls had a soothing effect on him and his low frustration tolerance and low anxiety threshold gave way to more stable ego functioning and a more spontaneous and relaxed behavioral repertoire. For the first time, he began talking in depth about his problems.

In his doll play, Elliot repetitively dressed and undressed the dolls. He was curious about the dolls' "bottoms" and their urinary, fecal, and reproductive capabilities. While he engaged in a desperate and fruitless search for the penis on the girl dolls, he was also able to verbalize his confusion.

Elliot insisted on taking walks. Typically, he ran at full steam and would hide behind bushes or trees. He played a kind of hide-and-seek and was relieved when I found him (testing me to see if I cared for him). He also risked injury. Several times he jumped from high places, darted out in the street, climbed precariously onto ledges, and fell down, scraping his knees. On one occasion he impulsively tried to jump off a ledge. Later he told me he wanted to "kill himself" (his words). I had to restrain him. These self-destructive, suicidal behaviors replaced his earlier attempts at genital mutilation. Now he was more depressed. Occasionally his exhibitionism knew no bounds. For example, he shouted out cheers, paraded around in a provocative

way, and did cartwheels everywhere. Even in the coldest weather he
wore gym shorts to his therapy sessions and enjoyed exposing his
legs and feet. Once he stood in front of the elevator and surprised a
group of people by dropping his pants.

In the next phase of therapy he seemed hopelessly in love with me
and also furious with me. He even asked me to be his father. When
he realized that I could not be his father, he became depressed and
angry (affects that he acted out in the therapy). Once he even coaxed
his mother to come into the therapy room and wanted the three of us
to hold hands, dance, and kiss. He pretended that he was our child.
Mrs. E. showed no empathy or understanding of Elliot's need to be
with his father. In the final phase of our therapy, Elliot was torn
between his dual allegiance to mother and to father.

In spite of the enormous stresses on him, Elliot was no longer
cross-dressing, nor was he entertaining the idea of being a girl. He
was able to separate from his mother and was beginning to see himself as a separate person. He was doing better in school and had made
some new boyfriends. It was at the point that Elliot was doing better,
and during her divorce proceedings, that his mother withdrew him
from treatment. Two weeks after the divorce was granted she let her
husband move back in with her, in effect repeating what her own
mother had done.

THE CASE OF ROBERT/"STRONGER"

At age four Robert paraded around the house in his mother's clothes,
wore her nightgown to bed, put on makeup, sat to urinate, and stated
that he wanted to be a girl. His parents did little to discourage this
behavior and regarded it as "cute." At preschool he told his age
mates that he was a girl.

Robert believed that he had a vagina. Whenever his penis became
erect he would "pull back his testicles . . . (and) bending his penis"
would threaten to "cut off' his penis with a knife. Robert told his
mother, "I want it to come off, it's ugly, I don't like it." Although
Mrs. D. seemed worried, she was also unempathic to the urgency of
her son's needs.

The mother believed that Robert's gender problems began when
his sister Leshauna was born (Robert was 11 months old). She said
that they were like twins except that Robert is feminine and Leshauna
is masculine ("Everyone mistakes Robert for a girl and Leshauna for a
boy"). She described Robert as having effeminate mannerisms that

are "switched off and on," and being "girlish-looking" ("other people see him as the girl and his sister as the boy"). At birth mother nicknamed Robert "stronger," an alias that underscored mother's feelings of helplessness and weakness as a woman and made her feel more firm about her female identity. The nickname provided mother with the strength that she perceived herself lacking as a female.

Robert, named after his father, was his mother's first pregnancy. The pregnancy was unplanned. Robert, weighing five pounds, was delivered by Caesarian section because he was breech. The mother reluctantly breast-fed Robert for three months. She described him as "very clingy to me. He didn't want to let go." Robert had an orthopedic problem that required him to wear a cast to the knees when he was 6 to 7 months of age, and a cast to midcalf between 7 and 9 months of age. After that he wore special shoes, which restricted his mobility and made him dependent on his parents. He was, however, walking by one year.

Robert was toilet trained by age 2½, never sucked his thumb or wet or soiled his pants, and was described as a cooperative well-behaved, "intelligent, sensitive, and curious" child. There was no evidence of developmental or behavioral problems. His first separation occurred at 3 months of age, when his mother took a three-day trip. She did not recall the separation as being particularly disturbing for Robert.

The parents are a black, middle-class, upwardly mobile, well-educated couple. The father is a quiet, reflective man regarded by his wife as "a mamma's boy," "pussy whipped," and a "wimp." The mother was described by her husband as an angry, vengeful, spiteful, argumentative woman who hates men. Although she admired her husband, she did not love him. She said, "We often say that maybe, after all the bills are paid, we'll go our separate ways."

The father was more concerned about his deteriorating marriage and his wife's inability to care emotionally for the children than he was about Robert's gender problem. Mr. D. stated that he had once threatened to take away their son unless his wife entered psychotherapy, because "you're a crazy, an unfit mother." He described his wife as furious and rageful during her pregnancy with Robert and practically a "witch" when she was pregnant with Leshauna. He viewed the marriage as quite stressful and recalled that his parents had disapproved of his wife-to-be and tried to discourage the marriage. When that didn't succeed, they tried to break up the marriage (a plan that eventually led to the couple moving to another city). Mrs. D. entered psychotherapy because of her "dissatisfaction with myself, my marriage, and anger and resentment towards my husband."

During her first psychotherapy she found out she was pregnant again! The therapy, which involved weekly sessions, lasted three years and terminated when they moved to another midwestern city.

Mr. D. was the youngest of three siblings, all of whom were male. He described his family as "a disgustingly male-oriented family" that was close-knit and "on an even keel." Mr. D. viewed his family as very loving and supportive and denied any gender problems in his family. He had lots of male friends and was actively involved in sports and other forms of vigorous activity.

Mrs. D. was the sixth of seven children. She recalled that as a girl "I wanted to be a boy." She was profoundly jealous of her brothers ("they could do everything I couldn't") and described herself as a lifelong tomboy. From an early age she resented her female status and hated her female body. She experienced her femaleness as enslaving her to an impoverished, empty, desolate life in which she could only sit back and watch men succeed. She recalled an incident in high school in which her counselor told her that because she was a girl she should only consider a career in home economics. She was livid with rage but could not respond to him. After that incident she "got the feeling that I couldn't work on my brains."

It was not without meaning that his mother would not let Robert alone in the therapy room and clung to him, stroking his body, caressing his head, wooing and cooing at him, and speaking for him. When I gave Robert some drawing materials, his mother intruded into his space, managed his play, and completed his drawings—handing them to me as if they were Robert's own creations and accomplishments. She could not bear to be separated from Robert and acted as if they were a single unit.

Mrs. D. sponsored feminist meetings at her home where she went into tirades about how men are bad, evil, destructive, and dangerous. Robert sat and listened attentively to his mother's lectures on the evilness of men and how they must be destroyed. Robert could recall his mother's discussions in detail. When his mother reflected on what my confrontation of these "discussions" might mean to her son, she tearfully stated: "I've taken a perfectly normal little boy and gotten it into his head that maybe it's not so keen to be a boy."

THE CASE OF BRIAN

After the birth of his brother Paul, Brian (now 4 years old) paraded around the house in his mother's clothes and told his age mates that he was a girl or wanted to become a girl. In his play, he assumed the female role and identified with the heroines. He spoke in a high voice, "had an effeminate manner," sat to urinate, and had a female cousin who also dressed him up as a girl. While this practice "nauseated" father he did not interfere with it.

When Brian awakened with a morning erection he became angry and would beat on his penis with his fists. He told his parents that he hated his penis and wanted to make it go away. He was frightened and angered by his erections. It was only with detumescence that Brian's anxiety lessened and he lost interest in harming his genitals. The parents were guilty about their role in Brian's genital abuse.

According to the father, Brian has "a very close relationship with his mother and he gets concerned if mother is left behind. I feel rejected because as a young boy he always went with me. We think it's related to the birth of his brother. I never associated one kind of sex with Brian when he was younger." Prior to his birth, both parents were concerned that their gender-role stereotypes would interfere with Brian's development as a male. Mrs. B. responded that "I had it in my mind just after Brian was born that we should keep him from becoming too macho. Richard [her husband] plays sports, is aggressive, and chauvinistic, and I didn't want it shoved on him [Brian] . . . In our marriage we were concerned that I would force feed him athletics and we've almost gone the other way." Mr. B. found Brian's girlishness repulsive, however, and he often stayed at work late into the night so that he would not have to see Brian's "effeminacy."

Both of Mrs. B.'s deliveries were experienced as uncontrollable traumatic events which she silently endured. When Brian was born there "was nobody to deliver him, it was surprising and scary as he simply landed on the delivery table while the doctor was out of the room." Her second delivery was more traumatic. In her eighth month, her water broke and she began hemorrhaging. Apparently Brian, who was then three, was sitting under the dining-room table when she "had a flush of blood which went all over Brian; he was scared and we didn't have time to console him"—as the family dashed to the hospital. After the birth of her second son, the mother was hospitalized for three days. She had little empathy for what impact the birth and her separation from him had had on Brian.

The mother described her pregnancy with Brian as normal. He was delivered by natural childbirth. Both parents agreed that they wanted a boy and were delighted with Brian's birth, but Mrs. B. was jealous of her sister, who was pregnant at the same time and gave birth to a girl. Brian was named after the father's brother and an old boyfriend of the mother who had died of leukemia at age 19.

Brian was not breast-fed because his mother was inhibited about breast-feeding and she did not want to be tied down. She guiltily explained that none of the women in her family had breast-fed their children. Mr. B. defensively stated, "Although Barbara didn't breast-feed her bonding was fine." Brian was toilet-trained at age 2½, when the family had taken several of the mother's sister's children—all girls—into her house for prolonged periods of time. The parents also noted that Brian never went through the "terrible two's" because they did not want him to be angry. Apparently they had heard that during this period of development children are likely to become strong willed, assertive, stubborn, rebellious, defiant, and angry. Both parents feared the consequences of Brian's anger and hoped that by stifling this aspect of his development they would not have to face the consequences of the so-called terrible twos.

Mr. B. was the third of four children. A tall, handsome, athletic man, he was emotionally sensitive and psychologically minded but had a need to control his wife. Mr. B. was the older male child (he had a sister three years older and a brother three years younger). The oldest child, a girl, had died at birth. His childhood was marked by rebelliousness, poor school performance, bed-wetting until age 16, abandonment anxiety (he was school phobic), angry confrontations with his father, and a reputation for being the "black sheep" of the family. During adolescence he was arrested for truancy and breaking and entering. He ran away from home while he was in junior high school. He once hit another boy so hard in the stomach that the boy was hospitalized. It was this anger that he attempted to shield from Brian. Mrs. B. thought her husband "was literally a bum . . . a provocative person." He recalled being a "disappointment" to his father, whom he viewed as a man "who endured his pain privately" (his mother had died in childbirth and his father deserted him), and always said in response to questions about his family, "I'll tell you when you're older, but he never did."

Although Mr. B. was close to his brother Brian (after whom he named his son), they competed viciously and their basketball games and racquet ball matches often ended in fistfights. Mr. B.'s emotional makeup was closer to his sister's and his mother's; that is, he tended to get tearful when hurt, flooded with emotion, and, at times, quite melancholy. He wondered if he didn't have "too much woman in me." Indeed, he viewed his emotionality as a kind of "explosive openness."

While growing up he was deeply influenced by his aunt (father's sister), who provided an important mirroring and idealizing relationship which bolstered his self-esteem and narcissism, making him feel special and rescuing him from a serious depression.

Mrs. B. was the fourth of eight children. She viewed her sisters (there were four, two of whom were twins) as "bubbleheads, confused, promiscuous, selfish, unable to care for their children" (the youngest gave their mother her three children to raise). While she viewed her brothers as sexually confused or emotionally crippled, she was closest to Benjamin who, at age twenty-seven, underwent a sex reassignment operation and was living as a transsexual woman. Mrs. B. is an attractive, intelligent, and outgoing woman who describes herself as always supporting the underdog, nursing wounded animals, and having the ability to spend hours talking to anyone in need. She had a need to make things right with herself and others. She was the only child in her family to separate herself from her mother and was designated as the only stable member of her family. In grade school, however, she was insecure and was teased about her looks and weight. However, as an adolescent she blossomed and was sexy and attractive. Whenever she was asked out by one of "the boys who teased me . . . the tables turned. I had such a feeling of power to say 'I wouldn't go out with you on a bet.'" As a result of the teasing, she said "I don't want my son to be cruel or torture someone who is not like him."

Mrs. B. was emotionally close to and identified with her father. Her home life was chaotic and her mother used her as a go-between to make peace with her father. She saw her mother as having a "magical sense" of control over her children who could not fully separate from her.

Like her daughter, Mrs. B.'s mother was the only sibling to move away from her family. They shared other similarities. They were both their fathers' favorite child, and they were both called on to calm their fathers' rages. Mrs. B. described her grandfather as "a raging, murderous man" who, when violent, needed to be tied down to a chair. The maternal grandmother (MGM) reportedly had to hide the kitchen knives from him as he threatened to harm other family members. Once he was tied down (usually to a chair) no one but the MGM would go near him. It was the rage that was traceable to two generations of men that Mrs. B. feared might infect her son Brian.

Mrs. B. was guilty for having separated from her mother. She viewed her mother as feeling inadequate and losing "her good feeling about herself when her kids weren't doing well. As the kids grew up and moved out, mother fell apart." As the only sibling who "broke away" from her mother she felt that she had emotionally killed her in the process.

Both Mr. and Mrs. B. felt that the chaos and confusion in their families involved considerable rage which "we want to spare them [their sons] from what we've faced."

Brian, a slight youngster with pale skin and almost delicate features, clung to his mother. While he showed an interest in playing boys' games and enjoyed boys' toys he labeled everything female. He called all the dolls "girls" even if they were obviously male dolls. He also talked constantly about his father's car and played with the toy cars. He was quite verbal and talked about his nightmares and fears of going to kindergarten. He was also meticulous and neat and concerned about making messes.

In our sessions he enjoyed beating me at board games and took delight in my failures while gloating over his victories. He did anything to win; breaking the rules and cheating were considered fair play. He always expected me to win and was always surprised and relieved whenever he beat me. His symbolic competition with father was evident in his play with me. Brian said that he would like to be "a butterfly only if no one touches me 'cause the powder would come off my wings and I couldn't fly."

The focus of our brief work (which was short-circuited by the parents who pulled him out of treatment when he no longer attempted to mutilate his genitals) was on his competitiveness, his need to win, and his jealousy of girls. To what extent his transsexual uncle actually contributed to this confusion remains unknown.

Brian's central conflicts focused on themes of castration anxiety and a fear that he would be punished whenever he succeeded. He employed reaction formation excessively and felt quite vulnerable. He was especially vulnerable to having his special powers (i.e., his maleness) taken away from him. He also viewed women as having special powers to give birth and was jealous of them.

While the family was reluctant to bring Brian in for further treatment (once his threats of genital mutilation stopped) they continued to see me as a couple, bimonthly for three years.

SELFOBJECT FAILURES AND GENDER IDENTITY: HATRED OF THE PENIS

While the initial stress that released the child's gender identity was the birth of a sibling or an experienced loss, the acute crises which caused each of the boys described above to masochistically attack their genitals was their experience of an erection. They were not only confused by the erections but the erections elicited feelings of anxiety, anger, fright, distress, and guilt (cf. Roiphe & Galenson, 1981). Indeed, with tumescence all of the boys felt out of control and were overwhelmed by feelings of panic, anxiety, confused body feelings, and heightened affective states (cf. Greenacre, 1953; Bauman, 1981).

None of the boys seemed to have developed a self-regulatory mechanism to monitor and control their feeling-states over their erections.

In no case did the parents (that is, the selfobjects comprising the child's intersubjective field) attempt to help their sons become aware of the normalcy of their erections and to feel pride in their genital functioning. To the contrary, the parents reactions to their sons feelings about tumescence varied from punitiveness and sarcasm to assuming a demeaning manner; parental reactions that left the children feeling unsupported and even more confused and anxious (cf. Miller, 1984). These reactions seemed to be related to a family agenda in which a preemptive cross-gender schema was communicated to the child (cf. Stoller, 1968). All three of the boys had a poor understanding of their sexual anatomy, were ignorant about the anatomical differences between the sexes, and were confused about reproduction. The parents made no effort to educate them about psychosexual functioning and, at times, supported their confusion and heightened their genital dysphoria. Indeed, the children may have come to believe that their male organ stood in the way of their being treated as valued individuals and that the only way they could be loved and protected by their parents was by sacrificing their penis. In the course of working with the three boys, several hypotheses emerged related to their anatomical (genital) dysphoria. These hypotheses included the following:

1. allaying their parents anxiety that as males (penis-maleness) they would be potentially destructive and dangerous toward their parents (Klein, 1975);

2. believing that the only way to be loved by mother (that is confirmed by the mirroring selfobject) was to be loved as females, and thereby assuaging the maternal selfobjects' threat of infanticide (cf. Bloch, 1974);

3. attacking the genital schematization of their self-representation (cf. Socarides, 1980) rather than the beloved object; in this sense retaliating without destroying the object and thereby preserving object ties (cf. Glenn, 1984);

4. complying with the joint parental transference to destroy their masculinity in order to preserve the parents' precarious self-representations;

5. feeling narcissistically depleted, secondary to the parental selfobject failure to confirm their self-system by showing pride and admiration in their male self (especially the body self), and

6. engaging in perverse sexual activity in order to shore up their precarious representational structures related to their gender-self system (cf. Stolorow, 1984; Brandchaft and Stolorow, 1984).

Essentially, all the boys experienced their penis as alienated from their body—self. That is, they acted as if their penis was disconnected from their body schema; an intruder, an attacking external object, which needed to be obliterated in order to reduce their anxiety and consolidate their self-experience. The boys' reaction to their genital self, and specifically to tumescence, must also be understood in terms of their chaotic and aggressive family environments, their overstimulated self systems, their heightened early genital phase, the intergenerational pattern of gender conflicts, their intense separation-individuation conflicts, the hystrionic and overdramatized communications of their mothers (which only increased their genital-self anxiety and precluded the development of a self-regulatory mechanism for monitoring their erections), and the negative parental transferences toward their male gender.

The releasors of their genital attacks were multidetermined. It is my hypothesis that as these gender-disordered children passed through the phallic phase, their parents' anxiety over their developing maleness may have created a potentially catastrophic reaction in them. What all of the solutions to the children's conflicts had in common was the need to sacrifice their genitals in order to preserve the object ties to their parents (cf. Chassequet-Smirgel, 1981). In each case the parents were oblivious to the pain their children suffered and what role they themselves played in that suffering (cf. Khan's [1979] notion concerning the pervert's need to enlist another person in the dramatization of the act).

All three boys evidenced varying degrees of narcissistic pathology (cf. Bleiberg, 1984). What seemed to differentiate these boys with genital dysphoria from effeminate boys with gender-identity disorders (who did not have genital dysphoria) may have been the uniquely sadistic parental selfobject milieu in which they were reared (cf. Tolpin, 1971, 1978). Children with genital dysphoria are seen as being raised in families in which high levels of sadism are directed especially toward phallic issues.

GENDER IDENTITY, THE SELF, AND
KOHUTIAN CONTRIBUTIONS

Although Kohut never formally addressed the issue of childhood gender-identity disturbances he did speculate on the origins and development of the gender-self-system, and his views on narcissism can be employed to help us understand some of the focal conflicts in early childhood gender-identity disturbances.

In his later writings, Kohut (Kohut and Wolf, 1978) discussed the effect of parental empathy on a child's gender and his or her self experience and stated that,

the parental expectations will, from birth onward, exert a considerable influence on the baby's developing self. The self arises thus as the result of the interplay between the new-born's innate equipment and the selective responses of the selfobjects through which certain potentialities are encouraged in their development while others remain unencouraged or are even actively discouraged [p. 416].

Expanding on these ideas, Ornstein (1981) has written that "there are situations in which the child's gender . . . (may) have created 'transferences' in one or both parents that exclude the child from empathic parental responsiveness from the time of his birth." A review of the parental transferences toward the children in this study confirm Kohut's and Ornstein's speculations. For example, in one case (Elliot) the father expressed homicidal behavior toward his son. And in two of the cases (Brian and Elliot) the fathers went through a phase of actively hating their sons and avoiding them. In another case (Robert) the father was emotionally detached and distant from his son and it was the mother who symbolically hated him and wished him dead as a male.

Additionally, all of the mothers were angry at men, disappointed in their fathers (to varying degrees), and pathologically jealous of men. Robert's mother wanted men dead; Brian's mother was frightened of masculinity and tried to undo it in her men; and Elliot's mother had the "balls" in the family. All of the women suffered from defective object relationships, experienced a sense of emptiness and rage, and were jealous and envious of males. From birth onward they must have communicated these ideas and unconscious fantasies to their children (Litin, Giffin, and Johnson, 1956), thereby introducing from early on the notion that masculinity was dangerous and dreadful. In each case, the fathers stood aside and allowed their wives to carry out their plans to use their sons to create a new kind of male.

Conflicts focusing on separation-individuation issues were also paramount in all three children (cf. Beebe and Sloate, 1982). The mothers and children ambivalently clung to each other. One mother spoke for her child, while another was spit at and struck by her child as he clung to her. According to parental recollections, the children (and their mothers) exhibited separation anxiety even prior to the child's second year. These conflicts over separation-individuation were focused around gender issues. While each of the boys occasionally clung to mother and could not tolerate too much separation (the same was true for the mothers) their "femininity" evolved out of conflict (in the intersubjective field of parent and child) rather than out of symbiotic fusion, imprinting, and a blissful symbiosis with mother (cf. Lichtenstein, 1961; Stoller, 1968).

While the children were able to separate in areas unrelated to gender identity (cf. Greenacre, 1959; Greenson, 1966, 1968; Stoller, 1974), each of the boys experienced a focal gender conflict related to the failure of their parental selfobjects to provide an empathic attunement to their developing gender identity. Kohut (1978) believed that too much parental influence or interference (i.e., a failure in empathy) could have a negative effect on the natural development and unfolding of the constitutional issues related to becoming a male or female (cf. Lang's [1984] concept of "nature's blueprint"). Stolorow (1984) has argued that "the empathic responses of selfobjects . . . play a crucial role" in the development of one's genital schematization, affect, and sense of self, which "in turn, facilitate(s) the evolution and structuralization of (the child's) nuclear self system." It appears that while self psychologists may have initially viewed the self as male or female ("nature's blueprint") as secondary to the formation of the nuclear self system they are not always in agreement as to what that means. Clearly the selfobject milieu plays a critical role in the organization of a child's gender-self representation, core gender identity, and gender-self system.

SELFOBJECT FAILURES AND GENDER IDENTITY DISORDERS

Notwithstanding the constitutional factors, and the unique contributions of the child (which play a role in the organization and activation of each of these psychic structures and mechanisms), the effect of the child's early selfobject milieu is critical to gender-identity development and self-cohesion. The way in which the male child's selfobjects respond to his body (take pleasure, or the lack of it) in his developing body image, his needs, and his overall self-experience will determine how his early experiences are organized around a nuclear self that is cohesive or chaotic, masculine or genderally diffuse. The child's early gender images and early gender-self experience are the creations of the mother-figure and are influenced by the mirroring selfobject function of the mother-figure. While the child's biological apparatus plays an organizing role in his nascent gender-self system (and gives it expression), those biological imperatives are overridden by social and parental forces (Stoller, 1968; Money and Ehrhardt, 1972).

Parental selfobjects also provide the context in which early forms of narcissism (that is, the grandiosity, exhibitionism, omnipotence, and idealization) are experienced and integrated into the child's archaic gender self-images and gender self-representations. There is evidence from our clinical case material that the mothers of our patients were unable to empathically link with their children's biologically and socially based maleness; and that the children experienced their mothers' selfobject failures in this realm as crippling to their gender-self development. The outcome was a faulty gender-self structure in which a quasi-, "as-if" feminine self-experience took root and a false self-system was erected.

The mothers' hatred of, and rejection of, their sons' emerging masculinity led to nascent feelings of disgust, hatred, fear, guilt, and terror in the boys concerning their penis—that is, the concrete symbol of their maleness. Because of the importance of the intersubjective realm for the young child, one may speculate that the mother's hatred of the son's genitality became the son's hatred. The mother's selfobject failure became the root of the child's impaired gender-self representation and his masochism. Such an experience would naturally lead to an impairment in the child's developing gender-self representation. Unable to be mirrored, because of their maleness, these young children would have no alternative but to either become psychotic, submit to the mother's infanticidal wish, or remove the dreaded insignia of maleness and allow the self to be mirrored for its female aspects.

Our clinical data suggest that all three children had developmental arrests related to parental failures in empathy and selfobject functioning. These selfobject failures led to breakdowns in the area of the child's gender self-experience; breakdowns that affected the child's organization of his gender-self image that later formed his gender-self representation and his nuclear self-system.

Mothers who hate their son's masculinity may be unable to mirror their son's archaic grandiose, exhibitionistic, and omnipotent needs because of their own impaired gender-self representations. Their children experience their mothers as either ignoring, rebuffing, or inadequately responding to their needs. These children feel empty, worthless, or bad, simply because of their maleness. Subsequently, the boy's gender-self experience may become confused and chaotic. When unduly stressed, especially by withdrawal, loss, or abandonment by their significant selfobjects, these children may experience their gender-self systems as enfeebled or fragmented. In some cases anatomic dysphoria may be the primary feature.

THE NUCLEAR SELF: ABSTRACT AND
ANDROGYNOUS VS. MALE OR FEMALE

The issue of whether the self (as a concept) is abstract and androgynous or male versus female is hotly debated by theoreticians
outside Self Psychology Circles (Stoller, 1974; Greenson, 1968; Person
and Ovessey, 1983; Fast, 1984). For Freud (1925), both sexes begin
with a bisexual identity which has a masculine and male cast. But it is
the girl or woman who must struggle to differentiate her femaleness
(cf. Lothstein, 1985). For Stoller (1968, 1974), both sexes are pro-
totypically female and feminine and it is the boy who must struggle to
differentiate his maleness by disidentifying from mother (Greenson,
1968; Rochlin, 1980) and identifying with father (Socarides, 1980). On
the other hand, Person and Ovessey (1983) have argued that there is
no substantive evidence that the original gender matrix is masculine,
feminine, or innate. Fast (1978, 1984) proposed a model of psychological differentiation which suggested that "during the first year of life a
child's gender-relevant experience is undifferentiated" and that for
children "all sex and gender possibilities are open to them." The
differentiation of gender-identity is viewed as part of a larger developmental process of differentiation, boundary formation and limit
setting for self-development. While Kohut's theory of self-development and the nuclear self is more parsimonious it is not without its
own problems.

One may argue that what Kohut calls a secondary phenomenon,
that is, the contents of the self, may be so inextricably part of the
primary nuclear self system that one can only differentiate gender-
self identity from the nuclear self system conceptually and not in fact.
Indeed, all three boys in this study showed some feminine traits
before the time when Kohut believes the nuclear self is said to coalesce. These findings support those found in the literature and reinforce the idea that parental selfobjects play a critical role for the child's
developing self system.

Given the evidence that gender-identity pathology can be manifested prior to the consolidation of the nuclear self (some reports
place pathology during the early part of the second year—cf. Galenson, Vogel, Blau, and Roiphe, 1973—and in our culture the newborn
is immediately labeled as having a male or female self) it would appear that the early organization of self-experience (prior to the coales-
cence of a nuclear self) must involve a male or female imprint. What
does it mean to speak therefore of an abstract or androgynous self?

In a previously published work (Lothstein, 1983), I argued that
gender-self structures begin to develop right at birth and are related

to parental wishes and transferences concerning the sex of the child and the family's expectations and goals for the newborn gender-self structure. The mother's gender-self images of her newborn become the child's gender-images and later coalesce to form his gender-self representation. This process is dependent on the normal or typical development of the child's ego functioning. In this sense parental perceptions of their child's gender, and their transferences to their child's gender, become part of the child's archaic gender-self images and later gender-self representation; a representational system that is directly affected by the intactness of the child's ego mechanisms regulating attention, concentration, object-constancy, frustration tolerance, and the capacity to bear anxiety.

There is a growing body of evidence that parental transferences concerning the gender of their child and specific selfobject functions of the parent that regulate the child's gender-self functioning, serve as the critical mass for the child's evolving nuclear self system. In this sense, what Kohut calls the secondary aspects of the self (that is, the contents of the self as male or female) are seen to play a more important role in the development of the nuclear self system. The term "secondary" is misleading to the extent that it has been interpreted by self psychologists to mean "less important." I am in agreement with Lang (1984) who believes that "an awareness of one's gender (ought to) occupy a central place in one's sense of self." A real self "must develop via selfobject relationships with real people" and such a self will be affected by specific selfobject transferences and failures related to genderal issues by exhibiting deficits in psychic structure.

I hope that all the above has raised some new questions for self psychology theory and will stimulate inquiry into the relationship between what Kohut calls the nuclear self and its contents; in this case the male or female imprint on the self. I hope also that I have demonstrated that what is labeled as "secondary" is nevertheless important and ought to become "interesting (to the) theoretical concerns of a psychology of the self."

SUMMARY

In summary, each boy was enmeshed in a quasi-symbiotic relationship with his mother, a woman who both hated and feared men. When these mothers became pregnant they wished for a male child whom they could control. Indeed, each mother had an agenda for managing her son's maleness. The mothers equated their sons' maleness with a destructive force which could destroy them. In this sense, by "feminizing" them they protected themselves from their sons' wrath and protected their sons from their own rage. The mothers also served a positive selfobject function; a function which involved soothing their sons' intense separation anxiety and allowing them to feel whole (that is, to experience a cohesive self). The fathers, on the other hand, were either absent or turned over their parental responsibilities to their wives. Having failed to rescue their sons from their enmeshment with mother during the phallic phase (cf. Abelin, 1980) these fathers passively supported the mothers' feminizing tendencies with their sons (cf. Tyson, 1982a,b). Consequently, the sons felt abandoned by their fathers and could not identify with them (an issue which would have implications for the father's selfobject function as an idealizing figure). The outcome was that these boys failed to develop along typical masculine lines (cf. Ross, 1982). It was the nature of the parents' unique selfobject relationships and transferences to their children, and the resulting failures in empathy (cf. Kohut, 1959) and attunement to the children's developing gender-self system, which led to the boys severe gender-identity pathology, and, specifically, to their anatomic dysphoria and genital mutilation.

REFERENCES

Abelin, E. (1980). Triangulation, the role of the father and the origins of core gender-identity during the rapprochement subphase. In R. Lax, S. Bach, & J. Burland, ed., *Rapprochement: The Critical Subphase of Separation-Individuation.* New York: Aronson.

Basch, M. F. (1981). Selfobject disorders and psychoanalytic theory: A historical perspective. *Journal of the American Psychoanalytical Association,* 29:337–351.

––––––– (1984a). Selfobjects and selfobject transference: Theoretical implications. In P. Stepansky & A. Goldberg, ed., *Kohut's Legacy.* Hillsdale, NJ: The Analytic Press.

––––––– (1984b). Selfobjects, development, and psychotherapy. In P. Stepansky & A. Goldberg, ed., *Kohut's Legacy.* Hillsdale, NJ: The Analytic Press.

Bauman, S. (1981). Physical aspects of the self: A review of some aspects of body image development in childhood, *Psychiatric Clinics of North America,* 4:455–470.

Beebe, B., & Sloate, P. (1982). Assessment and treatment of difficulties in mother-infant attunement in the first three years of life: A case history. *Psychoanalytic Inquiry,* 1:601–623.

Bleiberg, E. (1984). Narcissistic disorders in children. *Bulletin of the Menninger Clinic,* 48:501–517.

Bloch, D. (1974). The threat of infanticide and homosexual identity. *Psychoanalytical Review,* 62:579–597.

Bloch, D. (1978). *So the Witch Won't Eat Me: Fantasy and the Child's Fear of Infanticide.* Boston: Houghton Mifflin.

Brandchaft, B., & Stolorow, R. (1984). A current perspective on difficult patients. In P. Stepansky & A. Goldberg, ed., *Kohut's Legacy.* Hillsdale, NJ: The Analytic Press.

Chasseguet-Smirgel, J. (1981). Loss of reality in perversions—with special reference to fetishism. *Journal of the American Psychoanalytic Association,* 29:511–534.

Clower, V. (1977). The development of the child's sense of his sexual identity. *Journal of the American Psychoanalytical Association,* 18:165–176.

Coen, S. (1981). Notes on the concepts of selfobjects and preoedipal object. *Journal of the American Psychoanalytical Association,* 29:395–411.

Fast, I. (1978). Developments in gender identity: The original matrix. *International Review of Psycho-Analysis,* 5:265–273.

―――― (1984). *Gender Identity: A Differentiation Model.* Hillsdale, NJ: Lawrence Erlbaum Associates.

Freud, S. (1925). Some psychical consequences of the anatomical distinction between the sexes. *Standard Edition* 19:248–258. London: Hogarth Press, 1961.

Galenson, E., Vogel, R., Blau, S., & Roiphe, H. (1973). Disturbance in sexual identity beginning at eighteen months of age. *International Review of Psycho-Analysis,* 2:389–397.

Gershman, H. (1970). The role of core gender-identity in the genesis of perversions. *American Journal of Psychoanalysis,* 30:58–67.

Glenn, J. (1984). A note on loss, pain, and masochism in children. *Journal of the American Psychoanalytical Association,* 32:63–74.

Green, R. (1974). *Sexual Identity Conflicts in Children and Adults.* New York: Basic Books.

―――― (1985). Gender identity in childhood and later sexual orientation: Follow-up of 78 males. *American Journal of Psychiatry,* 142:339–341.

――――, Newman, L., & Stoller, R. (1972). Treatment of boyhood transsexualism: An interim report of four years' experience. *Archives of General Psychiatry,* 26:231–217.

Greenacre, P. (1953). Certain relationships between fetishism and the faulty development of the body image. *The Psychoanalytic Study of the Child.* 8:79–98. New York: International Universities Press.

―――― (1959). On focal symbiosis. In L. Jessner & E. Pavenstedt, ed., *Dynamic Psychopathology in Childhood.* New York: Grune & Stratton.

Greenson, R. (1966). A transvestite boy and a hypothesis. *International Journal of Psycho-Analysis,* 47:396–403.

―――― (1968). Dis-identifying from mother. *International Journal of Psycho-Analysis,* 49:370–374.

Harrison, S., Cain, A., & Benedek, E. (1968). The childhood of a transsexual. *Archives of General Psychiatry,* 19:28–37.

Johnson, A., & Szurek, S. (1952). The genesis of antisocial acting out in children and adults. *Psychoanalytic Quarterly,* 21:323–343.

Khan, M. R. (1979). *Alienation in Perversions.* New York: International Universities Press.

Kleeman, J. (1971). The establishment of core gender-identity in normal girls. II. How meanings are conveyed between parent and child in the first 3 years. *Archives of Sexual Behavior,* 1:117–129.

Kohut, H. (1959). Introspection, empathy, and psychoanalysis. *Journal of the American Psycho-Analytical Association,* 7:459–483.

―――― (1969). *Discussion on the panel of the development of the child's sense of his sexual identity.* Presented at meeting of American Psychoanalytical Association.

Kohut, H. (1977). *The Restoration of the Self.* New York: International Universities Press.

―――― (1984). *How Does Analysis Cure?* Chicago: University of Chicago Press.

Kohut, H., & Wolf, E. (1978). The disorders of the self and their treatment: An outline. *International Journal of Psycho-Analysis,* 59:413–425.

Lachmann, F. (1982). Narcissistic development. In D. Mendell, ed., *Early Female Development: Current Psychoanalytic Views.* New York: Spectrum.

Lang, J. (1984). Notes toward a psychology of the feminine self. In P. Stepansky & A. Goldberg, ed., *Kohut's Legacy*. Hillsdale, NJ: The Analytic Press.

Lichtenstein, H. (1961). Identity and Sexuality. *Journal of the American Psychoanalytical Association*, 9:179–260.

Litin, E., Giffin, M., & Johnson, A. (1956). Parental influence in unusual sexual behavior in children. *Psychoanalytical Quarterly*, 25:37–55.

Loeb, L., & Shane, M. (1982). The resolution of a transsexual wish in a five-year-old boy. *Journal of the American Psychoanalytical Association*, 30:419–434.

Lothstein, L. (1983). *Female-To-Male Transsexualism: Historical, Theoretical, and Clinical Issues*. London: Routledge & Kegan Paul.

——— (1985). *Maternal issues in female-to-male transsexuals who have delivered and reared their children*. Presented at the meeting of the American Psychological Association, Los Angeles.

Mahler, M., Pine, F., & Bergman, A. (1975). *The Psychological Birth of the Human Infant*. New York: Basic Books.

McDonald, M. (1981). Alternative treatment of a young boy with a traumatic psychosis: The rediscovery and reconstitution of the self. *Psychiatric Clinics of North America*, 4:509–532.

Meyer, J., & Dupkin, C. (1985). Gender disturbance in children: An interim clinical report. *Bulletin of the Menninger Clinic*, 49:236–269.

Miller, A. (1984). *Thou Shalt Not Be Aware: Society's Betrayal of the Child*. New York: Farrar, Straus & Giroux.

Money, J., & Ehrhardt, A. (1972). *Man and Woman, Boy and Girl*. Baltimore: Johns Hopkins University Press.

Ornstein, A. (1981). Self-pathology in childhood: Developmental and clinical considerations. *Psychiatric Clinics of North America*, 4:435–453.

Person, E., & Ovesey, L. (1983). Psychoanalytic theories of gender identity. *Journal of the American Academy of Psychoanalysis*, 11:203–226.

Pruett, K., & Dahl, K. (1982). Psychotherapy of gender identity conflict in young boys. *American Academy of Child Psychiatry*, 21:65–70.

Rochlin, G. (1980). *The Masculine Dilemma: A Psychology of Masculinity*. Boston: Little, Brown.

Roiphe, H., & Galenson, E. (1981). *Infantile Origins of Sexual Identity*. New York: International Universities Press.

Ross, J. M. (1982). From mother to father: The boy's search for a generative identity and the oedipal era. In S. Cath, A. Gurwitt, & J. M. Ross, ed., *Father and Child: Developmental and Clinical Perspectives*. Boston: Little, Brown.

Socarides, C. (1980). Homosexuality and the rapprochement subphase. In R. Lax, S. Bach, & A. A. Burland, ed., *Rapprochement: The Critical Subphase of Separation-Individuation*. New York: Aronson.

Sperling, M. (1964). The analysis of a boy with transvestite tendencies: A contribution to the genesis and dynamics of transvestism. *The Psychoanalytic Study of the Child*, 19:470–493. New York: International Universities Press.

Stepansky, P., & Goldberg, A., eds. (1984). *Kohut's Legacy: Contributions to Self Psychology*. Hillsdale, NJ: The Analytic Press.

Stoller, R. (1966). The mother's contribution to infantile transvestic behavior. *International Journal of Psycho-Analysis*, 47:384–395.

——— (1968). *Sex and Gender*. New York: Science House.

——— (1970). The transsexual boy: Mother's feminized phallus. *British Journal of Medical Psychology*, 43:117–128.

——— (1974). Symbiosis anxiety and the development of masculinity. *Archives of General Psychiatry*, 360:164–172.

Stolorow, R. (1984). Varieties of selfobject experience. In P. Stepansky & A. Goldberg, ed., *Kohut's Legacy*. Hillsdale, NJ: The Analytic Press.

———, & Lachmann, F. (1980). *Psychoanalysis of Developmental Arrests*. New York: International Universities Press.

Tolpin, M. (1971). On the beginnings of a cohesive self: An application of the concept of transmuting internalization to the study of the transitional object and signal anxiety. *The Psychoanalytic Study of the Child*, 26:316–351. New Haven: Yale University Press.

——— (1978). Self-objects and oedipal objects: A crucial distinction. *The Psychoanalytic Study of the Child*, 33:167–183. New Haven: Yale University Press.

Tyson, P. (1982a). The role of the father in gender identity, urethral eroticism, and phallic narcissism. In S. Cath, A. Gurwitt, & J. Ross, ed., *Father and Child: Developmental and Clinical Perspectives*. Boston: Little Brown.

——— (1982b). A developmental line of gender-identity, gender-role, and choice of love object. *Journal of American Psychoanalytical Association*, 30:61–86.

Volkan, V., and Kavanaugh, J. (1977). A nine-year-old transsexual boy and his family. Presented at meeting of the Virginia Neuropsychiatric Association. Williamsburg.

Zucker, K. (1985). Cross-gender identified children. In B. Steiner, ed., *Gender Dysphoria: Development, Research, Management*. New York: Plenum Press.

Zuger, B. (1966). Effeminate behavior present in boys from early childhood. *Journal of Pediatrics*, 69:1098–1107.

Chapter 12

On Boundary Formation

Russell Meares

Kohut's major theoretical innovation, the selfobject, has implications for treatment which are indeed "revolutionary" (Joseph, 1985). He described "patients suffering from specific disturbances in the realm of self" who experience objects as neither separate from nor independent of the self (Kohut, 1971, p. 3). Since the conception of others as an extension of oneself depends upon an immature sense of self-boundary, Kohut seemed, on the face of it, to be directing our treatment efforts toward maturation of the distinction between "self" and "nonself." My view follows such an implication and attempts to outline some forms of therapeutic behavior that might foster boundary formation. Doubt, however, is immediately cast upon the value of such an endeavor by Kohut's view that to treat others as selfobjects is not only a "disturbance" but also healthy—we all need, throughout life, people who are selfobjects to us (Kohut, 1977). It is necessary, therefore, briefly to confront the paradox with which Kohut has presented us.

The concept of the selfobject is complex. Although only two possible resolutions of the Kohutian paradox are approached here, it is not suggested that they are the only possibilities.

The first approach depends upon the difference between concept and function. The child *conceives* of the mother as an extension of itself so that to a large extent it relates to her as if she had no wishes, feelings, preoccupations, and so on other than its own. It is her *function* to take part in their engagement in a way that is appropriate to and necessary for its stage of development. The form of this function obviously changes during life. For example, a baby of ten to twelve weeks, when placed next to its mother so that it cannot see her face, shows extraordinary distress (Friedman and Meares, 1977). A face-to-face engagement is necessary at this age. At a later age it might be intrusive. Nevertheless, what is common to the respone of the selfobject is the effect of maintaining in the child a sense of unity and integration. Some of these responses give value and meaning to the child's expressions. This kind of response from others, as a kind of nutrient, is needed throughout life. In the same way that attachments are a central feature of the whole of human existence but separation anxiety is prominent only in childhood, the *functions* of selfobjects differ from the child's *conception* of selfobject. There arises, then, a possible interrelationship between separation anxiety, the selfobject concept, and an immature awareness of self-boundary (Meares, 1986).

A second approach to the Kohutian paradox involves a consideration of language. The developmental arrest affecting borderline and narcissistic personalities is generally agreed to occur during that period of life when Piaget considered the child has an incomplete sense of boundary between itself and its world. During this stage, the "egocentric monologue" is characteristic of the child's social behavior, particularly in the presence of the mother. Piaget (1959) described the child's behavior as follows:

> What he says does not seem to him to be addressed to himself but is enveloped with the feeling of a presence, so that to speak of himself or to speak to his mother appear to him to be one and the same thing. His activity is thus bathed in an atmosphere of communion or syntonization, one might almost speak of "the life of union" to use the terms of mysticism, and this atmosphere excludes all consciousness of egocentrism. But, on the other hand, one cannot but be struck by the soliloquistic character of these same remarks. The child does not ask questions and expects no answer, neither does he attempt to give any definite information to his mother who is present. He does not ask himself whether she is listening or not. He speaks for himself just as an adult does when he speaks within himself [p. 243].

It seems that it is the mother's function merely to allow this monologue to go on. As the infant chatters, it seems to be talking to itself, or else, as if there were little distinction between its thoughts and hers. To the objective observer, the infant is ignoring the mother.

Piaget believed, however, that awareness of the mother "penetrates into the intimacy of every wish and thought."

During the phase of the egocentric monologue, the child also conducts another form of conversation which is much more socialized and directed to events in the world around it. With maturation, this form of speech becomes predominant, leading Piaget to conclude that the other form had simply atrophied and disappeared. The Russian psychologist Vygotsky, however, came to a very different, and in terms of this discussion, very important view.

In brief, Vygotsky (1962) argued that the egocentric monologue does not vanish. Rather, it is internalized to become "inner speech." It has quite a different structure to socialized speech. It is not "speech minus sound," but is an "entirely separate speech function. Its main distinguishing trait is its peculiar syntax. Compared with external speech, inner speech appears disconnected and incomplete" (p. 138–139). It is to "large extent thinking in pure meanings. It is a dynamic, shifting, unstable thing, fluttering between word and thought" (p. 149). Deriving its characteristics from egocentric speech, Vygotsky also noted what he called "influx of sense" in inner speech. "The senses of different words flow into one another—literally 'influence' one another—so that earlier ones are contained in, and modify, the latter ones" (p. 147). This suggests a metaphoric element, and of links between components of thought based on association, analogy, and affect.

This inner experience, despite Vygotsky's use of the term "inner speech," is often wordless, depending much upon imagery. Its conversion into spoken words is an approximation of the experience expressed in associative language.

It has been argued elsewhere (Meares, 1977) that intimate relationships, among other things, involve the use of a similar form of language. It is not the language of committees or of that used for dealing with the daily events of the outer world. Since, however, intimate language is "inner" in Vygotsky's terms, what is "inner" is also "outer," since it is expressed. The boundary, as it were, dissolves. We enter a mysterious zone that is neither inner nor outer but both. It is a zone which, as Ryle (1963) points out, cannot exist in logical terms. Yet it is an experiential reality. It is the function of the selfobject, throughout life, to allow us to enter this place and to speak in a way which differs from that of an ordinary conversation.

What seems most basic to Kohut's approach to severe personality disorder is a potentiation of self-experience which is sensed as "inner" in comparison with "not-self," which is outer. I suggest that it is fostered by a particular kind of language. Before, however, proceeding to a preliminary sketch of some of the forms of therapeutic behavior which must encourage self-boundary formation, it is necessary to consider briefly certain aspects of this difficult subject.

First, we must consider the body. Self-boundary does not derive solely from skin sensation, yet body feeling is essential to it. Nor is it entirely psychological, although Sartre (1957) remarked that "the body is wholly 'psychic'" (p. 305) and not an anatomical thing. Rather, psyche and soma are mingled, so that self-boundary limits the totality of self-experience, including the bodily.

Second, boundary is not a "thing" nor is it immutable. It is better thought of as an experiential manifestation of the interchange between the individual and his or her environment, the most important component of which is social. Fluctuations in this exchange may result not only in changes in the dimensions of the sense of boundary (Meares, 1984) but also on the whole body-self experience (Meares, 1980).

Self-boundary is a metaphor. Although Schafer (1976) has been influential in his criticism of the spatial metaphor of self and such notions as "inner" and "outer," I have tried to show that his view has theoretical deficiencies and therapeutic disadvantages (Meares, 1985). In short, where he rejects the metaphor, I consider it fundamental.

Finally, self cannot be separated from its boundary so that all experiences of self involve, simultaneously, some sense of its boundary, however unaware we are of this. Since there can be no self without its boundary it could be suggested that the point at which the child discovers that there is some kind of demarcation between its own world, which is "inner," and that which is "outer," it learns that there is a distinction between self and not-self. The formation of boundary heralds the birth of self—a notion reminiscent of Mahler's metaphor of psychological birth. There is little concordance between major authorities on the age of this discovery. Mahler puts it at two or three (Mahler, Pine, and Bergman, 1975, p. 110); Piaget considered that it came much later, from seven to nine. Our evidence suggests that it is about four (Meares and Orlay, in press).

An important implication of these remarks, in terms of what follows, is that any therapeutic approach which tries to facilitate boundary formation at the same time fosters the evolution of self. Privacy and ownership as Goldberg (1983) has pointed out, are themes central to this evolution.

ASSOCIATIVE LANGUAGE

The "inner speech" described by Vygotsky might be seen as the "language of self." It is found in reverie, but blocked out by the stimuli of the outer world which demands attention and triggers goal-directed thinking. Such thought is linear and might be called "stimulus-directed." It is equivalent to secondary process.

Inner speech, which is "stimulus-free" has a shape that radically differs from that which is largely stimulus-directed. It wanders capriciously—a flux of images, ideas, and memories linked by analogy, affect, and other associations. In short, it is an associative language. It is by no means the equivalent of "primary process" since it has mature and adaptive functions (see for example Langer, 1942; Hobson 1985).

To foster what is inner is to enhance the distinction, or boundary, between "self" and "not-self." If we follow Vygotsky, we must try to encourage an associative form of therapeutic conversation. Seen in this way, Freud's basic rule is fundamental in a way that is quite different from its original intent. Rather than being a means to an end, the achievement of free-association may be a therapeutic end in itself (Meares, 1977). This, indeed, is the thesis of Kris (1983), who writes that his definition of the free-association process "deliberately describes the analyst's goal in the use of free-association method as the enhancement of the patient's free associations and not as the production of insight, nor as the development of a regressive transference neurosis and its resolution, nor as the reduction of symptoms or suffering" (p. 3).

To suggest that the facilitation of associative language and stimulus-free thought is therapeutic is also to imply that the promotion of linear thinking is untherapeutic. This is consistent with the findings of an experimental study of group function (Meares, 1973b). Nevertheless, much orthodox psychoanalysis is likely to potentiate linear thinking since the aim is often to translate the patient's productions into the language of secondary process (see, for example, Schafer 1976, p. 186). Winnicott (1974) was critical of such attempts to place the patient's thoughts in a straight line. He considered it necessary for the therapist to tolerate a succession of the patient's ideas and thoughts that, on the face of it, is nonsense. The therapist should not impose his own sense upon it "in a futile attempt to find some organization in the nonsense" (p. 65).

The unsuitability of a linear mode of therapeutic language is further suggested by the clinical situation. Those with severe personality disorders seem to have a diminished access to imagery and little ability to associate. Rather, they are characteristically dominated by stimuli. Early sessions often consist of catalogues of bodily sensation, or of the endless events of daily life. However, the patient seems to need such stimuli, fearing their absence. A sense of oppression is conveyed, as if the subject were caught in a system of "stimulus-entrapment." Samuel Beckett describes this system. His stereotypic character cannot achieve the sense of being "in his midst" and is "at the mercy of stimuli, 'clinging to the perimeter' of his self, afraid of being merely the reflection of others' radiations, merely a surface upon which the impinged" (Meares, 1973a, p. 65). The consequence for Beckett's character Malone is that he feels himself as "nothing but a series or rather a succession of local phenomena all my life, without any result" (Beckett, 1962, p. 75). Clearly, for such people a therapeutic aim must be to foster "stimulus-free" thought.

An escape from stimulus-entrapment is by no means easy. The therapist may begin feeling enmeshed in a stimulus-response mode of interaction that is difficult to evade. Freud (1923) however, pointed out one of the ways of minimizing this enmeshment. He recommended that the therapist himself change from the usual or mundane attentional mode in which attention is focused on salient stimuli, particularly of a social kind. Rather he should "defocus" and

> surrender himself to his own unconscious mental activity, in a state of "evenly suspended attention," to avoid so far as possible reflection and the construction of conscious expectations, not to try to fix anything that he heard particularly in his memory, and by these means to catch the drift of the patient's unconscious with his own unconscious [p. 239].

Since the therapist does not allow himself to be caught up in surface phenomena, the patient is less likely to be held in the thrall of immediate sensation. It is important to note, however, that the therapist in "defocusing" is not disconnected or cut off. Rather, as Freud implied, he is immersed in the whole context of the encounter. This paradoxical stance of engaged disengagement leads to the concept of empathy.

Audio tapes of therapists who have the ability to participate in the relationship with the patient and at the same time avoid entrapment in surface material show several characteristics of verbal behavior. One of these includes the intermittent utterance of various murmurs, grunts, and unformed sounds which make up one category of what Havens (1978) has called "simple empathic statements." Such an empathic therapist is not merely indicating that he is still there but is also, in broadening his attention span, "removing" himself from the immediate impact of the words that are said. As a consequence, his more complex empathic statements are not the mere resultants of immediate stimuli. The therapist, in concentrating on trying to detect an underlying flux of feelings, images, memories, and so on, rather than fastening on the "things" of the world—the day-to-day occurrences, the crises, and problems that come from outside—helps the patient to discover what is his or her own.

We are now led to the sense of ownership, between which experience and that of boundary there exists a reciprocal relationship so that where one is enhanced, so also is the other.

OWNERSHIP

William James (1962) remarked that for most of us the elementary psychic fact is "not *thought* on *this thought* or *that thought*, but *my* thought, every thought being owned" (p. 168). For those with severe personality disorder, however, the sense of ownership of experience is tenuous. A well-known example may be the case of Kris (1951). The man complained that he was unable to finish his thesis since he was a plagiarist. Kris took the trouble to discover that this was not so. He then concluded that the man wished to be a plagiarist in order to prevent himself from really being one. However, Lacan's understanding of the case was different and, to my mind, likely to be correct. The patient could not believe any thought could be generated from within himself as his own. As a consequence, everything he wrote must be the work of others (Lacan, 1977, p. 239).

Perhaps this case can be interpreted in terms of the Winnicottian false self. This concept needs brief examination since it is central to the notion of ownership.

It seems to me that Winnicott himself (1960) contributed to a misunderstanding of the false self system since he wrote that its function was defensive—"to hide the true self" (p. 147). In this way, it is seen as a pathological form of the normal "mask," or persona, which the social environment demands (p. 150). Through compliance to "the gesture" of the mother (p. 145), a false self is built which hides "the infant's inner reality."

I do not think this is all that Winnicott meant. My understanding of the false self system is different and derives from conversations with Bernard Brandchaft.

In those with personality disorder, the false self does not seem to be defensive. There is no sense of dysjunction with an inner reality. Rather, existence seems inauthentic. There is uncertainty of the genuineness of feelings, so that, as many patients say, they do not know what is "really me." Yet at the same time, they remark that such a statement is ridiculous since what they experience is all they have, and in this way, "really" who they are. What they convey is doubt that this experience is their own. It *feels* false. And also fragile, thin, and without vitality. Existence seems diminished of meaning. Such a situation might arise in the following way:

During the phase when separation anxiety is prominent, the child believes this existence depends upon his mother. He will do anything, even to the extent of sacrificing his own reality, to maintain the bond. The smallest disconnection from her may seem unbearable. When any of his expressions, whether of excitement, anger, fear, love, happiness, or misery, are unacceptable to her, as shown by some form of disconnection, he will reject these experiences, so that rather than remaining hidden, they are obliterated. A young man of 22, who still lived with his parents, described this situation: "I say I'm anxious. She says 'Of course you're not anxious.' So what I feel isn't real. So I'm only an actor."

Boundary formation and a sense of ownership of experience seem to be linked. How this might be so is suggested by the work of Piaget (1973). His argument, in brief, is as follows:

Before the formation of boundary, there is a limited sense of distinction between the outer world of things and an inner world of thoughts of those things. Rather, thoughts "are situated in the things," "objects alone appear to exist" (p. 152). Things, however, can disappear. In the sense that the child's experience can be removed by the disappearance of the objects of his thought, he does not "own" it. Next, we might ask, who is the author of his experience and from where does it come?

Piaget's findings led him to conclude that children's beliefs about the origins of their thoughts are similar or "parallel" to their ideas about the source of dreams. Dreams are made by their accompaniments (the night, the moon), by those who occupy the dream, or by an omniscient fantasy parent-god. The same may be so for thoughts, which are bathed in the mother's presence; her aura surrounds them. Since she is an essential ingredient, or accompaniment, of those thoughts, she may be construed as their author. Second, because she is so often in them, however indirectly, she may be conceived as their maker.

Under these circumstances, when the child's reality comes from others, it may not be very difficult to adjust his view, so that what a first impression seems to be so is given up in favor of a different "reality." However, the "reality" to which the child complies does not protect an "inner reality," since at this point there is no innerness. What is imposed is all there is.

This situation is extremely difficult to overcome since something like an "edit" system screens out all that is spontaneous. The therapeutic approach must obviously depend upon the uncovering and elaboration of *genuine* affect. This is to be distinguished from *habitual* affective expression, whether it be of a positive or a negative kind. What is genuine arises suddenly and immediately, but often in disguise. One aspect of Kohut's very important discovery of the significance of the "therapeutic error," signalled as Schwaber puts it, by an "affective shift," may be that it fosters the emergence of experiences of genuine emotion.

The elaboration of affect, however, does not depend solely on affect, which is an abstraction. Emotions are necessarily linked to images, memories, body feelings, and so on. The therapist helps to make these links. Such "interpretations," nevertheless, should not aim to tell the patient what he *really* feels or means. Rather, it is to help him discover, express, and value his *own* meanings. Hilde Bruch, who considered her approach had much in common with Kohut, put it this way:

> It is important to let a patient uncover the meaning of his own communication, with the therapist acting as an assistant in the process. If possible a patient should discover this meaning first [1974, p. 86].

> Most important, the therapist should not collude with the patient who always felt "that somebody else 'knew' what they felt but they themselves did not know or feel it [1982, p. 1536].

Hobson (1985) gives a beautiful example of this therapeutic approach. He was treating an aggressive, delinquent 14-year-old boy who, session after session, sat rigidly in his chair and glowered at the therapist—a picture of dumb insolence. Hobson, however, eventually made contact by conversing about cricket in an emotional way, full of the excitement of the game. Some weeks later the boy told about a dream: "I was by a dark pool. It was filthy and there were all sorts of horrible monsters in it. I was scared but I dived in and at the bottom was a great big oyster and in it a terrific pearl. I got it and swam up again."

Hobson's reply mirrored the boy's wonder and gave value to the experience: "That's good. Brave, too. You've got it, though, and pearls are pretty valuable" (p. 5). He said nothing more. To use Winnicott's word, he was not "clever," although he was quite aware that the monsters might represent sexual and aggressive wishes, and of the symbolic significance of the Pearl of Great Price. Nevertheless, in the following sessions the boy began to talk about his life, feelings, and frightening fantasies. He improved greatly and oriented in a new way toward his social milieu. Only once again, many months later. did the boy refer to the dream: "It's queer about that pearl," he said, "I suppose it's me in a *sort of way*."

In this case, therapeutic cleverness may have robbed the boy of his discovery. Sometimes, however, the effect may be worse—the patient may feel his thought itself had been stolen, as if a material particle of him had been removed. An example is provided by the story of a severe borderline personality who suffered intermittent quasi-psychotic episodes. His therapist was a gifted trainee who discussed a tape of one of her sessions with a renowned psychoanalyst. It was suggested that the therapist became more "active." Accordingly, she resolved to make further interpretations. The first of these was made in the next session. She noticed, however, that following her intervention, her patient's eyes moved away and down. Her words seemed to have made him dejected. He replied, in a dull voice: "I was just going to say that." As if she had taken from him what was his.

PRIVACY AND "THE SECRET"

Pierre Janet (1927) attributed enormous significance to the child's first attainment of what he called the "act of secrecy." At this point, the child realizes that his thoughts and feelings can be kept to himself and are not accessible to others. He discovers, in short, that there is an inner world, which is his own, and an outer one which is shared. Seen in this way, a study of the age at which children first know what it means to keep a secret may allow us to infer the age of self-boundary formation. The findings of such a study, involving forty children, suggest that this may generally occur between four and five (Meares and Orlay, in press). For those, however, whose personality disorder is a consequence of a developmental arrest before this time, the attainment of the "act of secrecy" may be tenuous. The issue of privacy is salient, and any revelation difficult.

The problem is illustrated by the dilemma of a young woman who, at our first meeting, stood in a corner of my room and refused to speak. At a subsequent meeting she tried to explain. Shy, ill-educated, and somewhat depressed, she said: "I suppose I'm scared that if I talk, there'll be nothing left to say. Say I told you all my thoughts, ideas and whatsit, it'd be like me piled up beside us, with nothing left to say."

She seemed to believe her ideas, feelings, and memories composed her and that, should they be lost, she would cease to exist. It was as if she attributed concrete substance to her thoughts. Her experience can be understood in terms of Piaget's postulate that, for the child, thoughts of things are in the things, so that in this way they have a material substance and can be lost or stolen.

In order to protect so fragile a sense of what is "inner," the therapist must not intrude nor in various, usually nonverbal ways, demand revelation. Indeed, it may be a valuable experience for the patient to know that he or she is able to keep certain secrets. The therapist should also be aware that brilliant and accurate guesses about the inner states and motivations of the patient may be felt as intensely persecutory (Meares and Hobson, 1977). The patient may experience the therapist as magical and omnipotent, able to enter those regions which are precariously held as private. There may be a feeling of violation or of theft of part of the core experiences of self.

Beyond the fragility of the private/public distinction in severely damaged patients, there may arise an aspect of secrecy which has a more positive aspect. The patient may harbor within himself a system of ideas or memories that is highly valued and affectively toned. Although never revealed, it is a central preoccupation of existence. An example concerned a man who had researched the history of a murdered queen but who refused to publish it since it was his own sacred and personal mystery. His thoughts of the queen were constant. She was more real, he said, than he was himself. Such a system of ideas, which might be called "the secret" (Meares, 1976), may become a generative one of self. Winnicott (1974) expressed this idea in the following way: "Even in the most extreme establishment of a false personality, hidden away somewhere there exists a secret life that is satisfactory because of its being creative or original to that human being. Its unsatisfactoriness must be measured in terms of its being hidden, its lack of enrichment through living experience" (p. 80).

Most patients, however, do not possess a system of secret experience as developed as that of the murdered queen. Indeed, it may not be entirely obvious to the individual himself. An example, so Alice Miller (1981) suggests, is perverse sexual fantasy and activity. In her view, the perversion may have a creative potential, recapitulating aspect of primal experience.

MATCHING AND DYSJUNCTION

Federn (1927), in his pioneering work on the subject of self-boundary, pointed out that the experience of demarcation between inner and outer worlds cannot be separated from body feeling. As a consequence, changes in this feeling fluctuate with the experience of boundary, so that depersonalization (or "estrangement") is always accompanied by changes in the boundary state (p. 42). His observation gives us a way of studying self-boundary through a consideration of depersonalization.

The origins of depersonalization are not known. Nevertheless, one might infer from clinical material that it arises as a consequence of an incongruence or "mismatching" between inner states and outer events (Meares and Grose, 1978).

What is important, in terms of this discussion, is that the inner states are particularly those concerning ideas, fantasies, and other experience of oneself, and that the outer events are those which somehow invalidate and overthrow these ideas.

An example is given by Hunter (1966). An ugly girl ran a puppet show. It was a great success. The children were delighted and shouted for more. At the end of the show, the girl stood up and revealed herself for the first time. There was silence, and the children seemed bewildered. Their reaction numbed her, and she had to be led away in a state of acute depersonalization. It seemed as if her experience of herself during the performance was not matched by the expressions on the children's faces when she showed herself.

In the therapeutic situation, dysjunctions occur when the therapist's interpretations do not match the patient's experience. Schwaber (1983) gives an example of such an occurrence. Schwaber's technique, however, depends on detection of mismatching through "affective shifts," so that the patient is given the opportunity to correct the therapist's view, in this way fostering a congruence between them.

Such an approach acknowledges that the therapist's attunement and empathic resonance can never be perfect. Indeed if it were so, therapeutic change would be impeded, for no difference can be found between self and other. The "optimal therapeutic error" is valuable since, without disrupting the necessary idealization, the patient learns that the therapist is not an extension of himself, nor does he know everything of his inner world.

What is important, however, in a process such as Schwaber describes, is the correction. Such an approach is by no means general.

A form of therapy still persists in which the therapist's interventions are directed unremittingly at the unconscious. This might go on despite the patient's protestations that he does not feel or think what the therapist contends. For the more mature patient, the response to the continuation of such an approach may be merely boredom or annoyance. For the fragile individual, however, the consequence may be malign. The discordance between inner and outer brings with it bewilderment, despair, and, at times, a depersonalization that persists beyond and recurs outside the therapeutic session. In accordance with the thesis that separation anxiety may be a manifestation of an immature concept of self-boundary, the patient's dependence upon the therapist grows rather than fades. The patient comes to believe that the therapist is omniscient and the only one who can save him. The patient himself feels increasingly worthless and helpless. A "persecutory spiral" develops, the only resolution of which may be suicide (Meares and Hobson, 1977).

SUBJECT-OBJECT DIFFERENTIATION

The development of a sense of boundary between self and the exterior world is paralleled by a process of subject-object differentiation in the inner one. In early life the infant does not have experiences of the mature kind described by William James (1962), in which the individual is "duplex"—"partly known and partly knower, partly object and partly subject" (p. 189).

Similarly, those with severe disturbances of personality development have a limited sense of distinction between their experiences and their awareness of these experiences. Rather, they seem to be inhabited by states of emotion, so that, for example, fingers claw, shoulders hunch, breathing becomes heavy. Emotion simply reads itself off. There is no space across which it can be viewed. The empathic stance may be helpful in creating this space, by means of which inner life is more truly experienced.

Empathy, as a process of "vicarious introspection" (Kohut, 1959), does not simply depend upon attunement to and immersion in the inner world of the other. This verges on mere identification, which may be an immature phenomenon. Rather, the empathic stance involves one's capacity to observe one's experience—to become a spectator, as it were, of one's identification. The notion of perspective is central. I have previously suggested that the function of the empathic stance is to help the patient project his inner experience as if on a metaphoric screen (Meares, 1983). This process is facilitated by the form of the therapist's language, which, as Havens (1979) has written, tends to be grammatically impersonal. The therapist, in "entering into" the patient's world, will remark upon the "film" playing on the visible screen. His comments will often begin with the word "it" (e.g., "it's difficult," "it seems there's something else . . . ," "it looks like . . . "). The "it" is the object—the projected experience. Through the decentration of the therapist, an intrapsychic subject-object distinction is encouraged.

The projection of experience as if it were visualized is also encouraged by the elaboration of metaphor: "The effect of metaphor is to create images, so that what is intangible and invisible is displayed. By the means of a sensitive awareness of resemblances and similarities, inner-states are 'set before the eye.' This 'can be called the picturing function of metaphorical meaning'" (Ricoeur, 1979, p. 142).

Metaphor, then is the "visibility of discourse." Metaphor, of a kind which is relevant here, uses the events of the outer world to portray what is inner. In so distinguishing expression and experience, subject and object differentiation is enhanced, and a perspective is gained upon the flux of feelings, images, and memories underlying the therapeutic conversation. And with this comes a growing sense of aliveness that contrasts with the lack of vitality, even deadness, which is characteristic of the early presentation of the narcissistic and borderline personality.

CONCLUSION

Kohut has radically altered our own view of personality disorder. The centerpiece of his theoretical system—the selfobject—gives us a way of understanding a range of clinical phenomena in a way not previously available. Moreover, his principal therapeutic instrument—the empathic stance—seems designed to overcome the central disturbance he defined. How neatly theory is married to practice is illustrated by a consideration of boundary formation. The empathic stance which depends upon, among other things, particular forms of language, affective attunement, and the facilitation of perspective, seems, on theoretical grounds, more likely than other forms of therapeutic approach to foster the maturation of distinction between "self" and "not-self" and promote the growth of a sense of "innerness."

REFERENCES

Beckett, S. (1962), *Malone Dies*. New York: Penguin.
Bruch, H. (1974). *Learning Psychotherapy*. Cambridge, MA: Harvard University Press.
———— (1982). Anorexia nervosa: Therapy and theory. *American Journal of Psychiatry*, 139:1521–1538.
Federn, P. (1927). Narcissism in the structure of the ego. *Ego Psychology and the Psychoses*. New York: Basic Books, 1952.
Freud, S. (1923). Two encyclopaedia articles on psychoanalysis. *Standard Edition*, 18:233–259. London: Hogarth Press, 1955.

Friedman, J., & Meares, R. (1977). Early analogues of separation anxiety. In E. J. Anthony & C. Chiland, ed., *The Child in His Family*. New York: Wiley Interscience.

Goldberg, A. (1983). *Self psychology and alternative perspectives on internalization*. In J. Lichtenberg & S. Kaplan, ed., *Reflections on Self Psychology*. Hillsdale, NJ: The Analytic Press.

Havens, L. (1978). Explorations in the uses of language in psychotherapy: Simple empathic statements. *Psychiatry*, 41:336–345.

———— (1979). Explorations in the uses of language in psychotherapy: Complex empathic statements. *Psychiatry*, 42:40–48.

Hobson, R. (1985). *Forms of Feeling: The Heart of Psychotherapy*. London: Tavistock.

Hunter, R. C. A. (1966). The analysis of episodes of depersonalization in a borderline patient. *International Journal of Psycho-Analysis*, 47:32–41.

James, W. (1962). *Psychology: Briefer Course*. New York: Collier-Macmillan.

Janet, P. (1927). *La Pensée Intérieure*. Paris: Maloine.

Joseph, E. (1985). *Presidential Address*. Presented at Self Psychology Conference, New York.

Kohut, H. (1959). Introspection, empathy and psychoanalysis. In P. Ornstein, ed., *The Search for the Self*. New York: International Universities Press, 1978.

———— (1971). *The Analysis of the Self*. New York: International Universities Press.

———— (1977). *The Restoration of the Self*. New York: International Universities Press.

Kris, A. (1983). *Free Association*. New Haven: Yale University Press.

Kris, E. (1951). Ego Psychology and Interpretation in Psychoanalytic Therapy. *Psychoanalytic Quarterly*, 20:21–25.

Lacan, J. (1977). *Ecrits: A Selection*. A. Sheridan, trans. London: Tavistock.

Langer, S. (1942). *Philosophy in a New Key*. Cambridge, MA: Harvard University Press.

Mahler, M., Pine, F., & Bergman, A. (1975). *The Psychological Birth of the Human Infant*. New York: Basic Books.

Meares, R. (1973a). Beckett, Sarraute and the perceptual experience of schizophrenia. *Psychiatry*, 36:61–69.

———— (1973b). Two kinds of groups. *British Journal of Medical Psychology*, 46:373–379.

———— (1976). The secret. *Psychiatry*, 39:258–265.

———— (1977). *The Pursuit of Intimacy: An Approach to Psychotherapy*. Melbourne: Nelson.

———— (1980). Body feeling in human relations: The possible examples of Brancusi and Giacometti. *Psychiatry*, 46:160–167.

———— (1983). Keats and the "impersonal" therapist: A note on empathy and the therapeutic screen. *Psychiatry*, 46:73–82.

———— (1984). Inner space: Its constriction in anxiety states and narcissistic personality. *Psychiatry*, 47:162–171.

———— (1985). Metaphor and reality: A response to Roy Schafer. *Contemporary Psychoanalysis*.

———— (1986). On the ownership of thought: an approach to the origins of separation anxiety. *Psychiatry*, 49:80–91.

———— & Grose, D. (1978). On depersonalization in adolescence: A consideration from the viewpoint of habituation and identity. *British Journal of Medical Psychology*, 51:335–342.

———— & Hobson, R. (1977). The persecutory therapist. *British Journal of Medical Psychology*, 50:349–359.

———— & Orlay, W. (in press). A Study of the Development of the Concept of Secrecy.

Miller, A. (1981). *Prisoners of Childhood*. New York: Basic Books.

Piaget, J. (1959). *The Language and Thought of the Child*. London: Routledge & Kegan Paul.

————— (1973). *The Child's Concept of the World.* New York: Penguin.

Ricoeur, P. (1979). The metaphorical process of cognition, imagination and feeling. In S. Sachs, ed., *On Metaphor.* Chicago: University of Chicago Press.

Ryle, G. (1963). *The Concept of Mind.* Middlesex: Penguin.

Sartre, J-P. (1957). *Being and Nothingness.* London: Methuen.

Schafer, R. (1976). *A New Language for Psychoanalysis.* New Haven: Yale University Press.

Schwaber, E. (1983). A particular perspective on analytic listening. *The Psychoanalytic Study of the Child,* 38:519–546. New Haven: Yale University Press.

Vygotsky, L. (1962). *Thought and Language.* E. Hanfmann & G. Vakar, ed. and trans. Boston: MIT Press.

Winnicott, D. W. (1960). Ego distinction in terms of the true and false self. In *The Maturational Processes and the Facilitating Environment.* New York: International Universities Press.

————— (1974). *Playing and Reality.* New York: Penguin.

Chapter 13

Self Psychology from the Perspective of Evolutionary Biology: Toward a Biological Foundation for Self Psychology

Daniel Kriegman

EVOLUTIONARY BIOLOGY, PSYCHOANALYSIS, AND THE DANGER OF MIXED METAPHORS

Numerous attempts have been made to utilize paradigms external to psychoanalysis to provide insight into psychoanalytic concepts. One of the dangers of such cross-fertilization is that concepts from different paradigms that appear to be similar may in fact be fundamentally different and thus lead to greater confusion, which is then obfuscated by pseudo-insight. Given this caveat, this paper will attempt to apply the paradigm of the theory of evolution to psychoanalysis. The ongoing paradigmatic shift within psychoanalysis from ego psychology to self psychology (Ornstein, 1981; Stolorow, 1983; Joseph, 1985) can be profitably conceptualized utilizing the following approach.

Many analysts, especially self psychologists, have difficulty with an evolutionary/biological approach to psychoanalysis because it appears to be associated with a narrow usage of the term "biology." "Biology" in the narrow sense conveys the somatic, the physiological, the biochemical—the study of the physical substrate of life phenomena. In this sense Kohut (1982) was correct in saying that psychoanalysis ought to be a psychology, true to the data obtained through vicarious introspection, and not linked in its constructs to psychophysiological concepts. Thus, as the science of complex mental states, it ought to divorce itself from biology in its narrow sense. "Biology" in the broad sense, however, means simply "the study of life." Psychoanalysis, under this, broader definition, clearly lies within the domain of biology and may justifiably be viewed in the light of "evolutionary biology."

Kohut's (1984) call for a psychoanalysis that is a "psychology through and through" is an important reminder of the essential nature of the psychoanalytic field. Yet, Kohut's cautionary note should not be construed as indicating that an evolutionary biological analysis is antithetical to the field of psychoanalysis. An evolutionary biological analysis is the study of how life was shaped by natural selection. It is an attempt to understand the *distal* causes (selective pressures) in the evolutionary history of species, those causes that shaped the phenotypes we see today. In understanding the relationship between these selective pressures and the *proximal* mechanisms (the existing mechanisms that control, shape, cause, and are the current phenotypic attributes), we are able to understand the adaptive value (in an evolutionary sense) of features of the phenotype. In so doing, we can perceive these features in a manner that sheds new light on their nature. An evolutionary biological analysis is an attempt to find the *distal causes* for *proximal mechanisms*. It is not an attempt to reduce the psychological into the somatic. Figure 1 clarifies this important point.

Using Figure 1, we can see where the confusion develops. Kohut presented us with the psychoanalytic arguments for the "reductionist barrier." He never claimed that the barrier could not or ought not be crossed. However, despite significant strides in this direction, the crossings continue to be clumsy at best and have not been helpful in understanding the psychoanalytic field. In saying that psychoanalysis should be a psychology proper, Kohut was really stating that it is not a *psychoanalytic* enterprise to try to reduce psychology to biology in the narrow sense; that mixing this nonanalytic enterprise with psychoanalysis tends to obscure and distort the data obtained from vicarious introspection and the psychological theories derived from such data.

The present evolutionary biological analysis is based, in part, on the belief that this barrier can *in principle* be crossed—that mental structures and patterns are shaped through evolution, which operates through somatic tissue via the transformation of the genetic code. In an evolutionary analysis, we are constantly aware of the existence of the somatic substrate, and when we use the word "biolo-

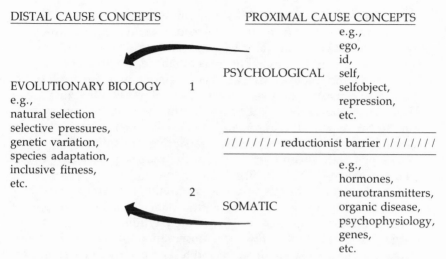

DISTAL CAUSE CONCEPTS

PROXIMAL CAUSE CONCEPTS

e.g.,
ego,
id,
PSYCHOLOGICAL   self,

EVOLUTIONARY BIOLOGY   1   selfobject,
e.g.,   repression,
natural selection   etc.
selective pressures,
genetic variation,   / / / / / / / / reductionist barrier / / / / / / / /
species adaptation,
inclusive fitness,   e.g.,
etc.   hormones,
               2   neurotransmitters,
                 SOMATIC   organic disease,
                             psychophysiology,
                             genes,
                             etc.

FIGURE 1

gy" we are simultaneously indicating both its broad and its narrow sense *without trying to cross the reductionist barrier.* In an evolutionary analysis of psychological phenomena, this barrier not only need not be crossed, but it need not even be approached. Both the somatic and the psychological must fit into the evolutionary biological (in the broad sense) perspective (arrows 1 and 2). In this paper I attempt to apply this claim to the psychological (arrow 1 only), and I do not attempt to cross the barrier. Mixing biological (in the narrow sense) constructs with psychological metaphors muddies the psychological waters, yielding a turbid vision of the human mind. Figure 1 demonstrates that the reduction of psychology to somatic factors (crossing the barrier) is simply not the same as an evolutionary biological analysis (arrow 1).

As we pursue the line of thought to be followed throughout this paper, we will not be trying to *reduce* psychoanalytic constructs to evolutionary forces. We may assume, however, that human psychology has some basis in our evolutionary history. What is being suggested is not a simplistic "evolutionism," in which every human trait is seen as an unfolding of prerecorded genetic instructions. Psychoanalytic theory has fostered major advances in our understanding of human behavior and psychology by providing a language and theoretical framework that enables us to envisage some of the patterns and structures involved in the internal workings of the human mind. While the patterns and structures referred to in psychoanalytic metapsychology are hypothetical constructs (Turner, 1967), for the purpose of an evolutionary analysis they can be considered to be as real as the physical structures that we readily analyze in evolutionary terms. Mental structures and behavior patterns, as well as physical structures, all can be profitably conceptualized in terms of their survival value and adaptive function. For example, intelligence is a hypothetical construct, and yet we can speak of its evolution just as we try to understand the evolutionary development of the upright posture or the opposable thumb. We can also consider the evolutionary development (selective pressures, adaptive advantages) of other ubiquitous patterns and structures in the human psyche, for example, repression (Slavin, 1985).

Like many other discussions and illustrations of evolutionary concepts, this paper draws on ethological data. Of course, data from other species cannot definitively indicate anything about human behavior or psychology. However, observation of animal behavior across many species can illustrate and test certain hypotheses in evolution theory. It is not the *data* from other species that can be applied to humans, but rather the logical structure of the theory of evolution—a logical structure that can be known through the correlation and analysis of data across many species. When we refer to reciprocal altruism among fish, we are not suggesting that people behave like fish. Rather, we are suggesting that evolutionary principles (for example, the adaptive value of a behavior pattern in regard to the "fitness" of the organism), which may be exemplified by other species, also apply to humans. Too often evolutionary theory is misused, and a behavior pattern in another species is taken to indicate that such a pattern must exist in humans. This misuse justifies a degree of caution in the application of evolutionary data and theory to human psychology. However, we must also be cautious lest we respond to the *"biological* blow, to human narcissism" inherent in evolution theory (Freud, 1917, p. 140) with defensive dismissal. We are, after all, members of the animal kingdom and evolutionary forces that explain nonhuman evolution apply to us as well.

FREUD'S USE OF EVOLUTION THEORY IN SUPPORT OF "GUILTY MAN"

In Freud's first published works (1878) he showed that there is a continuity between the nerve cells of lower and higher animals. This finding was contrary to accepted thought and supported an evolutionary viewpoint in which no sharp distinction is drawn between humans and lower animals. As a medical student Freud's studies focused extensively on evolutionary biology. This decisively influenced his vision of the animal nature and roots of human psychology (Jones, 1953), as could already be observed in his early neuroanatomical writings.

Many of Freud's vehement rejections of modifications to psychoanalytic theory can be traced to their failure to remain true to this evolutionary vision of the continuity between humanity and the rest of the animal kingdom. Freud may have been hypervigilant in guarding against the intrusion into psychoanalysis of ideas that would deny our drive (animal) nature, against those who would deny the "biological blow to human narcissism" inherent in the theory of evolution and his new psychology. Self psychologists continue to face this challenge (e.g., Ornstein, 1985).

Freud's psychoanalytic writings evidence this strong commitment to the notion that psychoanalytic theory ought to be developed within the framework of evolutionary biology (Slavin, 1985).

> . . . Charles Darwin . . . put an end to the presumption . . . that man is a being different from other animals or superior to them; he himself is of animal descent being more closely related to some species and more distantly to others. The acquisitions he has subsequently made have not succeeded in effacing both in his physical structure and in his mental dispositions the evidences of his parity with them. (Freud, 1917, p. 140)

Freud frequently referred to Darwin and evolution theory in justifying his drive/structure vision of human psychology (Sulloway, 1979). From this viewpoint, psychological structures are seen as being derived from the vicissitudes of drives (Greenberg and Mitchell, 1983). This biologically based conception forms the foundation of classical psychoanalytic theory and Kohut (1982) has referred to it as Guilty Man: "man as an insufficiently and incompletely tamed animal, reluctant to give up his wish to live by the pleasure principle, unable to relinquish his innate destructiveness" (p. 401).

This basic paradigmatic perspective is clearly presented in Freud's *Civilization and Its Discontents* (1930). Rational thinking, a form of ego control, and superego anxiety (guilt) are considered to be relatively recent evolutionary developments that compose an overlay superimposed on a more primitive and basic instinctual core. The metapsychological foundation for this perspective is presented in *The Ego and the Id* (Freud, 1923), which has been referred to as "the central paradigm of psychoanalysis" (Modell, 1975, p. 58).

Freud may have been trying to capture the experience-near construct we now refer to as the "self" when he originated the term "Das Ich" (literally "the I"), which in translation became the "ego." This later became a primary structure in his experience-distant tripartite metapsychology. Self-experience was then relegated to the synthetic function of this structure (Hartmann, 1939). In this model, the id ("Das Es" or literally "the It") is an impersonal, alien source of instinctual pressures that impinge upon the ego. According to A. Freud (1966) and inherent in Freud's work (Strachey, 1957, p. 6), there is a primary antagonism between instinct and ego. The Freudian picture of the human organism is of a creature ("the I") struggling with an impersonal antagonistic "It" composed of dark, unconscious, instinctual forces that threaten to overrun the ego. The struggle is only partly won and civilization achieved. The balance is tenuous. The repressive forces of the superego/civilization constantly must tame the threatening id by opposing it, "like a garrison in a conquered city" (Freud, 1930, p. 134). Object relational needs, empathy, altruism, and cooperation are all seen as transformations of our basic individualistic selfish instinctual nature.

Freud was clear on this point. The capacity for concern for others based on an empathic sharing of the other's experience, for example, in the form of compassion, was seen as a false facade over our true nature, that is, a reaction formation against sadism (Freud, 1915a, p. 129). "Reaction-formations against certain instincts take the deceptive form of a change in their content, as though egoism had changed into altruism, or cruelty into compassion"[1] (1915b, p. 281). Altruism, empathy, and aim-inhibited love (Freud, 1921) are achievements in opposition to our primary human nature (pleasure-seeking, full drive discharge) and certainly were not seen as having their own motivational source.

As psychoanalytic ego psychology developed, the focus turned to the ego and its functions and defenses, but this basic viewpoint was retained. Ego psychology can be seen as an extension and elaboration of Freud's evolution theory based assumptions. In the human psyche, biological drives are inherently in conflict with higher order thinking. Thus, ego psychology remains a drive/structure conflict psychology. On one hand, we have the phylogenetically primitive, self-serving, sensual pleasure seeking and aggressive drives. On the other hand, we have the rational, reality-oriented (gratification delaying) recently developed neocortex and the moral and cultural de-

---

[1]Strachey (1957) points out that the word "pity" or "compassion" could be used here as a translation for the German, *Mitleid*. which literally would be translated as "suffering with"—an excellent choice of words for a form of empathic union with another.

mands that also became possible with the increase in the complexity of brain structures and the development of civilization.

The gist of Freud's vision of guilty man is that this recent evolutionary overlay is like a "thin sugar coating" on a darker, more primitive and animalistic core. He took pride in bravely facing repugnant truths about our species. Kohut has pointed out the moralistic emphasis found throughout traditional analytic thought. Consider the pejorative tone in the following passage, in which Freud (1914) attempts to reduce parental love to its basic underlying essence, an underlying essence that also implies that parental devotion has inherent pathological aspects:

> [Parents] are under a compulsion to ascribe every perfection to the child—which sober observation would find no occasion to do—and to conceal and forget all his shortcomings. . . . [The child] shall not be subject to the necessities which [the parents] have recognized as paramount in life. Illness, death, renunciation of enjoyment, restrictions on his own will, shall not touch him; the laws of nature and of society shall be abrogated in his favour; he shall once more really be the centre and core of creation—"His Majesty the Baby," as we once fancied ourselves. . . . Parental love, which is so moving and at bottom so childish, is nothing but the parents' narcissism born again. . . [p. 91].

THE SELF PSYCHOLOGICAL VIEWPOINT

Compare that to Kohut's self psychological viewpoint. For Kohut, conflict exists—internal conflict, conflict between individuals, and conflict between generations—but rather than being an essential feature of human psychology, it is a "tragedy." It is an unfortunate byproduct of the failure of the human tendency towards empathic self-selfobject relationships—Kohut's (1982) concept of Tragic Man:

> Healthy man experiences . . . with deepest joy, the next generation as an extension of his own self. It is the primacy of the support for the succeeding generation, therefore, which is normal and human, and not intergenerational strife and mutual wishes to kill and to destroy—however frequently and perhaps even ubiquitously, we may be able to find traces of those pathological disintegration products . . . which traditional analysis has made us think [of] as a normal developmental phase . . . [p. 404].

Earlier in the same paper he uses Odysseus to exemplify "Tragic Man," describing him as: "striving, resourceful man, attempting to unfold his innermost self . . . and warmly committed to the next generation, to the son in whose unfolding and growth he joyfully participates—thus experiencing man's deepest and most central joy, that of being a link in the chain of generations" (p. 403).

Unlike Freud's individualistic drive/structure model, self psychology sees the primary motivational forces as deeply imbedded in the social matrix. While empathy can be used for "evil" (this point will be returned to later), the empathic capacity coupled with a yearning for inclusion in a self-sustaining, self-selfobject milieu suggests that cooperation, altruism, compassion, generosity, and the like may not be best understood as being in opposition to basic human nature— rather they may exemplify human nature.

Yet, was Freud not correct in seeing humans as "incompletely tamed animals" and to state that "men have no business excluding themselves from the animal kingdom" (1933, p. 204)? Does the abundant data not demonstrate human sexuality and aggressiveness, and when coupled with the theory of evolution, does this not provide one of the clearest arguments in support of the traditional analytic conception of Guilty Man? Must we not heed Freud's warning and be cautious lest we defensively dismiss the *"biological* blow, to human narcissism" inherent in evolution theory? After all, evolution theory is the only scientific theory of creation (Trivers, 1985), and it is the theory of "survival of the fittest"; not "survival of the most compassionate and altruistic." Does self psychology simply shy away from Freud's hard-won biological truths? The answer to these questions is no. Modern evolution theory can be used to show that Freud's vision of human nature was simply inaccurate. Kohut has demonstrated that the clinical data do not fit with Freud's harsh, moralistic view. This paper attempts to complement Kohut's clinical findings by showing that modern evolution theory (which was simply unavailable throughout the development of classical psychoanalytic thought) is more consistent with self psychology than with the traditional tripartite model of conflict-laden Guilty Man.

THE EVOLUTIONARY PERSPECTIVE

The overriding principle underlying evolutionary thought is that all life, in all its forms, structures, and behavior patterns, can be understood in terms of the built-in push towards reproductive success for the genetic material contained within an organism (Trivers, 1985; Dawkins, 1976). All living organisms can be metaphorically conceived of as participating in a gargantuan genetic relay race. The goal is for each organism to create and pass exact copies of pieces of its genetic "baton" to one or more fresh, healthy runners before the original runner expires.

All of the physical structures, internal psychological patterns, and behavior patterns of every organism in the race can be understood in terms of the advantages the structures and patterns provide to the runner in reaching this singular goal. To understand the myriad forms the runners take, one can study the obstacles and resources available to the racers on the course. Frequently the other runners are the obstacles and resources. The running patterns are enormous in their diversity, but each has the same aforementioned goal. Each of the current participants is the endpoint of an unbroken, four-billion-year-old chain of successful predecessors. In four billion years, not one of the current runners' direct ancestors dropped the baton! Yet, many of those currently in the race will fail.

The patterns of running—the physical structures of the runners as well as the techniques (behaviors, psychology) used to obtain resources and avoid pitfalls—are directly related to the specific parts of the genetic baton being carried. If a particular pattern is successful, then there will be more and more copies of its related baton parts and hence more and more runners displaying this particular pattern. There are always new patterns being tried out for the first time, for runners occasionally make errors in copying their baton parts. Most of these new patterns fail. These failures, as well as the failure of other, older patterns, litter the course. There are few rules in the race and only the one stated goal. Those racers who become distracted from the task at hand are soon "overrun" by others who maintained their focus on the goal. Mercy is rare—the struggle is relentless.

When Freud formulated the foundation for the classical psycho-analytic viewpoint, altruistic behavior and cooperation seemed to be inconsistent with such a competitive system, where the only driving force was "survival of the fittest." There appeared to be no specific selective pressures that would have made altruism itself adaptive. An organism was expected to be reluctant to forgo its primary instinctual selfishness. However, two important lines of modern evolutionary thought suggest that a cooperative empathic attitude toward others may confer on the bearer a powerful adaptive advantage, greatly increasing the altruist's fitness.

GUILT AND ALTRUISM: AN EVOLUTIONARY RESTATEMENT OF THE PROBLEM

Before we examine these evolutionary lines of thought, we must clarify the meaning of the term "altruism" as it is used by evolution theorists (Darwin, 1871; Hamilton, 1964, 1971; Trivers, 1971, 1985). Altruistic behavior increases the fitness of another organism while decreasing the fitness of the altruistically behaving organism (Trivers, 1971).

We are now at the crossover point between one theoretical system (psychoanalysis) and another (evolution theory). The assumption is that altruistic behavior as defined here refers to the same observational data base of human behavior that psychoanalysis has traditionally referred to as moral or guilt related. Most of the acculturated and civilized behavior that traditional psychoanalysis views as conflictual and guilt regulated is consistent with this definition of "altruism." As we proceed, it will be seen that we can increase our understanding of such behaviors and the psychoanalytic constructs we use to explain them by analyzing the adaptive/selective evolutionary pressures that shaped altruism.

Utilizing the evolution theory term "altruism," we can now recast the classical psychoanalytic assumption underlying our understanding of guilt. In the classical understanding, altruistic behavior is understood to be a result of a learned, higher order function that is in opposition to the more primitive and basic, self-serving sexual and aggressive instincts. In this conceptualization the evolution of the human cortex allowed for both the development of an ability to delay instinctual gratification and the introduction of the major influence of guilt. These developments, in turn, made altruistic behavior and civilization possible. As Freud (1930) put it:

> In the process of individual development . . . the main accent falls mostly on the egoistic urge (or the urge towards happiness); while the other urge, which may be described as a "cultural" one, is usually content with the role of imposing restrictions . . . [M]an's judgments of value . . . are an attempt to support his illusions with arguments. I should find it very understandable if someone were to point out the obligatory nature of the course of human civilization and were to say, for instance, that the tendencies to a restriction of sexual life or to the institution of a humanitarian ideal *at the expense of natural selection* were developmental trends which cannot be averted or turned aside and to which it is best for us to yield *as though they were necessities of nature* [p. 151, 156, italics added].

It is clear that Freud saw the civilizing (restrictive) forces as lying outside his biological system. They were somehow not part of nature, and it is the conflict between the natural (instincts) and the artificial, but necessary, restrictions (civilization) that leads to inevitable discontent. Yet Freud (1926) thought that the altruistic, loving, restrictive aspects of civilization were inherently necessary for human survival: "Our inborn instincts and the world around us being what they are, I could not but regard . . . love as no less essential for the survival of the human race than such things as technology" (p. 279). Thus, Freud saw civilizing forces, which created this essential love (in opposition to our "true" nature), as a *deus ex machina*. He could not conceive of a manner in which such a phenomenon could naturally (biologically) arise in the course of human evolution without turning to a contrived, Lamarckian explanation for its origins. In this explanation, hypothesized actual events in the prehistoric lives of a group of tribal individuals were somehow impressed on all succeeding generations (Freud, 1913; Holmes, 1983). Lamarckian theorizing is now known to be erroneous, though in Freud's day it was an integral part of evolution theory and was even espoused by Darwin himself (Sulloway, 1979; Brent, 1983).

In fact, until recently evolution theorists also had great difficulty accounting for cooperative and altruistic behaviors in both humans and other animals. Their solution parallels Freud's. In an attempt to account for such phenomena, both evolution theorists and Freud tempered the competitive picture of "survival of the fittest" (a picture consistent with Freud's depiction of the basic human condition) with the notion of selective pressures that shaped phenotypes that "were good for the species" (Wynne-Edwards, 1962). However, this argument is now known to be false (Trivers, 1985). Simply put, selection takes place at the level of the individual—or, more accurately, at the level of the gene; selecting genes that give rise to phenomena that increase those genes' representation in the future gene pool of the species. If a gene were to come into being that caused the organism to act "for the good of the species," as opposed to acting for the good of the genetic material carried by the individual, it would very quickly be outcompeted by selfish genes that took advantage of this altruistic gene's aid to the species.

Thus, the problem. Evolution theorists need to be able to encompass cooperative and altruistic behavior within a theory of selective pressures operating to create organisms that maximize their genetic self-interest. Classical analysts need to be able to explain the ubiquitous formation of civilization and culture within stable human groupings, without using Freud's Lamarckian or "for the good of the species"-derived notions. Another way of stating this is that the classical analyst must be able to account for the full range of human object relations without leaving the classical paradigm. Greenberg and Mitchell (1983) have shown that, so far this has not been done: the more accommodations of drive/structure theory are able to account for interpersonal/relational data, the farther they move from the classical paradigm. On the other hand, self psychologists also must grapple with this problem. The self psychologist does not see selfish ("selfish" in the sense of being pleasure seeking and unconcerned about or destructive to others, not in the sense of being simply narcissistic), driven behavior at the center of human psychology. Yet, self psychologists need to respond to the evolution-theory-based arguments about "survival of the fittest" without appearing to be naive idealistic deniers who are unwilling to face our true animal nature.

EVOLUTION THEORY'S SUPPORT OF SELF PSYCHOLOGY: ALTRUISM TOWARDS ONE'S KIN

We can now turn to the first form of the evolutionary perspective that is supportive of the self psychology viewpoint and that resolves part of this problem. The first form of the argument focuses on altruistic behavior directed toward one's kin. It was presented by William Hamilton in 1964 and provided the first major breakthrough in providing a solution to the evolutionary problem of altruism. This work has "turned out to be the most important advance in evolutionary theory since the work of Charles Darwin and Gregor Mendel" (Trivers, 1985, p. 47). For our present discussion, our use of Hamilton's solution will focus on his concept of "inclusive fitness." The overall inclusive fitness of an organism is not based on the individual organism's self-survival (personal fitness), but, rather, the survival of copies of an organism's genes in other individuals and in the resultant future gene pool for the species.

We defined "altruism" as behavior that increases another's fitness while decreasing the fitness of the altruist. Hence, parental behavior that benefits the child, often at considerable cost to the parent, is clearly altruistic. However, in analyzing the behavior of the parent, we must keep in mind that the child is related to the parent and therefore carries 50% of the parent's genetic material. Thus, the cost to the altruist (in this case the parent) in reduced *personal* fitness must be balanced against the degree of relatedness to the beneficiary in order to determine the effect on the parent's *inclusive* fitness. Altruistic parental behavior may reduce a parent's ability to survive or to produce other offspring while actually increasing the parent's inclusive fitness as the child carries copies of the parent's genes.

It is the maximization of inclusive fitness (as opposed to personal fitness) that is the singular evolutionary goal for all life forms. For a psychology to be consistent with our understanding of evolution, it must describe a psyche that is organized and motivated to achieve this goal. The biology of human offspring (assumed to be expressed largely through self-serving sexual and aggressive drives) may not be in conflict with the biology of the parent (assumed to be expressed through the parent's powerful tendency to become empathically involved and invested in the child's experience and well-being). A parent's genetic self-interest is maintained, in part, through giving to the offspring. To the extent that parents share genetic material with their offspring, they should be willing, able, and eager to "read" their children's needs and respond helpfully to them.

Let us digress briefly, to return to a point touched on earlier: empathy as a value neutral concept (Kohut, 1971, 1977, 1980, 1984). Thomas Kohut (1985) emphasized that empathy and altruism are markedly different concepts; empathy can even be used for evil. Thus far I have simply claimed that empathy as a tool for information gathering (a value-neutral concept) can be seen in the "ability to read the child's needs."

However, both parenting and self psychology as a *clinical* intervention are not simply based on empathy as a mode of observation—as a scientific tool for information gathering. Rather, the clinical use of empathy lies in its communication to the patient. What is seen as curative is the empathy-based selfobject function played by the analyst (Kohut, 1984). If the analyst were to communicate "scientifically" (i.e., objectively and accurately but without feeling or personal involvement) an understanding of the patient's experience, much of the selfobject function would be lost. It is the willing sharing of the patient's experience and the *wanting* to communicate this to the patient that is often an integral part of the patient's experiencing the analyst as a selfobject. An essential aspect of the selfobject function is this empathic *union*, which is intimately related to altruistic behavior motivated by compassion.

In an ethically carried out course of treatment, the aggrandizement of the analyst is not the goal. (See Kriegman and Solomon, 1985a,b for discussions of this issue.) Thus, the analyst's behavior meets the evolutionary definition of the term altruism: the analyst's self-interest (the relentless pursuit of the analyst's increased fitness) is forgone for the sake of the patient. Of course, the analyst is paid for this; but in many, if not most, cases, payment and ethical rules are not what prevents the compassionate analyst from taking advantage of opportunities to prey upon the patient's vulnerability and instead try to help the patient. More often, an ingenuous—and, I am claiming, biologically natural and inherent—desire to help the patient (compassion) is what motivates the analyst's moment-to-moment behavior and sustains the analyst's ethical stance. In this sense the analyst—

like the parent but with less motivation because of a genetic lack of relatedness (thus, the need for payment)—can be willing, able, and eager to read the patient's needs and to try to respond helpfully (in this case, with analytic empathy and interpretation), while willingly forgoing the pursuit of some of his or her own needs or wishes. The evolutionary origins of such a willingness to forgo the pursuit of one's fitness in the context of nonkin relationships will be more fully explored later.

Let us return now to our point of departure: understanding parental devotion to offspring based on inclusive fitness. Following Freud's appropriate insistence that we must not exclude ourselves from the animal kingdom, we should expect that in the biology of human beings—as in all species showing parental care—there is a natural, inherent, and direct tendency to act altruistically toward one's offspring (and to a lesser degree, because of a smaller amount of shared genetic material, toward all kin). Kohut (1982) describes this congruent fit between the needs of the child and the emotional responsive system of the parent as "man's deepest and most central joy, that of being a link in the chain of generations" (p. 403). Notwithstanding Kohut's biological disclaimers, he was appropriately following this evolutionary biological line of reasoning when he applied King's (1945) notion of healthy functioning to his conception of intergenerational relations. Thus, "man's deepest and most central joy" is seen as adaptive and healthy for it is the picture of an organism functioning "*in accordance with its design*" (King, 1945, cited in Kohut, 1984, pp. 187, 190)—a concept that lies at the heart of an evolutionary biological analysis.

EVOLUTION THEORY'S SUPPORT OF SELF PSYCHOLOGY: RECIPROCAL ALTRUISM

We turn now to the other form of the argument suggesting a strong direct biological basis to altruistic behavior. How do we explain the development of altruistic behavior that is not kin-directed? Again, at first glance altruistic behavior toward unrelated others appears to be antithetical to the basic self-serving survival interest that underlies evolution theory. However, the social evolution theorist Robert Trivers (1971), in what is already considered a classic paper (White, 1981), developed the concept of "reciprocal altruism," explicating the adaptive advantage of altruistic behavior towards unrelated others. He was even able to do this in regard to altruistic acts between members of different species, which, of course, is an extreme example of a lack of genetic relatedness.

The concept of reciprocal altruism stems from the idea that an altruistic act can at some point be returned to the altruistically behaving organism. For example, Trivers describes the relationship between certain host fish and unrelated cleaner fish. The cleaner's diet consists of parasites removed from the host, an act that can often involve entering the host's mouth. Trivers describes how a host fish will go through extra movements and delay fleeing when being attacked by a predator so as to allow a cleaner extra time to leave its mouth! It would seem to be the adaptive advantage of the host, at such a moment, simply to swallow the cleaner. Instead, the host delays its departure in order to signal to the cleaner that it is time to get out of its mouth. This type of altruistic behavior seems to reduce the fitness of the host in two ways: 1) it increases the chance that it will be eaten by a predator, and 2) it forgoes a meal of the cleaner. Yet, Trivers was able to demonstrate an adaptive advantage to this altruistic act: increasing the likelihood that debilitating parasites would be removed in the future. Guilt certainly could not be posited as the motivator of such behavior in the host fish; this kind of altruistic behavior is directly imbedded in the biological responsive structure and motivational system of the fish.

One cannot generalize from fish to humans. But what is demonstrated by such an evolutionary analysis are the necessary prerequisites for the evolution of reciprocal altruism: high frequency and reliability of association and the ability of two organisms to behave in ways that benefit each other. Reciprocal altruism is even more adaptive when there are frequent situations in which the cost to the altruist is significantly less than the beneficiary's gain. If this sounds like a perpetual motion machine, where the output magically exceeds the input, consider just a few human examples such as a traditional barnraising, the act of helping an unrelated lost child find his or her way back home, and most forms of human charity. In such situations the cost to the altruist is frequently far less than the recipient's benefit. People who can trade such acts will have a significant advantage over nonaltruists or those excluded from a reciprocal arrangement.

This evolutionary line of thought is powerful in posing a direct challenge to the classical analytic notion that "guilt" is necessary for civilization. Even though Trivers (1971) posits an important role for guilt in human social evolution, he points out that evolution theory cannot be used to "predict" guilt as central and necessary for civilization (personal communication). The prerequisites for the evolution of reciprocal altruism are present in our species and have been shown in other species to be capable of shaping extremely cooperative behaviors. (For a paradigmatic demonstration of reciprocal altruism, see Wilkinson, 1984.)

Trivers was able to show that altruistic behavior between human beings confers a powerful adaptive advantage on the altruist. A moment's reflection will demonstrate that much of human object relations exists within a complex web of kin and reciprocal altruism. In this analysis, rather than being an outcome of conflict brought into being by recent cortical evolution, the tendency to act altruistically is seen as being historically primitive. In fact, recent monkey studies (de Waal, 1982) suggest that reciprocal altruism existed at an early stage in primate evolution and in humans was a source of some of the selective pressures that led to the development of intelligence. Let us take a closer look at the evolution of altruism, cooperation, civilization, and intelligence.

THE EVOLUTION OF THE HUMAN CORTEX AND ITS RELATION TO CIVILIZATION AND GUILT

Trivers' presentation of reciprocal altruism suggests that such behavior and its underlying motivational system began to develop in the early history of our species or even earlier (with our primate predecessors or even with their ancestors). As kin altruism is even more primitive (ancient), there may have developed a tendency to utilize for reciprocal altruism the same cognitive and motivational systems that were employed for kin altruism. An admixture of kin and reciprocal altruism probably developed first among kin and was later extended to unrelated others. The following reconstructive evolutionary history of altruism and intelligence is consistent with both modern evolution theory (Hamilton, 1964, 1971; Axelrod and Hamilton, 1981; Trivers, 1971, 1985) and the human nature assumptions underlying the new psychoanalytic paradigm of self psychology.

Compassion, or sympathy for one in pain (the empathic sharing of the experience of pain and the desire to alleviate the sufferer's anguish), probably first evolved within the context of kin-directed behavior, because in a kin relationship an altruistic act increases the inclusive fitness of the altruist even if the act is not reciprocated. Therefore, the evolution of such behavior within kin relationships was not dependent on there first being a tendency for the recipient to reciprocate. The generalization of this behavior to *reciprocal* altruism among kin (and then to unrelated others) became possible when cognitive abilities were sufficiently developed so that the altruist could distinguish between those more likely to return the altruistic act (reciprocal altruists) and those unlikely to do so (cheaters).

The cognitive abilities necessary for the successful trading of altruistic acts are quite complex (Trivers, 1971). If powerful adaptive advantages were obtained through participation in a reciprocal altruism system, this must have created additional selective pressure for the further development of the cognitive abilities needed to engage successfully in trading altruistic acts without being cheated. Trivers suggested that reciprocal altruism evolved alongside increased cortical capacity and was a major source of selective pressure shaping its development.

Traditional conflict psychology sees altruistic behavior as a recent development brought into being *after* increased brain size began to lead to the formation of civilization: civilization, made possible by heightened cognitive capacities and the related ability to delay gratification, led to pressure to restrict instinctual behavior, resulting in altruism. In Trivers' analysis, the adaptive advantage of reciprocal altruism existed at the earliest stages in the development of human intelligence. This forced rapid enhancement of cognitive capabilities and the shaping of "civilizing" (social) tendencies in the individual. These adaptive tendencies enabled the individual to participate in a developing social order and thus to garner the optimal advantages of the successful trading of altruistic acts. As altruistic tendencies began to spread, the adaptive advantage of altruism increased. The following paragraph describes this snowballing effect, which is consistent with Axelrod and Hamilton's (1981) model showing how reciprocal strategies could arise in a population and ultimately outcompete purely selfish strategies, which would then be unable to reinvade the population.

The adaptive advantages of reciprocal altruism may have been a major source of the selective pressure that brought about intellectual advancement and as a result made social systems possible and advantageous. As increased cooperation became possible, those early humans who were able use guilt to control their sexual and aggressive behavior were able to attract altruistic actions toward themselves. Potential altruists were developing the cognitive ability to discern reciprocal altruists from cheaters. The cheaters could be identified, in part, by their selfish/instinctual behavior and their apparent lack of guilt, shame, or compassion. There was, then, an additional advantage to being able to participate successfully in the reciprocal altruism *system* that began to develop (an organized social grouping with rules to govern human relationships). This led to greater selective pressure for the cognitive abilities that would allow the participant to comprehend the subtleties involved in trading in altruistic acts without being cheated. As this cognitive capacity developed, it further enhanced the benefits of participation in an organized social system, and guilt became even more important, for it insured the individual's inclusion in the social group. Once individuals could be identified who displayed guilt and could be trusted to use it to temper their selfish behavior, the ability to remain in and participate in a reciprocal system—which because of this new, guilt-related stability could function at a higher level of efficiency—became even more important.

Thus, the capacity for guilt may be an important component of the reciprocal altruism system. It may have provided an important counterbalance to the pressures that selected for successful undetected cheating. Although it may have played a role in the further development and maintenance of such a complex reciprocal exchange system, it was not the *cause* of it or the force that enabled it to arise in our evolutionary past. Guilt developed along with other sources of motivation toward trading altruistic acts and functioned as a signal to others that "here stands a reciprocal altruist." The selective pressure shaping the development of guilt was the adaptive increase in one's inclusive fitness due to a fuller inclusion in the reciprocal altruism system as opposed to exclusion resulting from identification as a cheater. While some altruistic behavior may be influenced by guilt, the reciprocal altruism system (society) was not brought into play by the early development of guilt. Rather than thinking of guilt as the "cause" of altruism, in this analysis it may be more accurate to think of altruism as the cause of guilt!

These aspects of the emotional motivational system of the human *social* animal have not been fully accounted for in the classical psychoanalytic paradigm. Modern evolution theory suggests that the selective pressures making it likely that people would want to affiliate and cooperate (the empathic tendency, compassion, and the need to utilize others as selfobjects) were probably early developments *prior to guilt*. While guilt may have aided the development of highly complex, stable, and intimate social structures (which allowed for the frequent trading of altruistic acts without rampant acting out of sexual and aggressive drives), the selective pressure that brought about the development of guilt was the ability to gain full inclusion in, and the fullest benefits of, the reciprocal altruism system. This system—possibly in rudimentary form but probably already including the need for "human" community (the need for a self· selfobject milieu)—existed as a precursor to the development of guilt.

This is the exact opposite of the evolutionary path Freud thought the human species had traveled, and it is remarkably consistent with self psychology, which is built on the inherent basic capacity for empathy and the search for a nutritive self–selfobject milieu. It suggests that the traditional individualistic (drive/structure) psychoanalytic notion of guilt tempered selfish drives cannot fully explain most altruistic, cooperative, and communal social behavior (Kriegman and Solomon, 1985a). The tendency toward empathic union with others and altruistic behavior may not be a recent cortically based overlay in conflict with a more primitive biological core of self-serving sexual and aggressive drives, but rather may itself be based on a very primitive biological core.

SUMMARY

Within traditional psychoanalytic theory there has been a lack of recognition of the conflict-free motivational sources of the human tendency toward empathic union with others. Self psychology addresses this lack by focusing on the mutual interests that parents and children share and by analyzing the empathic transmission of this shared interest to the child as parents serve (or, tragically, fail to serve) as adequate selfobjects. In focusing on this aspect of human relations, self psychology appears to recognize a deep emotional wellspring, for example, compassion, that can give rise to altruistic behavior and that need not—and, Kohut (1984) argued, cannot—be understood within the context of a drive based conflict psychology.

We can also note that there is a similarity between the prideful joyful aspects of parenthood and the analyst's positive experience in the clinical setting (see Kohut, 1984, p. 187, 190, and p. 265, this chapter). This emotional experience—in this case between two unrelated persons—can also not be adequately understood in terms of a conflict psychology. I suggest that the human capacities for compassion and joyful empathic union were shaped by the selective pressures that created altruism (kin altruism and reciprocal altruism). It is the inborn yearning for empathic union with others, the natural parental tendency to succor the child, and spontaneous compassionate caring that account for the powerfully rewarding experience that can result from the intimate participation in the maturation and healing of an other through a lengthy empathic immersion in the other's psyche.

Modern evolution theory suggests that Kohut's interpretation of the clinical data may have the same degree of biological foundation in the human motivational system as we assume that instinctual drives have. Guilty Man, riddled with conflict, may in fact be, as Kohut viewed him, a result of the failure of the human tendency to seek out and maintain empathy based self–selfobject relationships. The theory of evolution suggests that there is a direct biological basis for this human tendency; that this tendency was selected for because of the adaptive advantage conferred on those who possessed it.

ACKNOWLEDGMENTS

Invaluable in the preparation of this manuscript was a matrix of wisdom, encouragement, and support provided by Dr. Malcolm Slavin, Mr. Barry Anechiarico, Drs. Murray Cohen, Joseph M. Schwartz, Robert Trivers, Paul and Anna Ornstein, Robert Stolorow, Helen Block Lewis, and Ms. Virginia DeLuca. I would also like to thank Mr. Richard Boucher, Administrator, and Mr. Dennis McNamara, Director of Operations, of the Massachusetts Treatment Center for the Sexually Dangerous Offender for their provision of institutional support.

REFERENCES

Axelrod, R., & Hamilton, W. D. (1981). The evolution of cooperation. *Science*, 211:1390–1396.
Brent, P. (1983). *Charles Darwin*, New York: Norton.
Darwin, C. (1871). *The Descent of Man and Selection in Relation to Sex*. New York: Random House.
Dawkins, R. (1976). *The Selfish Gene*. New York: Oxford University Press.
de Waal, F. B. M. (1982). *Chimpanzee Politics: Power and Sex Among Apes*. New York: Harper & Row.
Freud, A. (1966). *The Ego and the Mechanisms of Defense* (Rev. Ed.). New York: International Universities Press.
Freud, S. (1878). Uber Spinalganlien und Ruckenmark des Petromyzon. *Sitzungsberichte der kaiserlichen Akademie der Wissenschaften*. Mathematisch-Naturwissenschaftliche Classe, 78, III. Abtheilung:81–167.
———— (1913). Totem and taboo. *Standard Edition*, 13:1–161. London: Hogarth Press, 1953.
———— (1914). On narcissism: An introduction. *Standard Edition*, 14:67–102. London: Hogarth Press, 1957.
———— (1915a). Instincts and their vicissitudes. *Standard Edition*, 14:117–140. London: Hogarth Press, 1957.
———— (1915b). Thoughts for the times on war and death. *Standard Edition*, 14:273–302. London: Hogarth Press, 1957.
———— (1917). A difficulty in the path of psycho-analysis. *Standard Edition*, 17:136–44. London: Hogarth Press, 1955.

_____ (1921). Group psychology and the analysis of the ego. *Standard Edition*, 18:65–143. London: Hogarth Press, 1955.

_____ (1923). The ego and the id. *Standard Edition*, 19:1–66. London: Hogarth Press, 1961.

_____ (1926). To Romain Rolland. *Standard Edition*, 20:279. London: Hogarth Press, 1959.

_____ (1930). Civilization and its discontents. *Standard Edition*, 21:59–145. London: Hogarth Press, 1953.

_____ (1933). Why war? *Standard Edition*, 22:197–215. London: Hogarth Press, 1964.

Greenberg, J. R., & Mitchell, S. A. (1983). *Object Relations in Psychoanalytic Theory*. Cambridge, MA: Harvard University Press.

Hamilton, W. D. (1964). The genetical evolution of social behavior. *Journal of Theoretical Biology*, 7:1–52.

_____ (1971). Selection of selfish and altruistic behavior in some extreme models. In *Man and Beast: Comparative Social Behavior*, ed. J. F. Eisenberg & W. S. Dillon. Washington, DC: Smithsonian Press, pp. 59–91.

Hartmann, H. (1939). *Ego Psychology and The Problem of Adaptation*. New York: International Universities Press, 1958.

Holmes, K. R. (1983). Freud, evolution, and the tragedy of man. *Journal of the American Psychoanalytic Association*, 31:187–210.

Jones, E. (1953). *The Life and Work of Sigmund Freud. Vol. 1*. London: Hogarth Press.

Joseph, E. (1985). Address to The Eighth Annual Conference on the Psychology of the Self, New York, October 5.

King, D. (1945). The meaning of normal. *Yale Journal of Biological Medicine*, 17:493–501.

Kohut, H. (1971). *The Analysis of The Self*. New York: International Universities Press.

_____ (1977). *The Restoration of the Self*. New York: International Universities Press.

_____ (1980). Reflections. In A. Goldberg, ed., *Advances in Self Psychology*. New York: International Universities Press.

_____ (1982). Introspection, empathy, and the semi-circle of mental health. *International Journal of Psycho-Analysis*, 63:395–407.

_____ (1984). *How Does Analysis Cure?* Chicago: University of Chicago Press.

Kohut, T. (1985). Discussion of an earlier version of this paper presented at the Eighth Annual Conference on the Psychology of the Self, New York, October 5.

Kriegman, D., & Solomon, L. (1985a). Cult groups and the narcissistic personality: The offer to heal defects in the self. *International Journal of Group Psychotherapy*, 35(2):239–261.

_____ (1985b). Psychotherapy and the "new religions": Are they the same? *Cultic Studies Journal*, 2:2–16.

Modell, A. (1975). The ego and the id: 50 years later. *International Journal of Psychoanalysis*, 56:57–68.

Ornstein, P. H. (1981). The bipolar self in the psychoanalytic treatment process: Clinical theoretical considerations. *Journal of the American Psychoanalytic Association*, 29:353–375.

_____ (1985). Sexuality and Aggression in the Bipolar Self. Paper presented at the Eighth Annual Conference on the Psychology of the Self, New York, October 5.

Slavin, M. O. (1985). The origins of psychic conflict and the adaptive function of repression: An evolutionary biological view. *Psychoanalysis and Contemporary Thought*, 8:407–440.

Stolorow, R. D. (1983). Self psychology—A structural psychology. In J. D. Lichtenberg & S. Kaplan, ed., *Reflections on Self Psychology*. Hillsdale, NJ: The Analytic Press.

Strachey, J. (1957). Editor's introduction to "Civilization and its discontents." *Standard Edition*, 21:59–63. London: Hogarth Press, 1961.

Sulloway, F. J. (1979). *Freud, Biologist of the Mind*. New York: Basic Books.

Trivers, R. L. (1971). The evolution of reciprocal altruism. *Quarterly Review of Biology*, 46:35–57.

———— (1985). *Social Evolution*. Boston: Addison-Wesley.

Turner, M. B. (1967). *Psychology and the Philosophy of Science*. New York: Appleton-Century-Crofts.

White, E., ed. (1981). *Sociobiology and Human Politics*. Lexington, MA: Heath.

Wilkinson, G. (1984). Reciprocal food sharing in vampire bats. *Nature*, 308: 181–184.

Wynne-Edwards, V. C. (1962). *Animal Dispersion in Relation to Social Behavior*. Edinburgh: Oliver & Boyd.

Author Index

Subject Index

A

Abstract and androgynous self, 230–31
Accompaniment, need for attuned, 180
Adaptation between infant and caregiver, mutual, 70–75
  as abstract and general amplifier of variants in density of neural stimulation, 31–32
  affective communication, capacity for, 146
  affect-related information vs., 41–42
  celebration of positive, 47
  complexes, 32–33
  critical function for infant, 179
  experience of dysphoric, 49
  genuine vs. habitual, 245
  intensity dimension of infant, 35–36
  self-development and, 42–50
  studying facial expressions and, 29–31
Affective matching, 11–16
Affective maturation, 146–47
Alert activity, state of, 38, 40
Alert inactivity, state of, 37–38, 40
Alexithymic patients, 101

Alter ego transference, 147
Altruism
  as cause of guilt, 270
  cognitive capacities and, 269–70
  evolutionary perspective on, 261–64
  meaning of term, 261–62
  toward one's kin, 264–66, 268
  reciprocal, 266–70
Ambitions
  conflicts between attachments and, 195–209
  perceived as hubris, 196, 204–5, 207
Analysis of the Self, The (Kohut), 55
Analytic situation, tolerance of manic-depressive patient for, 93
Androgynous and abstract self, 230–31
Anger
  experiences of, 49–50
  facial expression of, in humans, 31
Anxiety, separation, 244
Associative language, 240–43
Attachments, conflicts between ambitions andd, 195–209
Attributions of object reality, 107
Attuned accompaniment, need for, 180
Attuned engagements, 178

281